Wasn't Me, Miss!

WASN'T ME, MISS!

Wasn't Me, Miss!

Wasn't Me, Miss!

Wasn't Me, Miss!

Wasn't Me, Miss!

Wasn't Me, Miss!

Wasn't Me, Miss!

'Wasn't Me, Miss!'

A Teacher's Tales

R.K.J. Adams

To Dawn

Best wishes on your journey,

Ruth x

First published by Rowham Morrex Publishing in the United Kingdom 2022.

Every effort has been made to trace copyright holders and to obtain their permission for the use of copyright material. The publisher apologises for any errors or omissions and would be grateful of any corrections that should be incorporated in future editions of this book.

This is a work of fiction. Names, characters, places and incidents are either the product of the author's imagination or are used fictitiously. Any resemblance to actual persons, living or dead, events, or locales is entirely coincidental.

Cover design by R.K.J. Adams (images Canva Pro)
Printed and bound in the United Kingdom by Mixam UK Ltd

A CIP catalogue record of this book is available from the British Library ISBN (Paperback UK) 978-1-3999-2136-7

Dedication

To my family who have been part of me, my life, my journey. Some are gone but never forgotten. Thank you for making me who I am. You have always believed in me, even when I didn't believe in myself.

Foreword

Michael Heppell is an international author of 'How to Be Brilliant', one of the top three motivational speakers in the world' and a Success Coach. His book 'Flip It' earned him a coveted Sunday Times No. 1 Best Seller title.

We all remember our favourite teacher. It's a popular security question, along with first pet and mother's maiden name. Your favourite teacher had the perfect combination. They brought a subject to life, were skilled storytellers and, above all, they cared about you. Teachers like that made you a happy learner.

In this book you will discover what makes a teacher a favourite. I know, if I'd been in her class, Emma Challis would have been my favourite.

Telling your story is difficult. What to put in, what to leave out. Will the reader want more or less? Will they care? In the coming pages you'll discover the delicate art of storytelling, told by a former primary school teacher, R.K.J. Adams through the eyes of her fictional character Emma. A teacher who cared. Spanning a career of four decades, including the best ones (the 80's and 90's) you'll enjoy a glimpse of what made this teacher so special.

Life has its ups and downs for us all. It's what you make of those experiences that counts. By taking a positive view, tackling challenges head on and getting out of her comfort zone, Emma will inspire you to be the best version of yourself. Even when she no longer teaches, you know that she'll always be a teacher at heart.

Michael Heppell

The Warm-up Act

A Moment In Time

'Good morning, everyone! Are you ready for your literacy lesson this morning? I hope you have your thinking cap on as you'll need it to write your story.'

Thirty pairs of eyes look at me as I pretend to put on a 'thinking cap'. I already know those children who are listening to me, copying my actions, who are compliant and will try hard to write their stories without a battle royale. I hear the few expected groans and my stomach churns as the battle begins. I look towards the usual suspects of the class who have shuffled on their bottoms to the back of the group. The little devils have moved, right under my nose. How can I get this small group of '*Desperados*' to write at least two lines again? Shall I threaten their playtimes, their lunch time? I need to be careful with my approach. I can't make a mistake today, of all days. I grit my teeth and continue with my questioning about what a good story should have. The answers flow and prove that some children in the class have been listening over the last few months. I am delighted with the responses and recap the answers the children have given me.

'Every good story should have a beginning. It should have some action in the middle and a great ending. There should be some interesting characters and some different settings.'

With the introduction completed, I feel that this part of the lesson has gone well despite having to move the gang back to the front of the carpet so I can keep my beady eye on them. I feel something touch my leg. I look down and there is a small hand on my tights, pulling at a snag. My eyes widen and I give a quick shake of the head to inform the child not to continue. The hand moves back to its owner, but I spot a leaving present in the form of slimy green snot smeared on my black tights.

I sneak a peek at our visitor. He hopefully hasn't noticed the snot incident. Yesterday I gave the class a full list of rules for behaviour in case of any visitors to the room. I promised the children extra Golden Time if they worked hard. I had omitted to mention green bogeys on tights.

The staff have been told not to look at the visitor, but I can't help myself. I glance again to check if he is still writing. He has a similarity to the Child Catcher from *Chitty, Chitty, Bang, Bang*. The irony is not lost on me. He looks pleasant enough, but I've heard he has been the most critical of the inspectors in school. He seems to have written reams, since nodding to me on entering the room. He had sat down on the only adult sized chair and placed his briefcase horizontally across his legs to act as a writing surface. He is still writing, his head leaning gently to the left.

I gulp. I am ready to send everyone back to their desks to write their story. A few bright sparks, the *'Eager Beavers'* will write novels with paragraphs, full punctuation and have character speech flying off their pencils. *'Snotty'* will get green slime all over his book … again. The *'Strugglers'* will forget finger spaces and mix capitals and lower case in the twenty letters they write. The *'Desperados'* will stretch out three words on each line to make it look like they have written a whole book. I feel a quiver in my voice as I send them off to their fate and mine.

The Child Catcher's ears must have been pricked by the noise as they move. Should I bring them back to the carpet or let it go? I freeze for a millisecond then clear my throat.

'I expect you to work quietly in 20 seconds from now.'

I slowly whisper the countdown to zero. The room falls silent. Perhaps I do know what I am doing after all, but I'll wait for my lesson grade from the inspector. I hear he only gives out 'Satisfactory' or 'Unsatisfactory' so there is no chance of a 'Good' or 'Outstanding'.

To my surprise everyone is working, the room is silent apart from the slight sound of pencils touching paper. I circulate to check on progress and to ensure that everyone keeps going. As I approach David, his hand shoots up, nearly hitting me on the nose as I go to lean down. My heart sinks and I wonder how I can quieten him without the inspector hearing. I am too late. He starts to bellow as normal,

'Miss!'

Smiling, I remember the next moments of the lesson; the teaching points I have been through countless times with children, in so many classes, in every school I've worked. The memories are racing through my head as I write my story; the ramblings of Emma Challis, née Slater, who taught for thirty-five years. My teacher's tales will have with a beginning, middle and end. There will be characters in the book, those people I've met along

2

the way and with whom I share my story. As for the settings .... there have been a few over the years.

My thoughts return to that literacy lesson. The 'Desperados' just want the lesson to be over, to run down the corridor half spilling their packets of crisps saved from breakfast, and to explode onto the playground to kick a football or to get into a tussle or two. I had wished the lesson to be over just like them. I had not been prepared for 'Desperado David' to make his move.

*This time I **know** what will happen next.*

The Beginning

Chapter 1
Dynasty And Destiny

When an uncle or aunty quizzed me about what I wanted to be when I left school, they always smugly added something about following in my mother's footsteps, giving a wry smile as they waited for my answer. I would reply most indignantly that I did not want to become a teacher. I had seen the long hours of study before I was seven, the holidays spent in school with my mother preparing for a new academic year, the marking, the collecting of yoghurt pots or egg boxes. There was always something going on in our house linked to my mother's teaching. We could not go to the countryside without searching for cones for Christmas art lessons or conkers for counting beads in maths.

'There were two sick in class today. One spewed on the carpet, the other over the pet hamster.'

My mother would come home full of stories which contained vomit, pee, poo or snot. It seemed that one child's orifice or another offered her a present almost every day in her class.

'Well, that's a first. One charming child pooed in a bucket that I'd left in the Wendy house by mistake. I couldn't find out who the '*Pooer*' was, but I've narrowed it down to three likely suspects.'

No! Teaching was not for me. When I had to contemplate the world of work, I never saw myself in a classroom. Besides wanting to avoid bodily fluids, I was extremely shy and the thought of commanding a class, performing on the classroom 'stage' was far too scary for a pimply teenager to consider.

If anyone in the family persisted with their career questions, I would say I wanted to work in a library. I have no idea why this notion came into my head except that it was an environment I felt comfortable in, quiet, serious and full of books which I loved. Sometimes I talked about being an accountant. I had always been good at maths, in fact I really enjoyed numbers and sums. A librarian or accountant would be a good career choice. There was also, most importantly, no snot or poo involved in either job. My mother seemed to talk endlessly about bodily fluids and having to clean children at school.

If friends asked me what I was going to do when I grew up, I played a joke, answering that I wanted to be a nun. I had watched *The Sound of Music,* so I created a fantasy and, after all, when I had been younger, I had wanted to be Julie Andrews. Being a nun would involve no board and lodgings to find. There was no work as such, all I had to do was pray. There would be no cleaning if you got a cushy number in the kitchen or convent and no snotty children. The problem was that people started to think I was serious about being a nun, or at least, playing up to my little joke. I kept up the pretence for over a year. Another positive reason for becoming a nun was the costume, whilst being unflattering to anyone, the habit would cover up any shape and size. It was black and white, and you didn't have to try to squeeze into jeans from Chelsea Girl or C & A. The downside, a huge one, was I had no religious bones in my body.

In my head, but never voiced was the joy I could have felt in being the British version of Debbie Harry from Blondie. Everyone wanted to be like her. She was sexy and risqué. The boys loved her. The girls loved her. However, I couldn't sing in tune and all the kids in school, who were interested in being in a band, were psychos wearing bondage, pretending to be Sid Vicious. Being painfully shy I should also have hated going on the stage. My looks were average at best so my dreams would be just dreams.

I wrote a letter to *Jim'll Fix It* as my next plan. I was convinced that I was destined to meet John Travolta, get married and enjoy the millionaire's life in New York or California. At the back of my mind, I sadly knew this was a fantasy which would never really come true. Looking back now there is great relief that Jim never fixed it for me, and I'm repulsed that I ever wrote to him!

Bubbling away was an idea I did not want to admit, even to myself at times. From around the age of fourteen I decided teacher training was a possibility, but I wanted no one to know especially my mother. She had no clue I wanted to be a teacher, nor had she put pressure on me to teach but I did not want to speak openly about this idea floating around in my head which would not go away. I had generally loved school, both primary and secondary, with the characters I'd met having a massive impact on me. I admired the teachers who had a passion for sharing learning with their pupils. There was something about them that was inspiring, and I felt a yearning stirring inside myself.

8

I had an appointment with the career's teacher. She was the first person to whom I had ever voiced my dream.

'I think I'd like to be a primary school teacher.'

She never flinched, never looked up from filling out my form and never nodded. I walked out of the room feeling brave. The truth was out, and it felt good. A few weeks later at parents evening, she informed my mother about my notion to teach.

'Emma told me she wants to teach but that is out of the question. She'll never be a teacher. She's too introvert and shy.'

My mother fought back,

'Yes. She is shy but she's bright and in all the top sets. I know when she sets her mind to achieve something, she is determined.'

The careers teacher continued, ignoring my mother's comments.

'Has Emma thought about working in Firkins? I know they are taking on school leavers at the moment. Working with customers might bring her out of her shell a little.'

Firkins was a local bakery. The bread, pineapple tarts and chocolate eclairs were delicious, but it wasn't a career either my mother or I had planned. With the small amount of confidence that I did have shattered, I had to admit some of what she had said was true. I was extremely shy and *"reticent to speak in class"*, according to my French teacher in my last school report. The thought of selling cream horns, a white bloomer or sticky Belgian buns left me feeling … empty!

'I should have a chat with her if I were you. Lower her sights. She is just not cut out for teaching.'

At this point my mother and Colin, my stepfather, both rose from their chairs in unison. They offered the woman no thanks for her time or acknowledged her. After they moved away from earshot, Colin gave his two penn'orth of wisdom.

'That was utter rubbish. If Emma wants to be a teacher, we'll support her all the way.

My secret was out. Colin and my mother knew. Mum was furious but not at my aspirations of being a primary school teacher. She was furious that a careers advisor, who had met with me for five brief minutes, had dismissed the thought of me being a teacher without even knowing me, my background and what made me tick. She had never taught me. She

9

didn't know the female role models in my life; three grafters who had come through hard times and who had made me determined to do what I wanted. All could be stubborn, worked hard and kept a roof over their children's heads. None of them wanted me to end up serving in Firkins. For other girls that was fine, a good, steady job but not for the three generations of women in my family. They wanted more for me. I wanted more for me. I'd seen those girls in Firkins mopping the floors at the end of the day when all the bread and cakes were sold. I was not going to be a cleaner!

I must explain why I didn't want to be a cleaner. I am not a snob, in fact, cleaning was in the family. It was in my blood, and it scared the life out of me even more than being a teacher.

In her forties my nan had become a tea lady and cleaner in the offices of a local printing company. My grandad had died suddenly in bed in late February 1961, so my nan had to make sure she worked to pay the rent and to put food on the table for her daughter who was twenty and her son, fifteen.

Nan was the matriarch of our family and had laboured away in factories for most of her life since the age of fourteen. Born towards the end of the First World War she was the middle child of three. Her mother, my great grandmother, had been in service as a lady's maid before she was married and was a very particular, smart woman even in her late seventies when I was born. Nan didn't quite have her finesse and the golden era of service was practically over when she was ready to find a job in the early 1930s. She didn't have the confidence to have taken her cooking or any of her practical skills any further in life other than to use them to make a happy home. She loved listening to 'Jimmy Reeves' or Matt Munroe on the radio, knitting, sewing and baking. These things together with home making were Nan's life.

I had never actually fancied following my nan into work as a cleaner. She had spent some of her younger days helping her parents. My great grandfather had several jobs after he had married but for twenty-six years, he had been the local primary school caretaker and my great grandmother had helped him to clean. She had also cooked the headteacher's meal every lunch time for years. In the evenings she polished desks and swept the wooden floors of the classrooms. Nan had grown up, knowing about cleaning duties and the pride in making rooms clean.

Nan had settled on the tea lady and cleaning work after a relative had mentioned the job to her. She had been there for years and talked fondly about the people who worked at the printing company. She seemed to revel in the glory of having a conversation with Mr John, the boss. She was always complimentary about the man, showing a loyalty to him for his kindness towards her. On her retirement he and his family organised a meal at a fancy hotel and some flowers and a hummingbird brooch. It didn't seem much to me at the time but to my Nan these gestures meant the world. It made her feel important for once in her life.

She worked in the days when there was a lunch break for an hour and a half, and the siren, locally known as *the bull,* would sound for the factory workers to get back to the grind right on the dot. There would be no chance of any extra precious minutes away from the factory floor. Nan would pop back home with one eye fixed firmly on the clock to make sure she caught the bus back to work in time. She would spend half of her precious lunch break travelling on the Number 2 bus, but she still managed to cook a lunch for me when I was a small child at primary school. I always knew what would be for lunch as it was the only food I would eat which caused no problems to my nan in her tightly packed schedule. Nan would always ask what I fancied but knew my answer already.

'Please can I have two slices of Spam, a dollop of Smash and some peas?'

When my meal was ready, I would re-enact Smash adverts from the television as I tasted the instant potato mixture. In my best alien voice, I knew the words off by heart.

'It means there is intelligent life on earth. Ah, Ah, Ah!'

I devoured lunch and always thanked her before returning to school whilst Nan raced back to work. As a child, I never appreciated how precious her time was but thinking back, it must have been hard to get home, get the meal on the table for me and grab something to eat herself before sending me on my way and she was running for the bus again.

Ironically when she retired, the younger lady who replaced her, only lasted a short time before resigning due to the work being too laborious.

11

So just three months after Nan retired at the age of sixty-two, she was replaced by a vending machine.

✓✓✓✓✓

The other grafter in my life was my mother. Having been the first person in the family to have hit the dizzy heights of Grammar School after passing the eleven plus, my nan and grandad did not know what to make of this independent girl they had created as she was academic but also a tomboy. She would spend hours in the garden, doing her homework or revising for some test but sometimes she would race off on her bike for some adventure with her friends from the local Methodist chapel or school.

Although she was clever and capable of passing exams, she only left school with 'O' levels because when she went into the sixth form, the timetable for her chosen subjects clashed. This meant she couldn't keep up with the work being set and quickly became disillusioned by the lack of support from the sixth form staff who did not sort out the problems. She left after struggling through with an impossible timetable, having completed just six months of the lower sixth form. Taking on a job in a laboratory testing the reaction of foods on metal bottle tops did not satisfy her nor did a job in the offices of a slaughterhouse, dealing with butchers' orders. She had set her heart on being a teacher.

In the fifties and sixties, it was an accepted practice for local education departments, to employ unqualified teachers who had shown academic ability at school. At the beginning of the autumn term in 1958, at just seventeen years old, Mum began working in a local infant class in the town. She was under the supervision of a teacher who was pregnant but not expected to go on maternity leave for a few months. During one of the teacher's pre-natal checks in early September the expectant mother was detained in hospital for high blood pressure. Precisely two weeks after commencing at the school, my mother was left solely in charge of a class of thirty-seven five-year-olds.

Although she had secured work in a school, my mother's story continued to spiral downwards after her disappointment at having to abandon her 'A' levels and a dream of teacher training college. Despite being warned by local folk who had knowledge of him, she married an amateur footballer in late March 1962, just a year after her father had died suddenly in bed at the age of forty-five. The weather was typical of that time of year with all the seasons in one day, an omen for what was already evolving.

Like many couples in the early sixties, married life commenced by living at my nan's house, in one of the bedrooms. Savings had begun in order to buy a house of their own. After a return to the lab, Mum had managed to get another contract in the school she had previously worked at when she discovered she was pregnant.

I had existed for a few short weeks when, on Boxing Day evening 1962, my father slipped out of the house. It wasn't an unusual occurrence, in fact it had become quite a regular thing, even before they were married for him to take off for a few hours on his own. On this occasion he had said he was going for a spin on his motor bike. Whilst my mother had popped upstairs to get ready to go with him, he had taken off into the darkness of that night; the Christmas lights still twinkling with all the promise and joy of the festive season and the excitement of what was to arrive in August 1963.

When midnight came and there was no sign of him returning, my mother made the decision to bolt the front door. My nan protested a little but was silenced by the stark reality of my father returning home surrounded by lies of where he had been or not returning at all. Her daughter's furrowed brow, pale complexion and tightened lips displayed determination which would not be altered by arguing with her. The lies had grown over the last year or more, in fact they had always been there as an integral part of my mother and father's relationship despite my mother refusing to acknowledge or accept this for many months. Whether he tried his key in the lock later that night we'll never know but he certainly did not return the following day or any other day after that. Perhaps my father had not wanted a summertime present? Perhaps he had feared growing up and having to share the responsibility of being a parent despite dreaming openly with my mother about having me and future siblings? Perhaps he just wanted to end the deceit of having an affair whilst married? Whatever his reasoning, my mother found herself two months pregnant, husbandless and alone. When she found out about the affair and that he had been cheating on her before they married, she was destroyed by his lies.

Skip forward a few months to me being born in August 1963 in my nan's back bedroom, surrounded by bedroom furniture that had been purchased for the marital home. My father refused to pay maintenance money regularly, as it was called back then. Mum's only choice was to pursue him through court every few months before he would begrudgingly settle some of back payment he owed, and the cycle would commence again. Mum dug heavily into the savings they had been making to buy a house. He made no contact except for one letter asking to see me a few months after I was born. He never turned up and I doubt he ever will, almost sixty years later. He may not be alive. I have no knowledge of him nor he of me.

✓✓✓✓✓

There is one story from this time of my birth which always makes me smile. My mother met a lady in the street who she had known since Grammar School. The lady is mentioned several times in this book as my first teacher at junior school and much later as a colleague. Back then, a couple of weeks after I had been born, Mum took me out in the pram and just coming down the steps of the local primary school entrance was Liz Wootton. The teacher smiled as she saw my mother, out with the pram.

'Oh, I see you've had the baby. Congratulations! Is it a boy or girl?'

'Thank you. I had a girl.'

Liz peered into the pram and made the usual comments associated with greeting a new mother. How was I? How was my mother? Finally, she asked my name. My mother, ever practical, knew she was talking to a teacher colleague.

'I called her Emma in case she is thick. Four letters to her name. I kept it short just in case.'

The two teachers stood nodding silently as they both considered this problem as they looked at me. Liz understood. Teaching someone to spell their name such as Christopher or Penelope could be tricky if they were not bright. I now understand why I was given a name with four letters.

✓✓✓✓✓

Life in 1963 was not a bowl of cherries for a single mother. Even though Mum had a marriage certificate and was the innocent party in this marital mess some of the neighbours looked down their noses at us purely because there was no husband or father present at home. Tittle tattle and the deception by the man she had loved, played heavily on my mother's mind alongside how she would manage to live now she had a child in tow.

14

When I was just two years old, Mum made enquiries at the education office to see if she could get unqualified teaching work again. Within hours, the local headmistress from Broomhill Infant School, just a few yards from my nan's house, knocked on the door to offer my mother a contract for a year. For the last three generations, all my family had attended either the infant or junior schools that shared the same site. Each school had a separate headteacher. My great grandfather had been the caretaker until his death at the age of fifty-nine; my great grandmother had been the cleaner. The school ran through the blood of more than three generations of my family.

Mum explained that she was a single parent. She had no-one to look after me and had been looking for just part-time work because she needed to balance babysitting costs with half a wage. The headmistress smiled and said not to concern herself. My mother was offered the opportunity to teach fulltime and take me to work with her in the pram. Back in 1965 schools were a different world with a school board rarely ever seen or mentioned. Nothing was ever questioned if the headteacher had granted a single, soon to be divorced mother a chance to bring her two-year-old daughter to school with her. My mother grasped the job with both hands and dutifully, each morning and afternoon the headmistress would greet her at the gates to the school, helping to lift the pram up and down the two or three steps so that Mum could take me to work.

Miss Wilson, her boss, was a strange, elderly lady with a face full of wrinkles and greyness. She was memorable for several reasons. She wore the same shabby clothes every single day, a pale grey jacket, matching pleated skirt and a finely knitted short sleeved top that had once had a pattern on it but with age and stains any prettiness had disappeared. It was well known that instead of washing her top she would wear it inside out when one side became too grimy. When she moved about the school an odour followed her. Around her scrawny, grey neck were a couple of keys hanging from a filthy piece of string. The keys were usually kept out of sight but if you ever caught a glimpse of them, when she was unaware, they appeared tarnished and even older than Miss Wilson. She guarded them with all her might and filth! Whilst she was this wizened old lady, in need of a twin tub, the kindness she showed to Mum in those few months was immeasurable.

15

From the age of two I was in school, helping my mum, being a good girl, keeping quiet and getting on with life as a toddler. I can't remember having the 'terrible twos' but I can't have been a perfect child. There are a few photographs from that time. I look at home in the middle infants' class. I seem to have spent most of my time in the *Wendy* house. The official name now, in our very gender-neutral world, is the play corner or imaginary role play area which often means it can be a post office, cafe or Santa's grotto. I liked *Wendy*, and whoever she was, I liked her humble abode very much. I spent my days in there whilst my classmates sat learning stuff that looked super hard and inaccessible to my little brain.

When my mother's contract at Broomhill, ended in the summer of 1966, she was approached by the headmistress of Whitegate Primary School a couple of miles away. The distance to the school was walkable and compared to the guild of old ladies at the local infant school, Mum was surrounded by some excellent teachers, many of whom were formally trained and were younger, full of enthusiasm for teaching. The downside was that the contract would be for one year only as the school had been given notice that it would be closing in July 1969. Although I was still officially too young to be in reception class at Whitegate, the headmistress agreed to me attending school with my mother.

I began to feel different to the other children. They called my mother 'Miss' and when they talked about their mums and dads, I realised I had no dad. The word meant a man who lived at home but there was no dad in my house, just my uncle. I did not want other children to know someone was missing from my family. I wanted no attention to be brought upon me so when I said, 'Miss, please may I go to the toilet?', it was said with a shy, quiet voice so no-one noticed a difference between their relationship with the teacher and mine. If I stayed quietly in the shadows, they might also not realise I had no dad.

Not drawing attention to myself came to a soggy humiliating end when my mother had to attend an interview for teacher training college. I had to go into another classroom with another teacher. Miss Evans had silver, white hair that gleamed and made her look beautiful even though she must have been in her late fifties or even sixties when I met her first. She had a lovely Welsh accent that sounded so wonderfully different to the voices of the Black Country that I was used to. She almost sounded like she was singing and always had a twinkle in her eyes as she bent down to speak to me.

I was so painfully shy that I wet myself rather than ask to use the loo. Miss Evans never chastised me or made a fuss but must have signalled to a classroom assistant to help. It was a lesson learned however and I never peed myself again after the embarrassment of making a puddle and crying. Years later when children in my class did this, I always remembered this event and understood their upset totally and with empathy.

The era of being an unqualified teacher at Whitegate came to an end for my mother in July 1969 when the school officially closed. She started to prepare for teacher training college to study for a Certificate of Education so that she could finally become qualified. She would be ten years older than the youths just finishing their 'A' levels and would be classed as a mature student. Mum did not care. She was a single parent to a soon to be six-year-old, with a long-time dream to be a teacher, some experience of teaching under her belt and the world of education finally at her feet.

My mother's world was also changing in other ways. She was now divorced. In late August 1968, just before she had started to work at Whitegate school, Mum read an article in the local chronicle about an RAF man, from the same town that we lived in, who wanted penpals whilst he was posted to Gan in the Maldives. In the 1960s, the RAF had a base there. It was paradise for many, with perfect sunsets, staggeringly beautiful beaches and good RAF camaraderie. However, Colin wanted a family life again after his wife had been unfaithful when he had been posted abroad a few years before. A penpal friendship blossomed between the two, and they hit it off straight away. He returned home briefly in the summer of 1969 which was a momentous occasion when he came to visit us for the first time.

Colin was a small man, claiming to be five feet and two inches but, in truth, he was around just five feet. His hair was golden, bleached by the sun. The white of his short-sleeved cotton shirt exaggerated his bronzed arms and face. When he walked in, I was playing on my 'Little Suzy' sewing machine. He immediately started to play with me, bending down to my level, looking into my eyes with his beautiful brown ones. Both me and my mother were besotted with him from that moment on!

17

A year later Mum started college with a spring in her step, in a long-distance relationship, and with a child finally about to go to school officially. My memories of Mum at college centre around the extremely long hours she put into her studies, holidays searching for items for teaching projects, and me being her model for clothes she made in textiles. She embroidered silver snowflakes onto pockets of a little grey pinafore and made me a red, velvet Christmas dress with white cotton lace on the collar and cuffs. From many visits to the local countryside, a few miles from the Black Country, she made a compendium of wildflower species for her science project. It was no surprise that she came away from college with a distinction after three years.

When she was qualified, Mum taught infant children in a newly built school. She continued to teach, mainly part-time from the 1980s onwards, concentrating on support pupils who had English as an additional language.

✓✓✓✓✓

So, my role models were all strong women, two had been cleaners, one a teacher. Any talk of work by the adults in my life was about cleaning or teaching. I am pretty sure that my life was destined to be spent in a cupboard full of mops, brushes and elbow grease or a classroom full of plasticine, Lego, lesson plans and snot. There was no escape, but which path would I be destined to take?

Chapter 2
A Primary Aficionado

The only problem Mum faced as she gained her place at college was childcare before and after school for me. She pondered this issue for weeks, trying out different scenarios in her head. Nan was too young to retire, and we needed her money anyway. My uncle worked long hours as a carpenter so he couldn't help. Everyone else in the family lived further away.

One day, out of the blue, weeks before she began, Mum was approached by a neighbour, Mrs Burton, the wife of the caretaker at Broomhill Infant and Junior Schools. Mr and Mrs Burton were long established in both schools and in the local community. Mr Burton had taken over as temporary caretaker when my great grandfather had died. A few years later he had secured a permanent job of both buildings. The couple had moved into my great grandparents' house long after my great grandmother had been moved out.

Mrs Burton had longed for a child. After many attempts to try for her own baby, she and her husband adopted a tiny boy. Now her son had grown up and although her maternal instincts had been satisfied over the years, Mrs Burton had always longed to have a little girl. I had known the couple since going to school with my mother.

'I was talking to your mum yesterday, and she was telling me about you starting college soon. I gather you are needing someone to look after Emma?'

My mother nodded.

'Yes, it's looking like I might have to forget the idea. I can't think of anyone to look after her before or after school. It will be an early start and I won't be back until after five each evening.'

'Well, I'm up early as Fred gets the boiler going just after six in the mornings and we are in school until after six at night. I'd love to look after her. That's what I've come to ask. I've talked it over with Fred and he's in agreement. Can I help?'

My mother knew the couple were reliable. Iris Burton refused any payment that Mum offered. It was sorted. Finally, she could relax about childcare. Every morning I would sit in the back living room of the caretaker's house, keeping warm from the old range, with Wendy a little old spaniel by my side, waiting for it to be time to start school. Mrs Burton would fuss over me and bring me toast or biscuits whilst Mr Burton came in for his breakfast after a few hours of being in the school building checking on the radiators and stoking the old coke boiler until it roared with anger at its daily duties.

This couple were comforting and familiar to me. Mrs Burton would always be dressed in a dark coloured jumper and skirt, with a flowery pinafore to cover her clothes. Her tightly permed dark hair would be combed and smart when I was dropped off at seven thirty each morning. Her glasses, with 1950's cat eye shaped frames, completed her outfit. Mr Burton would be wearing navy dungarees with a light-coloured flannel shirt. On his size twelve feet he wore polished black steel toe capped boots. As this giant of a man sat down for breakfast, he would touch his thick black spectacles, through habit rather than a need to adjust them. Those were halcyon days back then and a lovely, calm way to start the school day.

In the afternoons after school, I would hide from the teachers I didn't like until they disappeared. For most staff it was just a few minutes after home time. Others, more dedicated, would spend the next hour or so preparing for the following day's lessons. When the building was quiet, except for me and Mr and Mrs Burton, I would dance in a classroom they had yet to clean, pretending I was a famous ballerina or occasionally a teacher stood at the front of her class, telling some poor child off. I also used to pretend I was Judith Durham, the singer from The Seekers, belting out her songs at full volume.

My gratitude to Mr and Mrs Burton and what they did for me, and my mother will never end even though they are long gone now. I wish I had voiced my love for them back then but didn't. I just hope they know that I thought the world of them and little Wendy with her black velvet ears. Mr and Mrs Burton continued to look after me before and after school until I left primary. I even went on holiday with them once to their little caravan in the countryside. I thought I was in heaven.

When my mother went to college, I finally came to terms with the fact that there *were* other teachers in the world than just her. Some were harsh and nasty to children; others were gentle and kind like Miss Evans had

20

been. My first taste of having a teacher who wasn't my mother was terrifying. How I did not wet myself numerous times I am not sure, but it was the memory of humiliation and embarrassment that drove me onwards to never repeating that experience. I was, after all, a primary aficionado, having already spent nearly four years in school.

Miss Bagshot, my teacher, had a tiny head which seemed to sink into her rather large body. Her crimplene tops and skirts clung to each spare tyre she had. Her glasses made her eyes look tiny. She always looked tired, not helped by her pale complexion and her untidy short curly hair. I am not sure why she wanted to be a teacher apart from the long summer holidays and the status of teaching at the time. She seemed to dislike children and had a passion for making everyone uncomfortable. When I was told she had undertaken emergency teacher training for one year during the Second World War, I wanted to admire the fact she had rallied to the country's cause. Instead, I found myself thinking perhaps she had taught to avoid joining the land army. I truly hated being in her class. There was never any fun or play like there had been in the reception class with my mother. Those days were long gone. Miss Bagshot was strict and nasty with children, so I always tried to keep my nose clean and stay out of trouble.

One day I made a mistake in my writing and with a bit of goading by my best friend, Alison, I went up to the teacher's table to ask to borrow the rubber. The old bat was busy telling off another child for making a spelling error. I leaned forward, and my fingers reached for the rubber so I could get on with my work. Miss Bagshot had some magic sensor in the back of her head as she instantly turned towards me. Without hesitation or question, she banged my fingers onto the wooden desk with such a force that they stung.

'I'll not have thieves in my class, girl! Get back to your desk. How dare you take my rubber. I don't care who your mother is.'

Tears started to drip from my eyes as she began to chastise me for stealing her rubber. Having never stolen anything in my life, not even the rubber, as it hadn't been lifted off the table, I felt an injustice rise within me for me and my mother. She had mentioned her. What did she mean by her last sentence? I knew instantly to stop the tears. This lady did not want them and would criticise me and my mother for them. The sharpness of her voice warned me not to argue or cause a fuss because she would

21

see that as my weakness and use it against me like she did with other children. When I told my mother, later that evening, she comforted me and didn't tell me off for stealing a rubber from the teacher's desk. Later I heard her talking to my nan.

'She is a horrible woman, that Miss Bagshot! I'm not sure why she teaches. She doesn't like children. When I taught in the school you could always hear her shouting. She was forever smacking some poor child. She's a hateful old dragon!'

'If she touches Emma, she'll have me to deal with.'

'Yes, if she touches her again, I swear I'll hit her with a ruler myself! She'll care who I am!'

I guarded this secret, that my mother and grandmother hated my teacher too, in case Miss Bagshot changed her victim type! I was always careful never to call her '*Dragon*' openly but in my mind, she was a huge, green, scaly beast, with a long tongue that breathed fire. Her sharp, pointed claws could reach any child who dropped a pencil, tried to get a rubber off her desk or worst still, got a sum wrong.

I had learned to read a while before being an official pupil. When I was enrolled in the *Dragon*'s class, she insisted that everyone had to learn flashcards before being given a reading book. She scared me to death. The tone in her voice made me shake. I could hear and feel her breathing on my cheek from having to stand close to her when I was called to her table to read my words. Despite my ability to read well, Miss Bagshot refused to move me on to a book. I gave up on reading in school as Enid Blyton had caught my attention rather than reading flashcards with '*Peter*' '*and*' '*Jane*' on them. The final straw was when I supposedly could not read '*Pat the dog*', but I seemed to manage *The Faraway Tree* without any problems at home.

The worst possible lesson with the woman was Physical Education, often shortened and known by its initials, P.E. In *Dragon's* case these letters stood for Public Embarrassment. As there was no gym hall in the school all sports lessons took place outside. Woe betides anyone who forgot their P.E. kit. It was a weekly ritual of humiliation and belittlement when they were forced to do the lesson outside in their underwear. Looking back now it was a form of child abuse which Miss Bagshot revelled in but not a single parent ever complained. If you forgot your kit, if it had not been washed and dried that week, even if there had been a bereavement in the family, she made no exceptions for the Public Embarrassment lesson.

I was relieved to get out of the room, even just for a few minutes, to take the milk crate around to the other classes. When it was my turn to be *Milk Monitor*, I loved the responsibility. However, my hatred of milk, and being forced to drink it against my will, often made me retch at the thought of the cream gathering on the top when the bottles had been left to warm by the cast iron radiator.

During my year in *Dragon's* class, I found myself, along with my classmates and all other pupils at the infant and junior schools in a social experiment that was to rock the very core of both establishments. Although the schools shared separate buildings, the infant children were allowed to play on what was called the junior girls' playground. The older boys played on the junior boys' playground that was separated by a huge brick wall and wire netting on three sides of it to prevent footballs coming over to the infant and girls' playground, over the wall onto the road or into the caretaker's garden that sided on to both playgrounds.

One morning, without any notice of what was happening, a large number of new children appeared. Several double decker buses, full of these pupils, pulled up at the school gates. Chaos reigned as the children walked up the steps and into the front playground. We stared in disbelief. All the bus children were wide-eyed, and none had a smile on their little brown faces. Every single child had black hair. Most looked apprehensive and lost. The local education office, as part of a national experiment, had placed black children into white, working-class schools for an integration trial.

For days all I could hear were the immortal war cries, 'Fight! Fight!' being bellowed by some older boys as they ran onto the playground at break times. Although the girls' playground seemed quieter and safer it wasn't. A huge black Jamaican girl went around the girls' playground looking for fights. She had learning difficulties, by all accounts, and had an incredibly hard time at school. She picked up infant children like they were toy figures and violently tossed them aside after she had punched them a couple of times.

One morning, having caught her eye, she came towards me. I had been playing with my little friends. We all feared her as she roamed the

23

playground for victims. For some reason as she moved in to grab me, like I'd seen her do frequently with other infant children, she changed her mind at the last moment, came up to my face and laughed into my scared eyes. She rocked backwards and forwards, screaming hysterically as a group of children continued to goad her. In that moment she seemed as scared as I was. I ran as fast as I could towards the teacher. With the whistle between her lips, I wished her to blow it to bring playtime to an end. Just as I was within a couple of feet of the lady, the shrill sound filled the playground, and I knew I was safe.

Another incident to happen at this time was that one little girl, Kashmira took a shine to me. She had literally arrived from Kashmir the day before she appeared on the playground. She spoke no English and looked so bewildered that when I looked into her huge, deep brown eyes I felt terrible sadness. The beauty of her pink and green shalwar kameez made me fall in love with the exoticness of this tiny child. She was as shy as I was and we instantly befriended each other, walking around the playground holding hands. She seemed glued to my hip and followed me everywhere, even to the toilet!

On the third day of our budding friendship, for some reason, and without warning, she deliberately scratched my hand. It wasn't an accident but deliberate and to this day, I'll never know what prompted her to do so. The scratch drew blood and stung sharply. Just after it happened, I wandered around the playground on my own crying. The whistle blew and we went back into class. I was still crying; blood was running out of the wound and the teacher demanded I told her what had happened when she saw my hand. I blurted out the story and the instant I did, regretted it as Kashmira was called to Miss Bagshot's table. Without the chance to explain, had she been able to do so as she had no understanding of English, *Dragon* pulled her closer to the desk. The child's hands were turned over. Kashmira's tiny palms were smacked with the ruler two times. She screamed and her sobs were heard for the rest of the morning.

I had lost a new friend. I should never be forgiven. Her own hands were hurting far worse than my scratch which had stopped bleeding by now. My mother was told to take me to the doctor as the child had been in the country for just three days and no-one knew if she had had any injections before entering the UK. I was given a smallpox jab as a precaution. What a welcome to the country this little girl had been given.

24

She was a child, lost in a culture shock, transplanted from her own warring country to England and placed into an assimilation nightmare resulting in two little girls with a friendship lost, three sore hands and one injection.

Within a few weeks the children were gone, returning to their local school a couple of miles away. The social experiment had ended in failure. Later, when I was studying at college, I learned about the policies of multicultural education back in the 1960s and 1970s. I shuddered when the lecturer discussed how black children were bussed into white areas to be assimilated into school communities. My experiences were history; a sad, disgraceful social experiment that I'll never forget.

By the summer term all had settled down again. *Dragon* was worse than ever, shouting at children, smacking them with rulers on their hands or backside. Respite came on sports day, almost at the end of my time in her class. Each year the children from both buildings would be marched in twos, along the road to the local vicarage lawn, half a mile away. The rectangular piece of grass was a lush, vivid green where all the races took place. Enormous, coloured flowers of every variety filled the borders which surrounded the lawn. Pink, orange, yellow and red petals filled every possible space, and the air was filled with a divine floral perfume. It was in stark contrast to the hardness of the grey, concrete playgrounds we usually played in. Chairs had been placed on one side of the lawn for parents and visitors. Children sat opposite, waiting to participate.

The format for the afternoon was well-practised and had been the same for the last twenty odd years. The first event was a fancy-dress parade. It was such a colourful, joyful spectacle seeing children dressed in all sorts of paraphernalia, from the sublime to the ridiculous. In those days most clothes were still made at home so costumes had been lovingly sewn by hand or by use of a Singer sewing machine, keeping mothers in the area up until the early hours making their little darlings costumes to outdo the neighbour's child.

For this, my first occasion officially as a pupil, I wore a blue, shiny kimono brought back from Singapore for me by Colin. I had little cotton ankle socks on and blue flip flops. My hair had been made into a fat bun with knitting needles sticking out at diagonals each side. I had to be careful not to poke someone's eyes out as I turned to speak to my friends. I didn't win the fancy dress competition, nor did I want to. The winner

25

was called up to collect a small prize from the junior headmaster whom I feared.

Then the costumes were practically ripped off by each parent and we were all hastily prepared for *the* event of the whole afternoon, the country dancing. Our dancing outfits, which we had all been wearing underneath our fancy dress, were little green and yellow floral skirts or, for the boys, shorts. All were ancient, probably back to the days of my mother making them in sewing classes in the fourth-year juniors. The costumes were finished off with faded, short sleeved yellow tops. Off we went in our groups of six or eight, depending on which dance we had been assigned to demonstrate. We had practised for weeks. Many years later I'll mention country dancing again, but for now the music of 'Strip the Willow' was played and I danced on the vicarage lawn.

The races were then run, some just for fun but the final sprint events were always taken seriously. Afterwards, each child went up to a table placed nearest to the vicarage kitchen window and was given a drink of orange squash and a little biscuit, baked by the vicar's wife that morning. The whole afternoon was a heavenly distraction from Miss Bagshot. With the summer term coming to an end, I was soon to be leaving her class, bound for the junior school just across the playground from the infant building.

✓✓✓✓✓

The junior school was so different to the infants, with a separate headteacher and teachers who were younger, enthusiastic and seemed to like children. The headmaster, Mr Sutton, was the oldest member of staff and had been my mother's headmaster in the 1940s. She got on well with him back in the days when my great nan and grandad were still caretakers at the school. Mr Sutton was still a tall, very well-dressed man more than two decades later, in his final year at the school before retiring. He wore an immaculate suit, collar and tie, underneath his black cloak. On his dark grey hair sat a black mortarboard, balanced perfectly at just the correct angle.

Whenever he entered the room, the children were trained to rise quietly from their desks without dragging any chairs across the wooden floor. A welcome chant of 'Good Morning Sir' was given as a greeting to him. He listened intently to the salutation, twirling his handlebar moustache between his two thumbs and forefingers, as his eyes scanned the class for any dissidents. He commanded respect and got it in abundance from children and staff. Any foolish child who didn't respect him soon learned the hard way by being caned on the hands or backside in assembly in front of the whole school. In today's world this sounds barbaric but, in those days, back in the early 1970s, the cane ruled and the fear and humiliation of it stopped most children from committing silly misdemeanours. There were always children, mainly boys, who would fall foul of him, trying to get away with something. It was a futile game they played with Mr Sutton. Even in his final year of teaching, after so many years as a headmaster, he missed nothing. There was no mercy for any fool stupid enough to try to pitch their wits against him.

The headmaster's wife was far less loved. She walked around with a great deal of authority and her reign of terror was much to do with the fact that she was married to 'Sir'. She was a tall, slender woman with hair always placed elegantly into a pinned bun down the back of her head. I often wondered what she would look like with her hair down, but she never once broke her dress code. She wore finely knitted jumpers, pleated skirts and glasses from the 1950's with pointed top corners. Pearl earrings adorned her ear lobes, and a particular shade of pink lip stick was always worn on her stern lips. I wish I could report that I liked Mrs Sutton, but I feared her especially when we had to go swimming at the local baths. Beginning swimmers soon learned not to clutch tightly onto the pool side as she would walk along the edge of the baths, wearing her smart, white plimsolls which would crush any fingers she found in her way.

Luckily my first junior teacher was already known to me. Miss Wootton was young, had a passion for imparting information to her pupils, wanting them to do well. Ever since I had known her, she had the same fair complexion, light brown permed hair and blue eyes. She always wore hand knitted cardigans that either she or her mother had made. Sometimes she would wear a floral dress but, more often than not, she wore pleated navy skirts. As a painfully shy child I found her steadiness and calm approach comforting. She could be sharp with people who messed about. She had a quick wit, which was never cruel, but could be cuttingly sarcastic if required. The children respected her, and, within a few weeks of being in her class, we all seemed to start to learn in a way we had not done before with Miss Bagshot.

27

There were spelling, mental arithmetic and times tables tests every week. Miss Wootton quickly realised I could read, and I was given some of the Wide Range Readers which started to offer me more challenge. Gone was my fear to read to the teacher. A month later, Miss Wootton informed my mother that I had a reading age of over ten years old, just weeks after my seventh birthday. I was reading Enid Blyton books at home along with *Milly-Molly-Mandy*, *Pippi Longstocking* and *The Blue Door Theatre Company* series.

Miss Wootton had been an ancient history and classics student at university and her love of history rubbed off on even the die-hard children who disliked school. In her class I started to love learning and finding out about the world around me. I experienced my first ever school television programmes in her class and, to this day, one programme had a profound effect on me. It was about a remote island in the Western Isles called Barra. Little did I know that this programme would spark the beginnings of a passion for living in a rural Scottish community many years later. She continued to work at the school for many years. Later in my story, she will be mentioned again when I became a colleague of my beloved Miss Wootton.

One day, towards the end my first year in the junior school, the classroom door opened, and the headmaster walked in with a few other people that I didn't recognise. One was a lady visitor wearing a flowery blue dress and had grey, short hair. Her spectacles were modern. She looked extremely smart and smiled at everyone as she stood at the front of the class. We had all risen to greet Mr Sutton, but he told us to sit down which was very unusual as we always stood until he exited the room normally. He announced that Mrs James was to be our new headmistress and that she would be the headteacher of both the infant and junior schools. Mr Sutton, his wife Mrs Sutton and Miss Wilson were all retiring. I didn't know what the word meant but gathered from the smiles that the teachers were happy with this arrangement. It was the end of an era when Mr Sutton left. The school felt different immediately. *Goodbye Mr Chips* comes to mind when I reminisce about those times. Gone was his mortarboard, cloak and cane. Mrs James wore flowery dresses, carried a handbag and her weapon of punishment was a large white rubber bottomed plimsoll.

✓✓✓✓

28

When I moved into the second-year junior class, I was fortunate enough to be taught by another amazing teacher. Mrs Brown was a member of the local community as well as being a junior teacher and was very well respected. She was a small woman with bright red, rosy cheeks. Despite her kind, caring attitude to children she was no push over and the more disruptive pupils soon found this out to their cost.

Her lessons ran like clockwork, her class management was systematic and like the rest of the junior staff, she still followed Mr Sutton's orders, testing her pupils' learning every Friday morning. She allowed children to mark each other's tests in mental arithmetic and spelling but would quickly spot any errors when later going over the papers herself. Depending on how well you did in the test you were placed in a certain area of the classroom, given a number that corresponded to your place in class for the new week ahead. So, if you were told to sit in chair number 4 that meant you had come fourth in the tests. For two weeks once I was absent with some childhood illness and I was placed firmly at the front of the room which I hated. I liked to be further back. The system was very academically based, but it had worked for years and suited her classroom management.

After the tests were finished, Friday afternoons would be spent, preparing and cleaning our new desk for the week ahead. Each child would take out their belongings and move them to our new positions. A tin of furniture polish from home together with a polishing duster would be used to polish our desks ready for inspection. The room quickly smelt of bees' wax. When all was done, the last hour of the week was devoted to craft activities with the girls learning to sew and knit. The boys went into another class to learn about woodwork. Girls never had the opportunity to try their hand with saws or nails, nor the boys with cotton or knitting needles.

We still had to rise when the new headmistress entered the classroom and we all smirked when we had to say, 'Good Morning Madam,' until it became more familiar to our lips. Mrs James seemed more interested in the children and was more visible in the school than her predecessor even though she was running both schools now and had an enormous job to start to bring each school up to the present times.

I can't remember when I found out about 'the big school move' but when I heard the news, I accepted that it would be exciting. The old Victorian Broomhill buildings were no longer fit for purpose and the old boiler that Mr Burton stoked every morning at 6 o'clock was starting to be unreliable. The infant building had been ancient, dark and uncomfortable, rather like some of the infant teachers had been and the reception classroom still had a large open fire to warm it through with fire guards all around. The rocking horses in the room had long lost their paint. The furniture across both schools, despite our polishing and Mr and Mrs Burton doing their cleaning each day, was outdated and unfashionable. In the world of the early 1970s nylon and crimplene was popular and plastic furniture was in vogue. The old, wooden single desks in the juniors with dried up ink wells had been there since the school was built in the 1880s. The news was announced that the school was moving, lock, stock and barrel to a new site half a mile away. The children were elated, new staff overjoyed, and the old guard probably shook their heads in disbelief.

It was during the latter part of the school year in 1972 that a long crocodile line of children from the ages of eleven to five, walked in procession down the avenue to the new school, carrying piles of books and boxes. I can't remember how many times we made the journey, but the procession seemed to go on for ever. We walked in warm, dry weather for the most part. As we neared the day when we would vacate the old buildings, the rain started and the excitement of moving seemed to dissipate.

✓✓✓✓✓

After the Easter break, we were in the new establishment. No longer were we part of Broomhill. The name had been changed and we now attended Northwood Primary. I also had a new classroom and a new teacher because Mrs Brown had retired. It was sad to see her go as she had been so kind and such a good teacher. However, the excitement of the new building and, more importantly, the new green playing field felt like freedom after years spent looking at the brick walls and concrete playgrounds of the past. From the later Victorian era to the early 1970s, the playgrounds had seen hundreds of children enjoying their play, arguing, making friends, and lots of grazed knees. They had witnessed P.E. in pants, social experiments, a pram being wheeled through and so many more sights, I am sure. We now had two tarmac playgrounds and a

30

field that had been flattened and grassed months before. It was amazing. It felt as if we were in the countryside. The days of Northwood had begun.

On the downside, the building itself and the classrooms felt confined and small compared with the Victorian rooms and their vaulted ceilings. Often there had been a wooden folding partition that could be moved to create one huge room in which to hold assemblies or to teach many children in one space. At Northwood the rooms were tiny, ceilings so low I felt crushed by the height of them. Only a small storage area to the left and right of each classroom separated the spaces. With curtains replacing interior doors, the noise was horrendous. One wall in each room had glass windows from ceiling to floor and one door to exit or enter. In the past, if a teacher in the junior school had planned a recorder lesson, we would practise without anyone outside of the room hearing much of the din. Now we had to learn to whisper. We no longer sat in rows and columns but were sitting at carefully arranged groups of tables to encourage group interaction. This was hard for all children, even the quiet ones like me. We had always had to work in near silence but were now expected to speak to each other in whispered voices. I always went home with headaches in those first few weeks at the new school.

Everything was plastic or melamine, and nothing smelt of bees' wax polish anymore. There continued to be tests each week, but you stayed in the same seat forever. Exercise books and pencil cases were kept in plastic drawers in a tray storage unit. Little fingers strayed into other people's trays with crayons, pencils, hair bands and bits and bobs starting to go missing. Perhaps people were careless in classrooms that no longer smelt of polish or perhaps the temptation of being so close to other people's property was too much for some children.

'*Time is a healer*' is quoted often when trying to comfort people who have suffered a bereavement. Whilst no one had died, it felt, for a time, that I had suffered a great loss in my life. Mr and Mrs Burton continued to be the caretakers and I got to know the school building well very quickly. The rooms were smaller and my after-hours dancing antics and singing David Cassidy songs at the top of my voice were curtailed to a great extent. Staff seemed to stay longer and the lack of privacy between classrooms because of the lack of doors meant that the time spent waiting for a family member to pick me up seemed endless each day. Mr and Mrs Burton must have sensed this and suggested I started to vacuum. I was

31

almost nine and could be a bit more helpful now. They were both getting older so an extra pair of hands would be useful.

Moving to the new school had brought different challenges for the couple. They no longer swept the wooden floors but had to mop the new art areas that were shared between classes and vacuum all carpeted spaces including all the offices and staffroom. There was a large assembly hall in the middle of the school that doubled as a gym and a dining hall. If you had P.E. in the afternoon you had to watch out for the odd pea or piece of fishfinger that had been missed by the kitchen staff when they swept up the aftermath at the end of each lunch time. Meals were now cooked on school premises and the hour, and a half midday break became an hour. I was devastated as my culinary delight of the Spam, Smash and peas had to be scoffed in extra quick time, on the two days per week I was allowed to go home for lunch. Nan had more time to herself, but I had to run home and back so I could return to play before the afternoon session began. The school was no longer five doors down but a ten-minutes' walk. The consequences of this new building, and the effect it had on me, made me miss the old school and resent the newness of this place.

✓✓✓✓✓

As September came and a new school year began, I was now in the third-year juniors with a male teacher for the first time ever. Mr Merton was in his late twenties, possibly early thirties with black curly hair. There was not one morning when he looked ready to face the class. His chin was stubbly, his tie would be slight too loose, his shirts not ironed. When he lost his temper, which was frequent, his face would look like a tomato in need of a shave. His style of teaching was different to way the ladies of the '50s and '60s had taught me. He had an air of sarcasm which was cutting, and he used a P.E. pump on children who gave him problems. I was fearful of him, if I'm honest.

We started doing comprehension activities. The school had purchased a scheme called 'SRA' where you moved through a system of coloured cards that got progressively harder as you went through the programme. I loved the comprehension cards and was delighted to move to 'Aqua Level' which sounded exotic. I have always been easily pleased! In number work we were taught from a textbook using *Beta Maths*. This was the first time I remembered learning in this way. We moved through the book, completing exercises as we went.

32

Mr Merton liked to end most days by reading a book with chapters for the last half an hour. Some girls sat being hairdressers, plaiting or stroking their friend's hair. Boys prodded one another, pulling faces and tried not to laugh. However, within a couple of minutes everyone settled, listening to his stories. Although I wasn't keen on Mr Merton, he introduced me to a world beyond *The Secret Seven* or *The Famous Five*. Listening to him reading some of the classic children's stories such as *Carrie's War* by Nina Bawden, *Stig of the Dump* by Clive King and *The Hobbit* by J.R.R. Tolkien, set my imagination on fire.

During the year with Mr Merton, I first found out about death. One of my best friends had been ill since we had moved into Mrs Brown's class in the second-year juniors. She had caught the measles and apparently, when the adults were talking and thought I wasn't listening, there had been complications. Once Mrs Brown had asked my mum if she could take me to the hospital to see Lorraine, my little friend. I took a book for her but was only taken into the room for a few brief seconds as she had been tired and asleep. When we had moved up to Mr Merton's class, Lorraine had still not returned to school and whispering adults kept any knowledge of her condition to themselves.

Mrs James slipped into our class. Mr Merton looked straight ahead, never moving his eyes from a fixed position at the back of the classroom. For once his complexion was pale. It must have been decided that Mrs James would come for moral support as it was the teacher who broke the news. His gaze remained fixed as he spoke softly to us, informing the class that Lorraine had passed away. It was a kind way to put it but even I knew that being 'passed away' meant you were dead. I wanted to cry but the tears wouldn't come until later in the day when I could cry privately. Some of the girls did start to sob but I felt if I started, I wouldn't be able to stop. Lorraine would be missed but, she had left the class many months before and was now more of a memory than a real person.

✓✓✓✓

In these final couple of years at junior school, friendships were cemented forever. My closest friend had always been Alison, since we had begun at school together in Miss Bagshot's class. She was a pretty girl, taller than most in our year. Her long dark hair and hazel eyes made her stand out in a crowd. Being allowed to play at her house brought freedom which

I had not experienced before. Alison's family always made me welcome, and I loved to see how other people lived.

If I wasn't playing with Alison or one of my other friends, I could be found in Nan's back garden playing with the dogs or cats giving them rides in the boot of my tricycle. Failing that, I would be playing ball games up the old coal shed wall. My mum was still a single parent at this point. Life was not always easy, and we did not have money to waste, but my childhood memories are filled with long summer days, making perfume from rose petals, wrapping stones in newspaper to play fish and chips shops or lying on a red tartan picnic rug in my play tent, falling asleep in the heat of the afternoon sun.

If it was a rainy day, I would be inside playing 45s on my mother's record player that was in our bedroom, jumping on the bed and singing at the top of my voice, 'How can I be sure?' or 'Cherish' as David Cassidy blared away in the background. Note it was never Donny Osmond although I did secretly have a copy of 'Puppy Love'!

On moving into the final year at primary school, my teacher was Mr Green. He was a wonderful man, coming towards the end of his teaching days but who had a knack for giving his pupils enthusiasm for learning. Mr Green looked smart. His dark grey hair was carefully trimmed, not to long nor too short. He was always clean shaven and wore the same green-brown tweed jacket which had leather patches on the elbows. His crisply ironed, bright white shirt and collar sparked each morning. He was strict but had every child's respect, even those who disliked school. He never hit a child in my presence and rarely raised his voice.

My handwriting was terrible, and I think it was the constant bane of Mr Green's life, as he was always talking about it, urging me to improve. I could not, for the life of me, get to grips with the cursive handwriting that I had been practising since Miss Wootton's class. I hated it with a passion. The style stifled the flow of my writing and I got frustrated as I could not make it look neater. I felt a failure.

Our trip that year was to a living history museum near Bromsgrove. As a child, I had been lucky enough, since my mother had started seeing Colin, to visit stately homes, castles and any old buildings around the Midlands when he was stationed back in England after his time abroad. I loved history and when we heard that we were going to see some old building, my classmates groaned loudly but my heart was quietly singing.

34

That visit had such a profound effect on me and made me realise the importance of school trips. Some children, like myself, experienced these places every weekend, whilst for others it was unusual and an alien environment. Most children were almost certainly bored to tears, but I loved every single part of the visit. Parents evening took place a couple of weeks later and Mr Green mentioned the trip to my mum and Colin.

'Emma seemed enchanted by the place. She was like a different child. I have never heard her talk so much. She was the only one who appreciated why she was there.'

My mother told him that I had not stopped talking about the place and, as a family, we had visited the museum the weekend before parents evening. After many years and many visits later, I can still visualise the moment; a ten-year-old child walking into what was essentially the roof space of a grade two listed, fourteenth century hall. I stood staring at the exquisite carvings. The idea of those vaulted wooden beams, being seen by people who lived so many centuries before, thrilled me. I gasped and Mr Green had heard my reaction. What a teaching moment for him.

In his class I excelled at sport and was picked for netball and rounders teams to represent the school. One day it was announced that a house system was being introduced. We were informed that there were going to be captains and vice captains for girls' and boys' teams. I had never wanted to stand out from the crowd. I was shy and introvert, so I was absolutely shocked to learn that I was a girls' captain. Alison was also a house captain. I reeled at this news. This was my first time as a leader. I liked it!

The power, almost certainly, went to my head. My days were filled with dreaming up who would be good in our team for the inter-house netball competition. I can remember lots of bickering and lots of younger children sucking up to me because I was the girls' captain. I suddenly seemed to make lots of new younger friends who offered me their morning snack and even money to get into the team, if memory serves me correctly. I can't remember if we ever won a match, but we should have scored lots of points for arguing.

On one occasion I was chosen as the only child to represent the school in an athletics competition. My rapid rise to fame as a runner in school lasted all of thirty seconds. I was the fastest female sprinter in my little school but against girls bigger than myself, I failed miserably. As many

35

girls do when they are on the cusp of puberty, my enthusiasm for sport dwindled and, by the time I moved to secondary, I started to hate participating in P.E.

✓✓✓✓

Just after Christmas in late 1973 my great grandmother died. One of the role models in my life was gone. It felt like the end of an era. She had been born when Queen Victoria was on the throne and had been brought up with such delicate manners and attitude to life. The rock of the family, she had never seemed to flap or get anxious about anything. Even when there had been a chimney fire and I had been left in her care, in her late seventies she had managed to get help and keep us both safe. Having left the Midlands years before with her youngest child, my great uncle and his family, we were used to her visiting in holidays and staying at my nan's house. I loved to see her, and cherished time spent listening to her stories about the past. We travelled down to Northampton for her funeral and, on the way back home, there was an almighty storm with torrential rain. It felt as if the world was weeping at her death.

We moved house when Mum married Colin in February 1974, just a few weeks after my great grandmother's death. I caught a bus in the mornings to Mr and Mrs Burton's house, no longer having much time to knit or sew. There were just a few brief minutes now each weekday morning. The move meant that I was going to a secondary school away from Alison and my other friends. A visit one afternoon to my new school made me fearful for the future. It seemed terribly grey. There were grey walls, grey floors and even a grey/silver stripe in the tie we were going to have to wear. Nowadays children often have transition to high school commencing in the last couple of years of primary. A whole week of transition is usually organised towards the end of the final summer term for year six or primary seven leavers.

Alison remains my oldest friend and we have kept in touch over the years. In 1977, we spent part of the summer on a family caravan holiday in Rhyl and were together when a newsreader announced on the radio that Elvis was dead. We did meet again at sixth form for around a year, but her life was about to take a different path. She became a model, photographed by Lord Lichfield and moved to London where she still lives. Her friendship has always been special. We give each other space but know we are there for each other when needed.

Chapter 3
Stop the World, I Want To Be Debbie Harry!

The initial few weeks at comprehensive were exhausting. Firstly, there were teenagers everywhere. Northwood had been a school of just over two hundred pupils with no uniforms, a lack of sensible shoes and a world full of crimplene and handmade jumpers. Now there were one thousand, two hundred youths, many of whom were going through puberty with spots and little deodorant sprayed on their sweaty adolescent bodies. All girls were supposed to look the same in their white blouses and navy skirts and jumpers. The boys wore white shirts, black trousers and navy sweaters too. Girls never wore trousers, at least not in the early days of being at high school. The boys took great pleasure in looking up the girls' skirts as we climbed up and down the flights of stairs.

Uniform is supposed to make pupils feel part of a pack and to stop discrimination in terms of family finances. For the most part I have always been in favour of uniform but, at Woodfield High School, it did not strike me as being anything about equality. It was easy to spot the kids who had hand-me-downs, the kids whose parents had no twin tub, the kids who looked like they had been dragged through a hedge backwards. No-one at my secondary school had uniform from Marks and Spencer. If your family did have any cash, you were kitted out at the uniform shop a couple of miles from the school.

All of us had to wear a navy and silver striped tie. Everyone seemed to wear them in a different style. First years always looked smart, well at the beginning of the first term anyway. By the fourth year it was fashionable to wear 'kipper' tie style and have the knot as low down to your tummy button as physically possible. I hated wearing a tie for two reasons. By lunch time my tie tightened its grip around my neck like a boa constrictor and I could hardly breathe. The second reason was because of the games older pupils would play. They would flick the tie of any first year they happened to meet with such force that if a victim was unlucky, and tried to dive out of the way, he or she often got hit in the face if the *Flicker* caught them on the nose or mouth. I had also seen some older boys trying to strangle each other in rough play. I hated my tie and dreaded the older kids as they came towards me in a tightly packed corridor. This was where *Flickers* targeted first years mostly. 'Flicky first year!' could be heard as victims were picked out. If someone cried, told a teacher or tried to fight back they were selected even more. Trying to stay in the shadows as much as possible, causing no fuss was the best strategy by far.

The other ritual, which happened in the autumn term each year to first year pupils, was to grab hold of a youngster whilst they were in the toilets. Pushing a head down the toilet pan caused great amusement. Most times it was boys who would turn up in class with wet hair, shirt and jumper but very occasionally a rougher girl gang would hang around in the girls' toilets waiting for their prey. I avoided these girls too by lying low, latching onto someone so I wasn't alone. There was far less risk if you were in a pair or trio of being targeted by any gang.

Those initial weeks and months in the first year were unhappy. I was making friends, but I still felt alone and very vulnerable. At around that time, in the autumn of 1974, Eddie Holman re-released a record which was played constantly across the radio waves. I felt 'Hey there, Lonely Girl' was my tune.

✓✓✓✓✓

The comprehensive school dated back to around 1958 although it had existed on a previous site, just down the road, as a smaller secondary modern before that time. Some of the older staff had taught in the original building. Just a year or two before I started at high school, a group of younger teachers fresh from teaching training college had arrived, breathing new life into the place.

The school served several housing estates over a radius of a few miles. The catchment area varied hugely. A few children came from a new, modern estate with privately owned properties. However, most pupils lived on a large council estate, that over many years, had been nicknamed locally as '*The Maze*' due to the inability of visitors to find their way out once they had ventured into it. Back in the mid and late 1970s, the estate was known for several petty criminals who were neighbours to the hard-working families living beside them. A few pupils lived on the edge of the estate in high rise council flats. These kids were the athletes of the school due to the fact the lifts were always breaking down. It could have been a real melting pot to put children from the fancy new estate together with Maze youngsters but somehow it worked. All children were white;

38

no black or Asian families would have survived in the area. Local pubs were breeding grounds for the National Front.

There was a main teaching block which had four floors. Other original buildings were separate to the main one, connected by a small open walkway. There was a block that had offices and the assembly hall that doubled as a school canteen at lunch time. If you had a lesson in the hall which occasionally was timetabled, you were always distracted by the smell of cooking, the sound of pots banging or the cook playing her radio too loudly. A science block had been added together with one for craft, design and technology. Two more teaching blocks made up the site.

All the buildings at Woodfield stood at the end of a long driveway. Twice per day the journey was made to or from the school. To an eleven-year-old who was often numb with cold and frequently wet from numerous downpours, the driveway seemed to grow longer each day. There was a footpath on one side of it and on the opposite side was a huge playing field that in the autumn and winter months was waterlogged often. On the other side of the boundary fence was wasteland, supposedly full of mine shafts that also flooded. Years later houses were built on the wasteland, and I never quite understood where the water disappeared to or the mine shafts for that matter. Opposite this expanse of water was a public house that was always the talking point amongst the older teenagers in school and many bragged they had had a drink in '*Shippies*'.

The school had a playground area towards the back of the site where everyone would congregate for break and lunch times. The boys always played football on the tarmacked area whilst the girls gathered nearer the buildings leaning against walls to give their feet a rest from their platform heels.

It was at the back of the school, behind the playground, that pupils would wriggle through the metal fencing and vanish over to '*The Sana*' when they had enough of school. It was the site of an old sanatorium and a place kids could go to have a smoke and probably sex, given the number of underage pregnancies the school had back then. The area even had a mother and baby unit a couple of miles away for girls who could no longer attend school because they had babies and couldn't or did not want to attend their old school again after the birth of their child.

In charge of us all was Miss Wylde, the headmistress, who was a small lady in her late fifties/early sixties with silver, white hair. She always wore smart floral-patterned clothes when I ever saw her. Whilst she was a quiet woman her presence was felt throughout the school and when she occasionally walked into a lesson, there was instant respect for her. She had an unfortunate nickname due to the fact she had a false eye. Many of the pupils called her '*Cock eye*', but I never did. I felt it was an unfair name as she had a twinkle in her eyes that made her seem kind and approachable.

Once a year she would go through every single report book and sign her name neatly on the designated line. I often wondered how she kept her writing so neat. Signing her name one thousand, two hundred times was no mean feat. For a couple of years, she wrote a line or two of encouragement on my report which made me feel special and proud. I am pretty sure she would never have known who I was, but it was lovely to get a message from her in my report book.

Along with the two deputy headteachers she ruled Woodfield with a firm hand. One deputy dealt with pastoral issues whilst the other deputy spent his time creating timetables and was rarely seen except in special assemblies such as prize giving. Looking back, he must have done an excellent job as everybody knew what classroom they were to go to, at which lesson time and with which teacher.

Woodfield was organised into a house system with eight houses or teams which were named after local firms. The area, at the time, was heavy with manufacturing industries and the names were homage to firms whose history was linked to the heritage of the region. When Queen Victoria travelled through the area of the Black Country as a young princess at the age of thirteen, in her diary she described the area as, '*The men, women (sic), children, country and houses are all black.*' Nothing much had changed if you looked at some of the kids at school!

Each house had a house master or mistress, and I was lucky enough to have a complete legend of a man who had taught in the area since qualifying as a teacher many years before. He had been one of the teachers who had moved from the old secondary modern school to the comprehensive. He was nearing retirement Short in stature, he wore a grey suit, collar and tie. He should have looked smart but somehow, he was always covered in ash. As soon as the bell went for break or lunch he

40

would go to his office, shut the door and have a cigarette or two. He must have got through a fair few fags per day. If you knocked on his door, he would shout for you to enter and as you did, you would see him lower his legs off his desk and sit up straight. His room was full of nub ends and smoke. He also had a penchant for humbugs which I think he sucked to get rid of the nicotine smell on his breath in class. His humbug habit failed in making his breath smell sweeter and his nicotine fingers gave the game away completely as did the ash. Pupils, years before, had given him an endearing nickname which every generation of children called him '*Nasher*'.

Nasher took his status as legend to a whole new level one day, after having a fag or two in his house master's office. The story that went around afterwards lingered, and to this day I don't know if it was true or not, that he threw his latest nub into the wicker waste basket and went off to teach a maths lesson. Within ten minutes the whole school had been evacuated from the building, many having to come down a staircase right opposite his office. Smoke billowed out of his room, up the stairs and down the corridor of the main school block. I was on the top floor so had three flights of stairs to navigate as I and half of the pupils piled down the concrete steps, rushing to safety, yet heading further into smoke as the fire alarm rang loudly. We reached the second floor and were diverted through classrooms to the other staircase on the opposite side of the building. As I reached the bottom of the stairs and looked back along the long corridor towards his office the smoke was thick and black. We raced onto the school playing field, where teachers were hurriedly taking registers to establish if everyone was safely accounted for. Luckily one thousand, two hundred pupils and over a hundred staff were safe, apart from a few who were coughing as their lungs took in the fresh air. I think, after that, Nasher smoked outside, probably behind the metal bike shed where all the teenage smokers hung out.

A couple of years later there was another fire at Woodfield. This time, when the fire alarm went off, I was in the middle of a science lesson in one of the smaller classroom blocks that had just one storey. The teacher left the class, telling us he would go and find out if we had to evacuate our classroom. When he returned, he found an empty room. We had all run out of the building to the assembly point as soon as he had left us alone. This time some curtains in the main hall had caught fire. The cause was a couple of young culprits who had tried to find a secret place to have a cigarette. Nasher was not responsible that day!

✓✓✓✓✓

I remember those first few months at Woodfield for several reasons. Times were unnerving. I made friends during the school day, but home time proved to be a painful experience. Occasionally I would have someone to walk home with but for the first term and a half I often had to walk home on my own, down the winding drive and then up a steep hill and across town to get home. The walk, if a dawdle, would take around half an hour but on my own, I had to walk quickly and did the journey in fifteen minutes. The reason behind my sprints home, hopelessly out of breath and with aching legs was a shock to me. I was always followed by two girls who scared me. The first time it happened, I was totally unprepared, and I was left panic stricken afterwards. The girls were a year older and had been walking home behind me, when they started to laugh. One prodded me in the back and being naïve I turned around, thinking it was a friend. They just jeered and flicked my hair and tie, before walking passed me. The next time they saw me on my own they came up so close behind me that I could feel their breath on my neck. They didn't touch me but just laughed. That was it then. Each time they saw me they would come up behind, intimidating, laughing and frightening me until I genuinely felt that I would be physically hurt.

Back in 1974 the school was immensely tough. There were always fights happening in the playground, even before school sometimes and it could be boys or girls arguing. The girls were very rough fighters and would try to scalp each other, tugging hair or grabbing clothes. On one occasion a girl's underwear was exposed when another girl grabbed the blouse she was wearing and it ripped, showing her enemy's bra. The boys jeered and whistled until a teacher or two stepped in, parting the fighters. If the boys started fighting, they would turn into Bruce Lee trying to strangle each other with their ties, kicking and punching until blood was drawn by one or both assailants.

When the two bullies intimidated me, I was worried about getting into a fight more than anything. I was a shy eleven-year-old girl who wouldn't say boo to a goose. I could not handle a fight. So, my other choice was to run home. As soon as the bell would go, I would hare down the stairs and try to be one of the first kids up the drive. My lungs were bursting but I

42

had to keep going and it was only the stitch that would stop me. I ran up the hill, past three pubs, a primary school and a supermarket, over a level crossing and a few yards further to my house. If I made it to the first pub, I knew I was safe as neither girl had ever been seen running.

This journey home went on day after day until I had made strong friendships. My strategies changed to either dawdling at school, long after the bullies had gone or that I would walk most of the way with one of my mates, knowing I would be safe. I never told a soul about my daily fear and thankfully the bullies stopped following me after a while.

Another reason for feeling unnerved was that just a few weeks after starting at Woodfield, our world in the Midlands was turned upside down by the IRA pub bombings in Birmingham city centre. The tragedy was splashed over the local and national newspapers and television. Local Irish families went into hiding for fear of retaliation as the police hunted the bombers. The troubles in Northern Ireland felt more real now that bombings had happened so close to home, and we feared going anywhere in crowds for months after.

My other feeling of being unnerved was that I was no longer to be '*an only one*'. My mother was expecting her second child. The news was broken, out of the blue, at a fancy hotel, when I thought we were going for Sunday lunch. After a few shocked minutes, contemplating the age gap of almost eleven- and three-quarter years, I was delighted!

✓✓✓✓✓

One of the main problems with moving to high school from a small primary is the vastness of a school site when you are a first year and to find your way around to classes on time. From Northwood, where I had known every inch of the building, to a place that had several different teaching blocks, it was hard to navigate through all the corridors, full of teenagers and teachers.

Getting used to all the staff and learning their ways of organising their classes was also a challenge at first. Gone was the warmth of the primary school staff who taught every lesson, day in and day out, until you moved up to a new class the next September. I missed the familiarity of teachers but started to appreciate and enjoy having different ones throughout a school day and the in-depth knowledge they had of their subject.

My favourite subject at high school was mathematics. The head of department, Mr Evans, was an older, very experienced teacher who loved his subject. I shall never be able to thank him enough for what he gave me in his lessons. When I became a teacher years later, I found I loved teaching maths more than anything and I know that Mr Evans played a massive part in my passion for this subject. I realise that I am lucky. No matter what school I have taught in I have found children who hated maths. In many cases this feeling has been passed down to them from parents who have inadvertently spoken of their own fears about maths in front of their children. Having a teacher who has a passion for a subject makes such a difference. Mr Evans was my maths teacher for just two years, but I shall never forget him.

Later, my maths teacher was a lady by the name of Miss Lea. Her teaching style was less 'talk and chalk' and we always seemed to be working from textbooks rather than working through problems with her. No one had a choice of seating. Pupils were sat in rows according to reports she had heard about behaviour. Despite this being the top set for maths some lads did enjoy a little banter in the class, and she wanted them in her direct eye line. She placed me behind a cupboard. To see her demonstrate any work on the blackboard, should she ever do so, I had to lean right across the desk next to me. Luckily, I had been placed next to one of my friends Ann, so I could occasionally have the luxury of leaning right next to her to see Miss Lea. I knew why I had been placed behind the cupboard as she made it clear in the first lesson that she only trusted well behaved pupils to be out of her sightline.

It was true; I was very well behaved. What she didn't know was that I was football crazy. The Football Association had moved their live draws for cup matches to the exact time of being in a maths lesson. The football fans in the set were devastated until I turned up one day wearing my new birthday present, a watch radio. I kept my gift a secret until it was time to listen to the FA cup draw. Nervously I turned my watch on, hoping against hope that the sound would be inaudible to anyone except myself. The teacher could not see me as I lay my head onto my hand and wrist, appearing to everyone that I was deep in concentration with the maths exercise we had been set. I listed all the draws on a scrap of paper, half hidden by my exercise book. When the programme had finished, I leaned back in my chair, making sure I was still out of sight and whispered a draw result to the lad behind me. The next draw I read to Ann on my right. Slowly, and at first in almost silence, the messages got around to the rest of the class. Occasionally the noise would become a little louder if there was a particular juicy draw or one that involved a local team that could prove tricky. The teacher would roar at anyone who got too loud but overall, the plan worked well. This ruse continued every time there was a FA cup draw for two years. I learned from experience never to let a child sit behind a cupboard…ever!

I did well in most lessons and managed to work hard to be placed in all the top sets from an early age at high school. One of my favourite lessons was English. Over the years I had several English teachers, all of whom were excellent and full of enthusiasm for teaching. My favourite of them was the one I had in the fourth and fifth year, who was also head of English. Mr Rowe was a gentleman at the end of his career but as sharp as a pin in both the way he taught and in his discipline. He tolerated no nonsense and was a hard task master, but his lessons were so interesting that he rarely had to raise his voice. One day when I was around fifteen, Mr Rowe announced that we would be studying some First World War poems. Most of the class groaned inwardly and outwardly, and if I'm honest, I probably did also. So away from the comfort of familiar texts we went but our teacher knew what he was doing. He was a fine, principled man who gave us all something more than English lessons in those few weeks. He captured, motivated and inspired us and the class went silent. We were all in awe of those young lads not far from our own ages. Many of them lay dead in the mud of a foreign field days or months after writing their verses and baring their souls with such beautiful yet shocking words.

From the initial lessons in the first year to my last lesson in the fifth year, bar just one year with another teacher, I was taught French by an extraordinary lady who I adored and respected. There was something about Miss Gainsford I cannot explain other than she was extremely personable with a great sense of humour, and an excellent teacher. Her results were outstanding for a high school in a deprived area of the West Midlands. Many of the children had never been on holiday in England let alone to France so it was purely down to her teaching that her students learned French so well. This plain-speaking Yorkshire lass became a massive influence on my decision to become a teacher as she believed in the ramshackle group of kids in front of her, no matter what our backgrounds were.

For the third year I had another French teacher Mrs Mortimer who proved to be lots of fun even though she was strict in class. All the boys loved her as she was a good-looking young lady with long dark hair and gorgeous brown eyes. Despite the fact she was recently married, it was amusing to see her young fans suddenly develop an interest in French. She followed in her colleague's footsteps and was an excellent teacher also. One lesson in her class brings back a memory of her coping in difficult circumstances, something that will resonate with all teachers at some point in their careers. Lessons can be well planned, well-resourced and well taught but if something unexpected happens within a lesson it is the way a teacher copes that can make or break a situation.

It was an ordinary French lesson, nothing particularly special. The teacher had set some exercise for her class to complete so the room was quiet. Everyone was concentrating on what they needed to be doing. Suddenly a scream pierced the silence, followed by a strange laugher that filled the room. I can remember looking towards the direction of where the noises had come from, a couple of rows in front of me, and I was shocked they had been made by the school heart throb, Kenny Middleton. I had known the lad from the first day at school as he was in my tutor group as well as most lessons. He had striking good looks with a mop of blonde, curly hair. There was a sexuality about him which other boys did not possess as his voice had broken and the stubble on his chin and above his upper lip made him less boy and more of a man. My friend had a crush on him as did half of the school. I wouldn't have been surprised if some of the younger female teachers fancied him too. He was a third year but was rumoured to be 'going out' with a girl much older than himself.

As he continued to make a strange laughing noise, Kenny stood up for an instant, then without warning, collapsed onto the floor. His body began to shake, and I could see froth coming from his mouth. He was having a fit. We all sat in silence as Mrs Mortimer leapt forward to help the boy, calling a child to get the teacher next door and someone else to go to the main office for an ambulance. Miss Gainsford rushed in. Together they made sure the boy was made comfortable and didn't swallow his tongue. In those days using a ruler was acceptable practice and so a ruler was quickly found to place in the boy's mouth. They also

46

tried to calm us all down. Some girls wept quietly and the boys who had played football at break with the lad, looked on in shock. In what felt like hours but was in fact just a few minutes ambulance personnel entered the room and when appropriate sat the boy in a stretcher chair.

Both ladies looked drained as they spoke to us after the commotion was over. They calmed us down and allowed us to talk about what we had witnessed. We found out later that the boy had been too embarrassed to tell anyone about his recently diagnosed epilepsy. Rumours went around as to whether his parents had spoken to school staff but looking at these poor women no one had told either that they were teaching a youth who had fits because he refused to take his medication. Many years later, Kenny Middleton, the school heart throb and I would cross paths again, but that story is for later in my tales.

Another of my favourite teachers was a six feet four inches tall Welsh man who delivered his history lessons in a sing-song Welsh accent. Mr Griffiths was a no-nonsense teacher who soon had each class under control thanks to his physical presence but also his excellent behaviour management skills. He insisted that pupils were silent when he was speaking, and that the classroom was peaceful when we were given tasks to complete. I loved his classes and thrived on learning about the Picts, Jutes and Anglo-Saxons through to the Corn Laws in the Industrial Revolution during the four years I spent in his classes. I had a nickname for him at home which still stands today for some reason. I cannot remember why I called him '*Big Daddy*'. It was at the time when *The World of Wrestling*, as part of the *World of Sport* programme hosted by Dickie Davies, was on television on Saturday afternoons. A popular wrestler called '*Big Daddy*' was always the hero in his wresting bouts. His real name was Shirley Crabtree, but his wrestling name became very popular with his fans. My teacher looked nothing like Shirley Crabtree, but the nickname stuck, and I always had to be careful not to refer to Mr Griffiths as '*Big Daddy*' to my friends or the teacher.

One lesson I hated at high school was P.E. At primary school I had loved all sports. There was something about P.E. at secondary level that I despised. Maybe it was the fact I was going through puberty and embarrassed about doing P.E. despite being in a class full of girls. At the time I put my hatred entirely down to the fact of having to participate in a weekly communal shower routine that I dreaded. Even my mother had not seen me naked since I had been in the upper junior classes and now, I was expected to take all my clothes off and share a shower with girls that I 'barely' knew!

It really was too much for a quiet, shy girl who was prepubescent. Stories also went around amongst the girls that the boys had bragged about having a spy hole through to the changing rooms. It was all untrue but when a such a story is shared by young, impressionable girls, hysteria soon takes over from rational thoughts. I vowed to get out of having a shower for as many times as I could during those early weeks and months in the first year. My mother would write a note for me when I asked, and I was delighted when I had a monthly excuse and then a verruca. The damage was already done by then and I continued to hate P.E. for all my time at secondary school.

✓✓✓✓✓

One Sunday morning after what seemed to be hours and hours, we welcomed into the world my younger brother. I had so wanted a sister but after being called up to my mother's bedroom along with my nan, the midwife, my mother, and Colin looked at me as it was announced I had a brother. I had joked that I would put a baby boy in the dustbin as I was desperate for another girl in the family. On seeing this little baby boy with his eyes wide open, I said he could stay. It was a good job as he wasn't going back! Paul lifted his head up to look at me as I stared at this little human being. There was no way I could do anything but love him.

Colin was rather distracted for the few days that he had to look after us all whilst my mother remained incapacitated with the new-born member of the family. On the day after my brother had been born, I was in a maths lesson when a pupil knocked on the classroom door and entered the room. The teacher read out the message that the child had brought in. I was shocked when she called my name, and I was to take my packed lunch to the school office. I had never been called to the office before and I panicked that something was the matter with my mother or my brother. I ran down all the flights of stairs as quickly as I could and arrived at the office out of breath. I knocked on the door and burst in as soon as I heard the command to enter. I explained who I was, and the secretary smiled.

'Your stepfather's phoned. He's found out that he gave you some boiled ham that had been in the fridge for a few days. Apparently, it's green! Don't eat it as he's bringing some more sandwiches for you. Put your lunch in this bin.'

I am not sure if I should have heard the secretary's comment to her colleague as I left the room.

'That's the second father today who is in trouble with his wife because of a new-born baby. More rotten sandwiches!'

I closed the door and just in front of me was another young pupil approaching the office with a packet of sandwiches in his hand. He looked pale.

'Don't worry. Your father's tried to poison you!' I said as I passed him.

As time went on at school my friendships grew stronger. I had several friends. Ann who I have already mentioned was the girl whom I sat next to in Maths lessons and in my tutor group. My other friends, all from the same group were Dee, Mel and Dev.

Dee, aka, Denise was my closest friend at school, and we got up to all sorts of adventures. She loved styling her hair with the same flicks as Farah Fawcett, from *Charlie's Angels*. She was in love with Les McKeown, the lead singer from the Bay City Rollers so she went through a period of wearing trousers with tartan trims that were just a little too short for her like her idol's when we were out of school. She also loved Kenny Middleton on the quiet!

Mel would talk endlessly about her love for Pink Floyd and many of the older bands. Being the baby to three much older brothers, her love for music was far more mature than the rest of us. I swear that I had not heard of most of the bands she raved about.

Dev, short for Devina had a bubbly personality. She loved football and adored Kevin Keegan even more. When we got the chance to go to Wembley to see England play, we all gathered at my house to make a banner for the occasion. Not only did Dev love Kevin, but the three remaining members of our group were also rather taken with him and Trevor Francis, who at the time played for a local team, Birmingham City before becoming the first millionaire footballer when he transferred to Nottingham Forest. We spent the entire afternoon perfecting the slogan until it was right, *'Dee, Mel, Em and Dev, All Love Trev and Kev!'* When we got to Wembley and displayed the banner, it was only up for seconds before all the fans behind us complained that we needed to take it down as it was blocking their view higher up in the stands!

Being a teenage, there was usually some form of angst in the air. Often, it was about unrequited love for a pop or TV star. In my case I fell deeply 'in love' with a disco sensation. In 1977 the only name on anyone's lips was John Travolta. When the film *Saturday Night Fever* came out it was classified in cinemas as an 'X' category due to very strong language and sexual content. We were devastated. The music was blaring out constantly on Radio 1 and local radio stations, but we were too young to see the film. It was quite a surprise when one day Dee announced a plan for eight of us girls to sneak into the cinema. Her science teacher, a lady just a couple of years out of college, had suggested a plan after some of the girls in her science class had been overheard talking about the film they couldn't see. The teacher said she would accompany us under the guise of us all being over the age of eighteen. I was shocked at first at the plan and was worried we would get into trouble. After pleading with me and Dee explained the plan further, I too became convinced, that we might get away with watching the film.

We turned up outside the cinema, Dee, Mel, Dev, Ann, me and three other girls, all made up, all wearing platform shoes except the teacher who was so petite she looked much younger and much smaller than ourselves. The air reeked of cheap perfume and cherry flavoured lipstick. Somehow, we managed to get into the cinema with the smallest girl pushed to the front to pay for the tickets. When one of the group referred to her as 'Miss' we all coughed loudly to hide the mistake in case anyone heard. The lights went low, the film started, and the familiar music began to blast out of the speakers. There was John Travolta and we all swooned as he swaggered down the street. Eight teenagers, most under the age of fifteen, and one young teacher aged twenty-three, all fell in love that night.

✓✓✓✓✓

Teachers came and went but generally the staff at the secondary school were an excellent bunch, a mixture of teachers towards the end of their careers who had taught since the forties and a group of young teachers who brought life into the school and a lot of enthusiasm. The eclectic mix

50

worked and in general, for me, a shy child who loved school and wanted to do well, I thrived, and my results went from strength to strength.

One shocking incident happened in the latter half of my time at the school. We started the academic year with a form teacher who was a new member of staff. When we walked into the room as the bell went at the start of the school day, there stood a young teacher with light brown, curly, shoulder length hair with tight black corduroy trousers and a wine-coloured velvet jacket. He was the first male teacher I had ever seen not to wear a tie. He looked like a *Rock God* and naturally all the teenage girls, including myself swooned at him, falling in love instantly. He could have been Robert Plant's younger brother. The boys in the class were all in awe of his stylish fashion sense. These were the days of flared trousers, platform shoes and small leather bomber jackets. He took the register and just as he had finished the bell went for the first lesson. None of us wanted to leave the room as we were all thinking of the year of fun, we would have with our new form teacher.

The next morning the tutor group lined up ready to enter the classroom to swoon or stare at this guy, his fashion style and his bottom. The bell went and we waited for the door to open in anticipation, pushing to get a glimpse of *Mr Rock God* again. Instead, we were greeted by my French teacher, Miss Gainsford and one of the craft teachers. Register was taken despite lots of whispers going around the room until finally a lad put his hand up and asked where the new form teacher was.

'He left,' was the short response.

We all stared at each other; mouths wide open at the thought that Robert Plant's younger brother had left after one day. Gossip went around that he had been forced to leave on the first day when it was found out he had no teacher qualifications. Gone were the days of unqualified teachers. *Mr Rock God* must have told a few lies in his application and interview. He was never seen again … sadly!

Teenage hormones began to kick in and amongst our year of girls the love angst turned to boys at the school. One girl had an eternity ring given to her by one of the lads. She was the centre of attention for days as it made her stand out from the crowd. I often wonder what happened to the couple, but I do know that they got married a few years later, not long after leaving school.

Some girls were in love with the John Travolta of our school discos, the lad who had collapsed in an epileptic fit a year or so earlier. Now that he was on medication and his secret was out, Kenny was back to being the school's heart throb. The first time that he turned up in a white suit, black shirt, white waistcoat and shiny black shoes everyone in the room, kids and teachers alike were stopped in their tracks. All eyes were on him as he took to the dance floor, brimming with confidence and oozing charisma. As 'Night Fever' played, his body moved in perfect rhythm to the music and he seemed lost in his own fantasy, captivating every single person who watched him that evening. For now, he was our John Travolta. In less than a year he would be a punk!

The journey to adulthood led some teenagers down a different pathway in life. Whilst no-one ever seemed to comment or question the boys and their sexual encounters, for the girls who went along this pathway there was only one outcome. Some girls saw it as a natural step their own mothers had taken whilst others were as green as green and had not worked out what had happened to them until it was too late. The first girl in my tutor group was thirteen when she became pregnant. At fourteen she had her baby and a while later returned to school on the first day back after the summer holiday, but it was immediately obvious she was no longer a school pupil but a woman with a child and we never saw her again in school. In total we had five pregnancies with four babies born and one termination in my tutor group. None of my friends fell to this fate. Apart from a couple of lessons at primary school and one memorable high school 'Design for Living' lesson in which a condom was produced and talked about, I am sure most of these girls were as clueless about pregnancy as I was. Our tutor group became notorious for being the 'pregnancy class'. As soon as one girl disappeared, another one's tummy started to expand, and the gossip would grow just as the tiny embryo inside her grew too.

My bedroom was my sanctuary, music was my life. My radio and record player were my most treasured possessions. I was obsessed with listening to the charts and watching *Top of the Pops*. My own collection of records varied from New Wave with groups like The Police, Blondie and the Buzzcocks to Neil Diamond and Abba. I adored Debbie Harry,

52

her style, her attitude and her hair. Out of school I wore tight black corduroy trousers. My hair was lightened by a peroxide perm. I danced around my bedroom, trying to look as cool as she did. I wished I had her confidence. Of course, I was kidding myself. Debbie Harry was considerably thinner than me and much better looking but when I put on my leather jacket, I was in my fantasy world.

The golden age of disco music was still glorious, and, with the arrival of *Grease*, John Travolta shot to mega-star status. A new dawn beckoned full of the Sex Pistols and Johnny Rotten, The Stranglers and The Clash. The lads who were big influencers on the school playground started wearing safety pins and chains, trying to get away with small items of bondage too when they could. They, and a few girls from my year, called themselves names like *Sid Snot* and *Nancy Spunk*. I avoided them as they had a habit of spitting on people.

✓✓✓✓✓

Much of school life in the last year at Woodfield centred on what everyone would do when they left school. There were a few pupils like me who had dreams of going to college or university. For most kids there was a necessity to get a job to support the family finances. In 1979, the job market for school leavers was limited and unemployment rates were rising. Traditional industries, which had been the main route for most school leavers in the past, were just beginning to decline and this trend would continue with the death of many manufacturing trades. Somehow, against the odds, some of my friends began to find jobs.

Dee went to work full time in the local chemist where she enjoyed a Saturday job for a couple of years, washing bottles, sorting out stock and helping the dishy pharmacist to dispense medications. A couple of years later she would marry the man and moved away from the area, down south. Eventually she moved back to the Midlands and has always remained in touch via the annual Christmas card.

Dev got a job in a bank and sadly after the last day at school I never saw her again. By now she had an older boyfriend and had distanced herself a little from our group. We had not seen much of her in months, outside of school.

Mel could not find work. When she left school, she signed on the dole. I bumped into her towards the end of my time at teacher training college,

53

five years later. She was working in the office of a local taxi firm. Her life seemed less sorted than the rest of us and although she sounded happy enough, I never could tell if she was.

Ann got a job working for the local electric board and spent many years there. She moved a few miles away, closer to the countryside when she married. After being made redundant from the place she had worked since she was sixteen, she became a classroom assistant. She was made for the job. Had her circumstances earlier in life been different, she would have made a fine teacher.

When my turn came to see the careers teacher, she asked me what I wanted to do. I blurted out my dream to her and she had dismissed my idea to my mother and Colin without hesitation at parents evening. I still remember the words which have played in my mind over the years. I should never be a teacher. I was too introvert and shy. Teaching was not for me so I should forget this notion. Had I thought about working in Firkins? I had no other plan. Teaching was what I wanted to do. I constantly asked myself if I wanted to be a teacher just because my mother was a teacher and I still was unsure if my desire to teach was dynasty or destiny, or perhaps a little of both. I did sense a change in the air for women. The country had its first ever woman Prime Minister.

I wanted to give the notion of teaching my best shot. I was painfully shy, but I could improve perhaps. I could try to study harder, and I was determined to revise as much as I could. With just the bat of an eyelid, the main exams were upon us. To add to the pressure, the high school had no sixth form unit so I knew that if I wanted to gain 'A' levels of any description I should have to move schools after my exams. The group of girls I had belonged to for almost five years, began to separate as we started on the next steps in our lives. Some friendships were sadly lost forever.

✓✓✓✓✓

The sixth form unit I attended was part of another high school. I missed the staff and pupils at Woodfield but settled into a different world, one with no uniform. That is not exactly true as there was a uniform of sorts revolving around jeans.

Two years at sixth form were a blur which seemed to revolve around revision and exams. The aim was to get two 'A' levels needed for entry to teacher training college and my life was devoted to this goal. Lessons and the standards expected were hard and I struggled at times, especially with maths which I had always loved so much. English lessons were best as the teachers were thorough and knew their subject well. One of my French teachers went off ill, never to return and so half of the lessons were missed. I never took general studies seriously but enjoyed some of the visitors who came to speak to all the sixth form.

Away from other school buildings, the sixth form block seemed very grown up to the schools I had attended before. The common room was a busy place, strewn with sixteen- to eighteen-year-olds, pretending to study but often chatting or playing about instead. When the stereo system was brought into the common room, for the first few days, it was a sensational hit. However, battle lines quickly became drawn as war broke out over the music played. If it was a Rockers Day the music would be bands such as Iron Maiden, Rush or Led Zeppelin played at full volume, whilst on a Mods Day The Jam, Clash and Stranglers would be blaring out for all to hear. I confess I remained neutral in the politics as I liked most of the music that was played. If a Blondie song was put on the record player, I was in heaven but I equally listening to a band the Rockers played frequently; Dire Straits would become one of my favourite bands as an adult.

Battles for the stereo between the Mods and Rockers intensified to the point that someone complained about the atmosphere in the sixth form common room. The record player was removed as a punishment for a week. Conversations started up, the Mods and Rockers mixed and to be honest, despite me being a massive music lover, I did appreciate the quietness for once. We needed to study.

My application, to a local teacher training college, went smoothly. A few weeks later I found myself treading the same steps my mother had taken for an interview. One of the lectures asked the first question.

'Can you explain why you want to be a teacher?'

I answered in the only way I could. The words came easily. I wanted to show the world that this quiet girl who had started life in a one parent family could do well against all the odds.

'I want to make a difference in children's lives. Not all children start life the same for a number of reasons. If a child can get a good solid education and achieve to the very best of their ability, it can make a massive difference to his or her life as an adult and ultimately as a parent.'

Both interviewers nodded.

'Tell me about a teacher who has inspired you.'

'I should like to tell you about a teacher I had when I was six. Her name was Miss Bagshot. I called her *'Dragon'* in my head. She was unkind to her pupils; punishments were harsh, and she was unfair. She would humiliate children and never showed any compassion for anyone.'

A frown appeared across the faces of both interviewers. Their eyes narrowed. They clearly had not expected this answer, but they allowed me to continue, both staring intently.

'I learned so much from the experience of being in her class. It is important to show you care and have empathy with your pupils. Motivation and inspiration are far more powerful than chastisement and punishment. I think the relationship between a teacher and a child is key to building a firm foundation for learning.'

They nodded in unison. The frowns disappeared and had been replaced with smiles. They now understood my odd subject matter. The rest of the interview went without incident. As I walked out of the building, I felt my mother's presence. Her shadow was large, but I realised that I wanted to be a teacher because that was what I truly wanted to do, not because I was following in my mother's footsteps. When I realised this knowledge about myself, I felt easy about my choice of career.

On receiving a letter offering me a place at the college, on the condition of gaining two 'A' levels, I was determined to get the qualifications. However, I entered the English exams with high hopes, French with moderate hopes, maths with no hope and the general studies exam with no care.

When I collected my slip from the school on results day, I hesitated to read it. What would happen if I didn't get what I needed? I hatched a plan to move to a college to re-sit my exams. I should get to teacher training college eventually, no matter what this paper said. Glancing at my results an enormous weight fell from my shoulders. I could move on with the next part of my life. I breathed a sigh of relief.

Chapter 4
So, It Begins

The summer of 1981 was full of the Royal Wedding between Charles, The Prince of Wales and Lady Diana Spencer. Street parties and commemorative tackiness followed. When late September arrived, I began my Batchelor of Education degree.

I always considered my college days to be a means to an end. I wanted to get my training over as soon as I could so that I could teach. I stayed at home, listening to Blondie, UB40 or The Police, didn't live the social life expected of students and never got drunk. I thought the whole experience would be rather like my life at that time ... boring!

Somehow college was never mundane. There was always some school project to get involved with, some lesson to plan or some resource to create for teaching. My greatest achievement, from all my visits and teaching practices in numerous schools across the Midlands, was to learn to create a worksheet on a banda machine in three colours. There were no photocopiers back then. The smell of the chemicals was overpowering. The euphoria of using three coloured inks on one worksheet may have been related to the odour overtaking my senses rather than my technical skills!

Our college ran courses for three age ranges: nursery/first schools, primary/middle schools or upper/secondary, linked to the fact that the college was in a local authority that had a first, middle and upper school system. The first few weeks at college were spent visiting primary and secondary schools to assist with each student's decision as to which pathway they would choose. I already knew where I belonged. I wanted to be a primary teacher. My natural leaning was for the nursery/first school option. Even though I opted for a younger age group to specialise in, my teaching certificate after three years stated I was qualified to teach three to twelve year olds.

After the first few weeks, our year split into the three groups, and I rarely saw many other B.Ed. students except during educational psychology or philosophy lectures. My group was the smallest by far; nine students who were to specialise as nursery and first school teachers.

Although I was a nervous, and extremely quiet student, my grounding in education would stand me in good stead throughout the years. The nursery/first students learned to teach in a much more practical way than the other two groups. Their studies were more theory based and they rarely undertook 'real' teaching apart from when we were all on teaching practice.

These were the days that were pre–National Curriculum where we were expected to produce schemes of work for every subject and individual lesson plans for every teaching practice we did. One of the many joys of teaching in a primary school was that you had to teach every subject. My favourite subjects remain English, maths, history and P.E. My least favourite subject has always been music, which even surprised me, given the fact I wanted to be Julie Andrews, Debbie Harry or, in later years, Cyndi Lauper. It's not the singing. I love singing, even if I was rarely in tune. It was not the music appreciation, listening and talking about different kinds of music. It was understanding crochets and quavers and the like. I knew how to play the recorder from my junior school days and learned some simple guitar chords at college. However, nothing conquered my feelings of inadequacy to teach music.

The tutors were pleasant enough but, for the most part, they remained distant in their relationships with us all. Some were older characters who loved to tell stories and often went off script. We would begin with a lecture entitled 'The acquisition of language' but twenty minutes into the session, we could be listening to a tale about the lecturer's holiday in Greece. Although they always had interesting stories to tell, and there was a vague link to subject matter, it became annoying when they quickly moved on to the real topic for the last half hour of the three-hour stint to cover what was needed and give out an assignment.

The only memorable lecturers were ladies. Deborah organised and taught the whole first/nursery unit of study. She had an energy and passion about teaching young children that no other lecturer possessed. Her style of delivering lectures was inspiring. Her child-centred approach and her ability to share her passion of teaching with student teachers will stay with me forever. Lectures always referred to child development and what was appropriate practice in the classroom. When I reflect on her passion, I wonder what she would make of the world of education in the 2020s; the pressures placed upon children at such young ages to all perform at the same level, at the same speed to meet a certain criterion created by education gurus.

The other lecturer of note was a P.E. specialist called Fiona who taught her subject brilliantly, making each student take part as a child and as a teacher. In her early forties, she was fanatically fit with a trim figure. She wore a black leotard and white tights in every lesson. I felt conscious of my body in front of her. I was shorter and much stockier than her. I wanted to please her and when I taught in front of her, she gave me encouragement and praise. The only thing that spoilt my lessons was my dancing ability. I had always loved dancing and singing as a child but only on my own, without an audience. I had no ability whatsoever. When asked to learn dance steps Fiona could spot my problems a mile off. After many sessions with her she must have become exasperated. On one occasion she asked me to sit out of the practice because of my "two left feet". Hearing Fiona utter those words in front of everyone completely devastated me.

Whilst at college we visited two 'special schools': one classed as an 'M' school and one a 'S' school. The 'M' school was for children with moderate learning needs who generally found spelling, reading, writing and arithmetic difficult. Severe special needs schools had children with profound physical and mental disabilities. It was the first time I had ever seen such profoundly disabled youngsters. I had begun teacher training in the year that recommendations from the Warnock report of 1978, were made into an education act. Little did any of us realise how much impact Dame Mary Warnock's work would have on our careers. It would become standard practice for children with additional needs to fully integrate with their mainstream friends. I was privileged to work with families and their children with a range of needs over many years: significant hearing loss, autism, physical, emotional or mental needs, and even a child who was blind. Years earlier many of these children would have been prevented from attending or from mixing socially with friends at mainstream schools.

The people in my year had a mixture of backgrounds and experiences. Some were mature students who had worked in industry for years and had either been made redundant or had chosen a different career path later in their working life. Some were in their late forties or early fifties. Others were younger and because of various reasons had not chosen teaching as a profession when they left school. The final group of students were like me, just finished school themselves and had decided on becoming a teacher earlier in life. I was a painfully shy teenager, the youngest student in my year at college. I was not yet an adult but no longer a child.

A few students left after the first few weeks, deciding that teaching was not for them. Others lasted until the first teaching practice was over. A few people quit college at this point, whilst others clung to their hopes and were given extra support from lecturers. One student lasted until halfway through the second year but eventually had to leave as she could not meet the standard expected in classroom practice. There was also a shocking incident when a student was escorted from the halls of residence for assaulting his girlfriend. The numbers on the course dwindled until everyone who was truly committed to teaching had been discovered and those who were not left.

We began lectures. I found education sessions fascinating and learned lots. I often could hide in larger gatherings, never having to speak but in our first/nursery group there was nowhere to hide in the shadows. I felt out of my comfort zone, teaching small parts of a lesson to a group of adults but something drove me on. My first ever teaching session was based on the theme of colours. I began with a poem by Christina Rossetti, 'What is Pink?' I practised and practised reading the poem beforehand and prepared my colour props. When I sat down, at the end of my ordeal, I felt relieved yet triumphant that I had conquered my nerves. My cheeks were bright red, and my forehead was damp, but I had done something significant that day. I had started my teaching career.

Many more days were to be like this one, teaching parts of lessons to my fellow students. Mostly, the performance would be to the other eight colleagues in my group. When a video camera was introduced, we taught our first children. A small group of infants were brought to college to take part in some mini phonics lessons. The experience was terrifying, especially when we had to analyse each other's performances after the children had left. There was something about teaching children that day that made the session bearable. Their responses were natural, unrehearsed and often unexpected. As I caught the bus home on the afternoon, after the first videoing session, I wanted to sing. Working with children had been wonderful.

✓✓✓✓✓

My first teaching practice was at a school just a couple of miles from home. I was placed in a second-year junior class at the upper age range of my specialism. The class teacher was a happy-go-lucky chap in his late twenties. He had a wicked sense of humour and was loved by his pupils for his jovial nature and his love of football and sport. He had not long become a father, and this showed in his creased shirts, the faint smell of sick and the bags under his eyes. He was popular in the staffroom, sharing baby stories or tales about his latest visit to the football club he supported through thick and thin. From the tales of his team's great tragic losses week after week, it sounded more likely that he supported them through thin rather than thick. His name was Steve and he seemed very grown up to me, an eighteen-year-old.

Steve's class were a mere nine or ten years younger than me. In my first few lessons with them, they ran rings around their naïve teaching student who was green behind the ears. Later I was to realise that this is the game all children play when faced with a supply or student teacher. My naïvety showed but Steve never criticised me, merely pointing out things to try next.

By the time the four weeks teaching practice was upon me, I had been visiting the school for eight months. My lessons and subject schemes had all been signed off at college by the lecturers and approved by the headmaster and Steve. My first ever whole class lesson was on the water cycle. As the least scientific person you could meet, I had researched and researched my topic. Before the children entered the room, I wrote on the blackboard for the first time since being an infant child. My writing was crooked, shockingly poor and totally incorrectly sized. Steve reminded me that Rome had not been built in a day.

In came the children and sat at their desks. After greeting them, I began.

'Does anyone know why it rains?'

There were lots of answers.

'It's because of God crying.'

'Miss, it's because of the clouds.'

'My mum says it never bleeding stops.'

The '*Eager Beavers*' waved their hands madly in the air every time a question was posed. The '*Middlers*' avoided pushing themselves

61

forward. The *'Quiet Ones'* sat there wanting to hide. I recognised them easily. I remembered to include all the children in the discussion. By the end of the lesson the children had learned a few new words, produced a class display and had not killed each other. I went home shattered and with an over inflated sense of being a teacher. There was still much to learn!

On the second day of my teaching practice disaster struck. Steve had phoned in sick. Whether he was ill or if the baby had kept him up on too many occasions, he was absent. The headmaster entered the room to inform me that Steve was not coming to work just before the school bell rang that morning and asked me,

'What lessons are you teaching today?'

'Only one lesson. It is thirty minutes, reading a story at the end of the day.'

His nose twitched slightly as he frowned. He clearly had hoped for a different answer to the one I had given. Together with Keith, the deputy head, he shared the lessons that day. On the third day the headteacher popped his head around the door.

'I have meetings today and Keith is teaching. Can you cover this morning?'

I nodded. Thankfully I realised he might use me as a supply teacher. So, for the next three and a half weeks, I taught every lesson instead of the specified fifty percent of the timetable. When my tutor came to observe, he was delighted I was teaching full time. His report stated I had done well to cope with the situation. Occasionally the headteacher or Keith would pop their heads around the door for a few seconds probably to ensure no one was killing each other.

The class were learning about the weather. What I had not appreciated, in the slightest, was how weather played a part in classroom behaviour. On one occasion the children had no outdoor break because of the rain. After their lack of freedom, they were tetchy and argumentative with each other and me. On windy days they would come into class *'as high as kites.'* Older teachers would talk about the weather in the staffroom, whilst sipping their tea or coffee. It seemed a deeply serious topic of conversation on the merits of different types of weather.

If it snowed …

'I can't stand the thought of all those wet socks drying on the radiators.'

If it was sunny …

'I can't stand the smell of those sweaty bodies. I must teach a lesson on personal hygiene and use of deodorants.'

If it was windy …

'Good luck today. They'll be on the ceiling!'

If it rained …

'God help us all. Don't use anything sharp this afternoon if they have no lunch time outside. They'll kill one another.'

As a teaching student, I dreaded every kind of weather! I vowed never to teach the topic of weather again. I hated rainy days with a passion.

By the time Steve finally returned to school, I had three days left. I really resented his presence. For a few short weeks it had felt like I had my own class and had conquered all nerves about controlling behaviour. My report from the school was made up, no one had seen me teach apart from my tutor, on just one occasion. I passed and that was all that mattered.

The second year of training commenced with more school visits, projects to complete and lectures to attend. The topics became interesting and practical, for the most part. I realised that I enjoyed being at college and the life of being a student teacher. There was a great sense of being an adult, going to the refectory at break and ordering a sausage sandwich with brown sauce. Ambient music played in the background. I missed the battle of the stereo.

My second teaching practice was in a very different school to my first one. I was placed in a class of five- and six-year-olds with a class teacher called Kate. She had been teaching about ten years. Her husband worked as a third-year junior teacher in my first teaching practice school, so she knew Steve well. I felt immediately at home and comfortable to teach in front of her. She was in her early thirties and chatted away to me as if I were a colleague rather than a student. She was easy to talk to and was enthusiastic about having someone to help. Her approach was down to earth, and she was realistic about teaching. Relationships were important in her class. The nervousness I had felt working with Steve disappeared and I started to relax and enjoy working with her. During my time at the school, I changed all display boards in the class, taught all lessons I should teach, and Kate was there every day to hold my hand, guiding me along the infant teacher path.

It was an entirely different world to my first practice yet only three miles away. Apart from two white children, every child in the class was of Pakistani origin. A large proportion of the class were boys who loved to attend school in Pakistani army uniform and wanted to play guns all day long. In any conversation, whether it be on maths or topic, one of the boys would always slip in a reference to being in the '*Pakistani army gang.*' They wore their badges proudly on their khaki, uniformed chests and banged their hearts when they mentioned their gang. Kate gave constant warnings about pretending to shoot each other as they would sneak a gun built out of Lego into a game or return from the playground with a twig or two up their sleeves to attempt a battle if they finished tasks early. Many had little or no English, but they knew the phrase '*Pakistani army gang'* very well and I found myself smiling every time the words were uttered, even though I should have encouraged them not to fight. Kate wanted them to learn English to get the best start they could, but she celebrated the children's culture and liked them to teach her Urdu.

It was the first time I had ever seen school signs that were written in several languages. I wanted to learn more about the children's backgrounds, understanding that knowledge brings familiarity and breaks down barriers that have built through prejudice. Children would bring in food from home for staff. Food is always a way to celebrate differences and similarities. It was probably this teaching practice that started my passion for curries. Living near to the Balti district in Birmingham meant many pleasant evenings in Pakistani and Bengali restaurants over the next thirty years.

During a lesson in the first week of my practice I noticed several children scratching their heads. Stupidly, I thought nothing of it. When more children joined in with the communal scratching the next day, I mentioned it to Kate. She rushed off to the school office. When she returned, she had some news.

'The secretary has called Nora!'

I was naïve and fell hook, line and sinker for the notion of a person named Nora being telephoned for some reason.

64

'Who's Nora? What does she do?'

Kate had a deep, husky voice from years of smoking. Her wicked laugh made me wonder what was so amusing. I must have looked extremely gormless as I stood there scratching my head.

'Nora, the nit nurse of course!'

The reality of the scratching dawned on me quickly. Not only had head lice found some smaller heads to live on, but they had found a home in my hair, and Kate's too but she did not know it yet. I could not wait to get to the chemist that afternoon after school to buy a nit comb and some Suleo shampoo. I vowed never to bend over and be close to a child's head again. Naturally it wasn't the last time I had little visitors stay. Snot, sick and nits would be recurring themes, no matter where I taught in the years to come.

The headteacher was a serious man who seemed to have the worries of the world on his shoulders. At the time I could not understand his actions when he banned me from staff meetings. We had been told at college to make sure we stayed for all meetings and that schools would be disappointed if we did not participate. One lunch time he walked into the staffroom, full of adults and as he sat down, he spotted me in a corner.

'Emma, pick up your sandwiches and get out. Just go now!'

Everyone turned and looked at me as I stood up with my sandwich in hand and picked up my bag. I was too stunned to speak. My cheeks burnt with humiliation. I wanted to make myself invisible. He scowled as I hurried past him. Towards the end of lunchtime Kate found me crying in the classroom. His sharp manner had been shocking and had taken me by surprise. The teacher apologised for his behaviour. She too had been taken aback by his words.

'I am so sorry, Emma. The head shouldn't have spoken to you like that. He's tetchy at the moment, and he took it out on you.'

'Why was he so rude?'

'Swear you'll keep this to yourself! You swear?'

I nodded.

'There are lots of financial pressures at the school due to the numbers on roll falling. He thinks there may have to be some redundancies. You mustn't say anything. We've been warned about discretion and confidentiality. Please keep it a secret.'

The headmaster must have realised he had snapped at me as he took me out of class that afternoon and explained himself why he had an emergency staff meeting that lunch time. After that I was invited to all meetings and never left out. Perhaps he realised his sharpness or maybe Kate had quietly spoken to him, saying he could trust my discretion. In the end no one was made redundant, the roll rose after a couple more families moved into the area and the school was saved, for a while. I vowed never to speak to any student I had in the way that headteacher had spoken to me.

The teaching practice was soon completed. My reports were good, and even I could tell that my lessons were improving. When my practice ended, I was genuinely sad to leave, apart from the outbreak of head lice which was still rife in the school. Kate had been generous in sharing her class with me, her teaching tips and ways to get rid of nits.

✓✓✓✓✓

My last teaching practice came just before Christmas in my final year at college, and it was an unpleasant experience from start to finish. My first practice had been in an old Victorian classroom, similar to my own primary school before the big move. My second had been in a 1960s building with low ceilings and smaller teaching spaces. This third practice was back in a Victorian building with high, vaulted ceilings but the room was too small for the thirty-nine pupils who sat like sardines in rows as there was no place to group tables for so many children. It was difficult to move around the class. If someone put up their hand for help, whilst sitting at their desk, it could take minutes to move children and chairs to get to a specific child. Health and Safety people would have had a field day if we needed to do a fire drill or to get out of the room if there had been a real emergency.

I took an instant dislike to the class teacher, who I secretly nicknamed *'Wilma the Witch'*. She was older than Steve or Kate and had been teaching for over thirty years. If anyone saw her in the street *Wilma* looked normal. She was of average height, a predictable curly bob hairstyle and presented herself well, always looking tidy and smartly dressed. There was, however, something about her face that irritated me. She always had a smirk whenever she spoke. Her huge, bulging blue eyes sparkled as if she found everything amusing. Many years later I realised why her eyes were so prominent when I saw something that reminded me

66

of her. She had an illness but even with this knowledge, years later, it was not the reason why she was such a thoroughly unpleasant person. I pondered if she had been born void of empathy for her fellow humans. Why did she dislike people so much? Her sarcasm was sharp and targeted at no one in particular. Everyone faced the barbed comments that flew from her tongue; pupils, staff and student teachers could not escape. In fact, her sarcasm and criticism of myself seemed to give her immense pleasure. She reminded me of Miss Bagshot in the way she talked to pupils. I shall admit that I feared her as she felt my teaching was not good enough and when I copied her methods exactly, *Wilma* still criticised me.

'That lesson was dreadful. Why did you use those awful comprehension books?'

'I'm sorry. I'll find other materials to use.'

She had used the books in every comprehension lesson I had seen her teach.

'Have you not got an original thought in your head?'

'I'm sorry. I'll use something different next time.'

Try not to cry. She would love the tears and think she had won.

'Do you realise those children listened to you talking for ten minutes?'

'Sorry. I'll try to keep my lesson introduction shorter next time.'

Did she not realise that in her last lesson, the children had listened to her for forty minutes?

I seemed to do everything incorrectly. When she spoke to me, I always began each reply with the word 'sorry'. My teaching commitment was to cover ninety percent of the timetable. Naturally she insisted I taught full-time whilst she tittle-tattled around the school, running down one member of staff or another.

To add to my woes my tutor was someone I had a run in with shortly before my teaching practice had commenced. She sent a letter less than a fortnight before the practice was due to start, requesting an essay be completed at very short notice. Originally, she had told us the essay was postponed until after the teaching experience but forgot to ask her boss's permission to change the date. She invited each student to an individual meeting to soften the blow. When my meeting time came, days before the assignment was due in, and less than a week before I was teaching full time, I went into the session furious. Never had I spoken to anyone in an

67

office of superiority in such a way but I found my voice and could not hold my anger at her incompetence.

'You had to know your mistake weeks ago. You can't have forgotten the procedures for changing assignment dates.'

'Calm down, Emma. I can sense some hostility. Are you having boyfriend trouble? Is it the time of the month?'

'Calm down? You must be bloody joking! This is purely your incompetence, nothing to do with me. How dare you suggest it is my fault I am angry. I'm not angry. I'm furious. You have let us all down. I shall make an official complaint about you after the teaching practice. Stick your essay where the sun doesn't shine. You'll get it on the date you told us weeks ago.'

Slamming the door behind me, I could still hear her weak excuses. When I arrived home, I was still shaking. I found out later that every other student had also refused to hand in the assignment. The divide and conquer plan, in meeting with us individually, had failed as we had all stuck to our guns. A letter arrived after two days, with a poor excuse, poor apology and a new date for the assignment after the practice had finished. She was a vicar's wife and a part time vicar herself. I had blasphemed a few times during our meeting and did not regret it in the slightest! I was stuck with this woman as my tutor for the last teaching practice with *Wilma the Witch*.

The teaching practice dragged. The tutor came, observed me teaching and gave me feedback, clearly mindful of how she spoke to me. I was polite but cold, determined to do well, not giving her any chance for negative comments. Had she failed my lesson, I swear I should have hit her!

In the final two weeks of term, *Wilma* who was also head of infants, decided the annual Christmas play needed perfecting. This meant that many lessons were stopped, and my hundred percent timetable was ceased. I sat in the hall, supervising children who were bored with rehearsals and her incessant high-pitched whine full of sarcasm.

'Dear, if you're going to be an angel, look angelic, don't pick your nose.'

'Has that king, the one with the large mole, got a problem with hearing?'

'Mrs Phillips, I have repeatedly asked you to make sure they come on the stage in the right order. Can you not follow an instruction?'

Under her breath she tutted, sighed and moaned every time we went into the hall. No one took any notice of her. The public performance went well. *Wilma the Witch* took the praise and thanks from the headmistress for her contribution. The claps for her achievements were short, whilst other members of staff had roars and cheers. When the final day came, I had no thanks or encouragement from *Wilma* to spur me on for my final two terms. I was glad to finish.

In February 1984 Torvill and Dean enchanted the world with their *Bolero* ice dancing routine, completing their goal to win an Olympic gold medal for their performance. My goals were to finish college, get the degree and find a job. Most of the students, myself included, attended generic interviews at the local education offices. A few lucky people got permanent places in schools. Several job adverts came up in the local area and I applied for them all but got no response.

So, I left college, waiting for my results after three years of study and had no job. My only other option would be to stay on for a fourth year to get the honours degree. It was compulsory for the students in the year below me to do that. Had I been born a few weeks later, four years would have been my fate. The thought of another moment as a student filled me with utter dread. I just wanted to teach and had had enough of essays, exams and being on the other side of the blackboard.

The Middle

Chapter 5
'Wasn't Me, Miss!'

As soon as I awoke on the Thursday morning, the day before all the schools broke up in the area for the long summer holidays, I was conscious that I was still unemployed. Although most of the other third year student teachers shared my predicament, I felt that I had failed. There was nothing I could do now until a school contacted me.

After lunch I settled on my bed with a book to read and must have dropped off to sleep. I was awoken when the telephone rang downstairs. These were the days of one landline phone, and if you were fancy, you might have an extension upstairs. We did not have one, despite Colin working for British Telecom after he had left the RAF. My mother called up the stairs to me that I was wanted on the phone. I hurriedly jumped off the bed and went downstairs, still a little sleepy. I mouthed to my mother,

'Who is it?'

She tried to mouth back a name, but I wasn't familiar with it. I picked up the receiver and greeted the caller.

'Hello Emma. My name is Miss Martin. I am the headmistress of Park View Primary School. I have your name from the education office list as a probationary teacher. Would you be interested in teaching a mixed middle and top infant class?'

My heart skipped a beat. I replied that I would be very interested.

'I'd like to invite you for an interview. Could you attend at 4 o'clock that afternoon?'

'I should love to attend but I've just missed the bus and there isn't one for another hour. I can't get there in time. I would be late.'

'That's not a problem. I can come and pick you up in about twenty minutes, if that's okay?'

I thanked her for her kindness and accepted her invitation immediately, giving her directions to get to my house. The next twenty minutes were spent in a mad whirl. I had a quick wash, put on my interview clothes, sprayed on some L'Aimant perfume and brushed my hair. As the car pulled up outside, I just had time to check myself in the mirror.

Miss Martin greeted me when I got into the car and immediately struck up a conversation. We chatted all the way to the school about teaching practices and which college I had attended. She was easy to talk to. After arriving, she told me she was retiring the next day and that the deputy was going to be the acting headteacher for a while. I was disappointed as I had felt comfortable chatting to her. What she did not tell me was that there was a battle between the education authority and the local community to keep the school open as the numbers on roll had dropped significantly over the years. A decision would be made by the end of the next term.

I was greeted at the door by a tall, balding man in his late fifties who was friendly and welcoming. The pale grey suit he wore accentuated his tanned complexion and for an added touch he had carefully placed a contrasting handkerchief in his breast pocket. The headteacher went off to her room, leaving Pete Moore to show me around the school. We did a quick tour of the building, and he answered my questions about what reading scheme was used, what maths scheme, all the questions that I would need to know if I passed the interview when it started. The headteacher must have gone to get her questions in order.

We retraced our steps back towards the school offices and were continuing to chat about how I had attended the local comprehensive as a teenager, when he stopped at a room which we had passed a few minutes before. He drew back the curtains to expose a large rectangular room with windows the full length of one wall.

'So, this is your room,' Pete announced grandly.

Had I misheard him say *my room*? What about an interview? I was puzzled and confused. In fact, it had been odd since the telephone call less than two hours before. Pete continued talking, ten to the dozen, full of his plans for the next term. How could I check my understanding of the situation? I didn't want to look foolish. I was a naïve probationary teacher who had misunderstood what was happening. There was nothing for it. I needed to be bold.

'Did you just say this will be *my room*? I haven't had the interview yet.'

My voice was full of apologies in case I had misheard what had been mentioned a few minutes before. Pete smiled,

'Miss Martin interviewed you in the car, she signalled that all had gone well and that I could offer you the job. You will come, won't you?'

This time I knew. This time I understood. This time I realised that I *had* been interviewed in the car. I felt an enormous weight lift from my shoulders. I was elated. Pete offered me a lift home. He chatted away about his holidays in Spain, his wife, his grown-up children. I felt a distinct liking for this man who was easy company. I must admit that I did not listen to everything he said. My head was spinning with the news I had a job!

Friday was the last day of term and the end of the academic year, when schools broke up for the six weeks holiday. I had a job. It was to be a temporary contract for one term because of the unknown future of the school but at least I had a job from September until Christmas. I was able to visit on this last morning to meet my class and witness Miss Martin take her final assembly. She was presented with flowers, gifts and cards to celebrate thirty-nine years in teaching. I could not comprehend that amount of time. I was just twenty years old. My coming-of-age birthday was still three weeks away. Thirty-nine years in teaching coming to an end and I was just beginning.

The school was on the edge of the catchment area for my old secondary, Woodfield. It was a significantly deprived area with all children coming from council dwellings which were houses, high rise flats or maisonettes. Many children lived in the Maze. Families had, for generations, been low skilled, manual workers. Increasingly many were unemployed, as much local, longstanding manufacturing businesses had closed over the last few years. There were low aspirations for education and employment amongst some parents, grandparents and even great grandparents. To enthuse any child to want to do well at school would be an uphill battle. I was in seventh heaven; this was just the kind of school I wanted to work in. I wanted to make a difference. My mission sounded grand and perhaps my ego was over inflated, but I would try my very best.

The summer holidays were spent, as they would be for many years after, preparing for the new school year. There was something soothing about making coat peg labels, tray labels and labelling exercise books. It made me feel prepared. I was informed which days the school would be open during the summer holiday for me to get my classroom ready. My classroom ... that sounded so grand and so surreal. On all my teaching practices I had 'borrowed' the classroom and the pupils. Now I had to think how I would set a room up, where the furniture would go and where children would sit. Thankfully in my first school all the types of exercise books were chosen for me as I would not have had a clue about what I wanted in terms of lined or unlined, large squares, small squares or any squares at all for that matter. I spent every single day that I could preparing my room that summer.

In 1984 there were no training days or time set aside for planning. So, on the first day of term, in September, at precisely 9 o'clock the bell rang and in came the children. I helped them all to find their coat pegs using the shiny new labels I had made and in they came to the classroom. My first class was so small compared with classes I had had on teaching practice. There were just eighteen pupils, with a mix of fourteen middle and four top infants. I already knew that such a small class was a luxury, but I was still overawed by the task ahead of having responsibility for the education of these little humans. I saw eighteen pairs of eyes looking at me in anticipation of what I was about to say, hanging on my every word. I greeted them with a welcome, reminded them of my name, how I expected them to answer the register and off we went in alphabetical order. This was it. I was finally on the other side of the blackboard with a 'licence to fill' their heads with learning. Just as I was daydreaming someone disturbed me from my thoughts. An older child's head popped around the curtain.

'Excuse me, Miss. Everyone is waiting for you in assembly.'

It was the one thing I had to remember, and I had completely forgotten, assembly! With an extremely red face, I took my class into the hall, trying to creep in without making a fuss or too much noise. All eyes were on me for a second time that morning, a hundred pairs of smaller eyes and four pairs of adult eyes, looking at the useless probationary teacher. I just wanted to melt into the background. My drumroll to the world of teaching had been wrecked at the first beat.

The rest of the day was spent in a daze. The lessons went as well as could be expected and the children responded to my instructions, which was a bonus. I had learned most names by morning break and the rest by lunch time. By home time at half past three I felt exhausted but happy. School had always been part of my life. The difference was that I was being paid to teach. My wage packet at the end of the month felt like I had won the football pools!

The children in my class showed various levels of enthusiasm or interest in learning. There was a mixed group of five pupils who finished every task at breakneck speed, and I soon realised that I needed to plan work at a higher level for the *'Eager Beavers'*. Most of the *'Middlers'* plodded along, remaining on task when asked to do so. A few children, the *'Strugglers'*, needing reassurance and constant reminders of what to do. Their basic skills such as reading, handwriting and counting to five were very poor for their age. Most just wanted to please but couldn't do the work. Then there were a few who could do the work but couldn't be bothered, the *'Desperados'*. I felt as if I was in a cowboy movie, ready for pistols at high noon, when I asked them to write.

All the children in my first class, except one were well behaved. The boy stood out in several ways from his peers. Firstly, his behaviour was challenging. The other reason he stood out was that he was the only black boy in the school, in an area of white working-class families, many of whom held very strong views on families with different backgrounds. Prejudice was rife and difference was not tolerated especially of a single man with dreadlocks and his two small children from Birmingham who were of African Caribbean descent.

Looking back to that school, it was no wonder that the boy was angry. He would have almost certainly faced racism, name calling and bullying at Park View Primary, but it was never heard or witnessed in class. The playground would have been a breeding ground for the National Front. There were no policies on bullying, racism or equal opportunities which would shock teachers nowadays. Back in the mid nineteen eighties, there were still many repeats on the television of programmes such as *Love Thy Neighbour* or *Till Death Us Do Part* which modern audiences would refuse to watch after a couple of minutes. I regret not listening closer to playground chatter. The boy never mentioned the fact he had been called *'Nigger'* or *'Wog'*. These names, and far worse, were commonly used by the folk in the area and their children would have copied adult chatter on matters such as race. A child isn't born racist. He or she learns hate from their elders and words that can act like knives.

Parents and some staff found it strange that a father was able to bring up two children without their mother. They were ignorant of the details in which Joe's father had taken full responsibility for his children. He had saved them, moved area to avoid the drug dealing world his children had lived in with their mother. Having split with her ex-partner, her life had spiralled out of control and her two young children had needed rescuing from a future destined for a children's home or fostering. Joe's father had stepped in when the children were on the point of being taken into care. It was hard for a woman to be a single parent; I knew this from my own experience. It was a million times harder for a father. People saw his Rastafarian hat and the dreadlocks on his shoulders. They did not see a parent desperate to give his children a good start in life.

The boy, Joe, would fly into a temper when he struggled with his work, and he would become violent towards children or myself. He would rip up his work and stamp on it. Chairs and even tables would go flying in his rage. Everyone would get out of the way. No-one had explained about behaviour of this kind back at college. Psychology lessons were about Skinner's pigeons or Chomsky's research; the nature versus nurture lectures had contained nothing on how to miss a flying exercise book or chair.

The days before Individual Education Plans meant that children like Joe would turn up to lessons every day, struggle if something was difficult and then he would literally 'kick off' at anything in sight which was often my shins. I didn't know how to handle these situations. He would swear and rant, then tears would fall and eventually quietness. I would be given a sanitised version of a playground incident and like a fool, I accepted what Joe told me. Perhaps I was scared to hear the truth: the name calling, the monkey noises and the constant chants to 'get back to the jungle'. I tried adapting my lessons to be more practical for him, with less writing and we found a happier medium at times.

Fifteen years later, I read of a court trial about a man being found guilty of a carjacking and holding a woman at knife point. I was horrified to see Joe's name as the criminal. It was him; same unusual surname, correct age and the old temper Joe had years before. How did a young boy like Joe grow up to threaten his victim like that? What drove him to commit such a crime?

He had been an angry boy tormented by prejudice. When he was calm, he was affectionate and funny. He knew love but lived in a world of hatred. Whilst he was still in my class, his father announced one day that

Joe's birth mother had died. He was a little boy who was crying out for help. His grief for the separation from his mother and then her death along with growing up with intense racism were too much for a child of six years old. There was an incredible injustice for children like Joe who slipped through the nets of education, deemed to be a '*naughty boy*'. Had Joe gone to my old primary school he would have had the cane or plimsoll on his backside for his behaviour towards his peers and staff.

A child's behaviour is a form of communication. Kicking, punching and lashing out at anyone who came into his sight was Joe's way of telling the world of his unhappiness, the unfairness of his life and the taunts he often encountered on the playground. Luckily, he was never caned. I was glad Pete's attitude to corporal punishment was laid back compared to some headteachers. It was still legal to hit a child in school, but he talked to anyone who misbehaved, trying to find out what was going on in the youngster's head. Pete hardly raised his voice unlike his colleague in the next room.

Mr Simmonds was much younger than Pete, but he never invited me to call him by his first name. He would walk past me in the corridor every morning without speaking or even acknowledging my existence. He wore a khaki tweed jacket with brown patches on the elbows, a tweed tie that matched and similar coloured corduroy trousers. His white shirts stood out from the rest of his attire. His clothes made him appear older than his true age which was late thirties or early forties. Simmonds was a good-looking man, with a fine jaw line. His sultry Mediterranean looks could have earned him major roles in movies, had he chosen a career in films. However, his personality was devoid of charisma. He spoke with superior tones, mostly moaning about his class and the laziness of youths. In his few conversations with children, he showed no emotion nor kindness. He had no empathy for anyone. I made sure I never sat in his chair in the staff room nor dared to drink from his mug. I was as fearful of him as the children were, and especially of his wooden walking stick which he carried everywhere, He had no need for such an item as he was a physically fit man, but I found out how he used it from the conversations children had with me when I was on playground duty.

The only other two teachers were in their late forties and, until recently both had been unmarried. June was the colleague who was to oversee me. Her ginger hair looked home cut, using a basin as a template.

She never took any pride in her appearance, wearing the same two jumpers with the exact same pattern, one a faded blue and one a pale green. These jumpers were teamed with a pale polo neck which ensured no flesh was ever seen apart from her face and hands. Day in and day out, her trim figure seemed buried in the long unfashionable skirt she wore. She was recently married and was more interested in her pursuits outside of school than within it. Her life, with that of her husband, revolved around church. She was a fervent Christian and told me she was praying for me after school on my first teaching day. I wondered if she was concerned about my teaching ability but in fact, she prayed for everything, the child who had nits, the joy of fireworks and that she would be able to leave teaching and become a minister soon. Her heart was not in teaching, and I don't believe it had been for years. After school I often heard her crying through the curtains that separated our classrooms. I never interfered but decided it was easier to either take myself off for a walk to the library up the road for half an hour or to leave early on these afternoons. I would catch a glimpse of her, through the gaps in the curtains, standing in the classroom, hands held with palms facing up to heaven, speaking and crying to Christ.

The only teacher who helped me and I could relate to was Maggie. She lived with her mother and had never married. She was on the cusp of fifty and her life was devoted to teaching. Although she would frown at spending money on beauty, secretly I felt Maggie could have been a pretty lady had she worn a little make-up and had her hair styled longer than her usual short greying mop that had once been mousey. It was a 'sensible' haircut, and her clothes were 'sensible', but I sensed Maggie wanted romance and to look attractive. Occasionally she would have a blouse opened perhaps one button too much, revealing a little more of her bosom than she should.

The only problem I had with Maggie was that she would want to chat to me for hours after school which delayed me in preparing for the next day's lessons. I sometimes would dread her footsteps coming along the corridor as I had nowhere to hide and was her 'prisoner'. She loved to impart her knowledge and experiences to me. Then she would move on to stories about her love life. I sometimes wondered if the tales had been made up for her young audience as often, they would sound like a Barbara

Cartland novel. I could not say I was busy or that I was leaving when she appeared at the curtain. I was the victim of her loneliness.

So, Maggie, June, Pete and Mr Simmonds were my colleagues who made for an interesting bunch. I must admit that I enjoyed being with the children at playtime rather than being in the staffroom. One break time Maggie banged on the window. The playground was at the front of the building and from the staffroom much of the space could be viewed. Without a word spoken, the three older members of staff jumped up, left their cups on the coffee table and ran through the front door which was next to the offices and staffroom.

'There's a runner,' Maggie nodded, indicating the way the 'runner' had gone.

Pete and Mr Simmonds raced to the gate and stepped onto the pavement. The runner was nowhere to be seen.

'There was some sort of altercation between Paul Baxter and Stephen Smith. It's any guess what it was about but Smith took off in a huff.'

Pete took Paul Baxter to one side to establish what had gone on between himself and the other boy. It seemed, from Pete's brief explanation, back in the staffroom, that it was nothing of great importance. I felt guilty at sitting there, drinking coffee and this must have shown on my face.

'Don't worry, Emma. We often have runners and they always come back.'

Just as he had finished speaking, there was a loud knock on the window. Pete smiled.

'See, I told you!'

Stephen Smith was indeed back on school premises. He was one of the first of the older children to speak to me on the playground, in my first few weeks of being at Park View. He seemed a pleasant enough lad and polite with it. His appearance gave an indication of his life. He was the second youngest of seven children and was in the final year at primary school. At ten years old he was the last of the five boys in the family and the 'hand-me-down' jumper which he always wore had been patched in several places, now with gaping holes in parts of the body and sleeves. It was faded green in colour, having been hand knitted many moons before and worn by four other sons before him. His hair was poorly cut and usually unkempt. He had two sisters, one older than himself. The other one, who was in my class, was the youngest of the entire family. He and his sister, who also wore the boys' old clothes looked different to the other children in school. Claire's hair hung in one untidy plait down her back. There were no pretty bows or ribbons as other girls had. Her hair was tied with an elastic band. Money was scarce for many families at Park View Primary. However, parents were proud of the way in which they turned their smart, clean children out to school each day. Stephen and Claire were never smart and certainly never clean.

The boy had a reason to hang around my classroom door at break time. He felt protective towards Claire and would look after her if he was not involved in a fight or absconding. When committed to his brotherly duties, Stephen would chat to me and make a point of saying hello. I paid little heed to his attention as I was too busy getting ready for the next lesson. One morning breaktime he dawdled a little longer than normal, but I carried on with my class chores and within a few seconds of passing the time of day with me, he had gone off with his sister to play.

Playtime passed quickly, as did the next lesson and it was soon time to send the children to wash their hands for lunch. It was June's turn to do 'lunch duty' which involved making sure the children were polite and orderly as each class was called up to collect their meal from the canteen staff. Once the children were settled and eating their meals, the duty teacher was able to collect his or her meal. It was tough choosing where to sit. There was always the worry of a grubby, snotty hand messing with your lunch if you needed to leave your meal for a few seconds to get cutlery or to stop the noise in the canteen.

As June took great pleasure in offering up a grace for the meal, the children would sit for five minutes, peeping through supposedly closed eyes and praying hands to see what had been written on the menu board. I left my class with her and went in search of my much-needed ham sandwiches and smoky bacon crisps. I was starving. A lesson on halves and quarters, talking about cutting sandwiches, had made me think about my own lunch more than once in the last hour. My bag was tucked underneath my desk, in a small recess where legs should normally fit. It was bursting with papers, some of which looked out of place and sticking up higher than I remembered leaving them. I made a mental note that I

82

should keep my bag tidier. I took out the papers and put them into a pile on the table. I eagerly searched for my lunch but knew instinctively it was not there without emptying the contents onto my desk. There were no sandwiches, crisps or a KitKat that I remembered I had also placed in my bag that morning. I knew I had picked them up; they were not in the kitchen at home. I looked at them on the bus and had contemplated the idea of having the KitKat on the journey but had persuaded myself to wait for the pleasure at lunch time.

I went to the staffroom empty handed and in need of a coffee. I was alone at first but when Pete entered the room, he gathered something was wrong. I had tried to hold the tears. I felt pathetic that I was hungry. I could manage a few hours without food and would have a meal when I returned home. He told me to follow him, and we made our way to the canteen. Cook made me a cheese sandwich and I instantly felt better. Pete asked me if anyone had been in my classroom that morning. I shook my head and then stopped for a moment.

'Stephen Smith hung around at break for his sister. He stood in the doorway but no-one else.'

He nodded. Could it have been Stephen? I thought back over the weeks. Sometimes he had asked me if I had any snack or lunch and I had told him. It would be unfair to think it was him without proof. Pete and I agreed not to specifically question the boy. The meal had been stolen, of that there was no doubt, but it could have been ninety-nine other children in school that day.

I returned to my classroom earlier than usual before the end of lunch. I had been so depressed about my sandwiches when I left the room, I had not noticed the metal bin, a couple of feet away from where my bag normally was placed, at the side of the desk. There, in the bin, was a KitKat wrapper, the empty bag left from my sandwiches and the remains of a screwed up smoky bacon crisp packet. Someone had eaten my lunch in my room. When the children returned for the next lesson, I explained to the class that I was sad and the reasons why. All the children shook their heads when asked if anyone knew anything about my lunch going missing, and all looked guilt free, except one.

The next day, at morning break, Stephen popped his head around the classroom door as he waited for Claire to collect her coat from the cloak room. I never said a word to him as I glanced up from my desk, gave him a nod and looked down at a piece of work I was marking. Without warning he spoke,

'Wasn't me, Miss!'

I never looked up, never replied or acknowledged his words. The afternoon before, Claire came up to my desk when her classmates began their work, tears streaming down her face. With a look of guilt, I instantly knew why. She whispered to me that her big brother had stolen my lunch for her as she was hungry. I knew she was telling the truth; the pair never brought any snacks and had no breakfast. Stupidly I had been reduced to tears for thinking I would starve for missing one meal. The last food Stephen and Claire had eaten was the school lunch the day before.

I would hear that phrase, 'Wasn't Me, Miss!' countless times over the years. The words always haunted me. When a child made that uttering, they would almost certainly be lying. The image of Stephen and Claire would never leave me.

✓✓✓✓✓

Life on the Maze was hard and often was unusual to anyone who lived just three miles away, like me. On one rare occasion I was asked to accompany Pete to attend a house whilst there was a hymn practice at school. Pete was concerned about one of the older boy's attendance and, as his younger brother was in my class, he wanted me to tag along.

The house was a five-minute walk from the school, just into one of the streets at the entrance to the Maze from the main road. As we approached, I could see a ramshackle gate, tied with a piece of blue rope to hold it in place. Pete lifted the rope, opened the gate for us to go through and managed to put it back without it disintegrating. As we walked up the path towards the house, the boy from Pete's class could be seen standing with his back to the window, arms raised, cheering at something. Someone must have seen us as we approached the front door. Muffled sounds came from within as Pete knocked. A few seconds later the father appeared barefoot, his string vest visible beneath a set of braces which were at full tension to hold up a pair of stained black trousers, two sizes too small for him. A cigarette hung from his bottom lip and an old, discoloured cap balanced on his greasy locks as he shouted,

'Come in Mr Moore.'

He continued to bellow even though his wife was only about four feet away from him,

'It's the teachers, Mother.'

'Mother', a thin, pale faced woman, dressed in a faded blue house coat sat down hurriedly, trying to look like she had been sitting on the old settee for ages, attending to her sick child.

'We have come to see how Kevin is. His brother, in Miss Slater's class, didn't seem to know why Kevin was away from school today.' Pete explained.

It was Mother's turn to answer but our eyes both went to Kevin who was now lying on the settee, with his pyjamas on. His mustard-coloured jumper was clearly showing under his pyjama top which had been so hastily buttoned up incorrectly. Half of one trouser leg was visible also. The boy had clearly put on weight since the last time he had been seen in school a week before as his pyjamas were straining at the seams with his additional weight gain.

'It's like this Mr Moore, Kevin's got a fever so I'm keeping him off school 'til he is well enough.'

It was true that the boy was red in the face. He was sweating profusely. Pete was diplomatic. He explained the importance of Kevin attending school and that he hoped to see him as soon as he was well.

We left and before we had reached the gate to tackle the rope, Kevin was back cheering at some football match or other he was watching on the video recorder. Pete sighed as we reached the pavement, gate now back in place with the rope to keep it shut. Walking away from the house, he declared,

'Well, at least the chickens were all still under the kitchen table for once. Last time I went in they were running around the living room!'

Like it or loathe it this was life on the Maze.

✓✓✓✓✓

My first parents evening loomed after the autumn half term break. For some reason teaching a class of children was far less scary than having to talk about a beloved child to his or her parents. I prepared by making notes on each child which took me a whole week of evenings to write. As the planned date became ever nearer, I began to have a dream that would plague me for the next twenty- five years. No matter how I fought off the nightmare by being prepared, the dream always came.

I would rush into a classroom that I did not recognise, late for parents evening. All the parents would look up at me as they sat there waiting for the teacher. No exercise books would be ready to view, and I would be totally unprepared. At the point where I was about to sit down, my mouth would go dry, I would feel exposed as I had not changed into appropriate clothing, my hair was uncombed and I would not be able to think of what I should say, mixing up children with the wrong parents.

In case my dream came true, I went overboard with preparations. All the children's trays would be cleaned out, everything laid out ready with name cards on the top of each pile of books. My notes would be checked and checked. It was exhausting. The parents evening went well and there were no problems. One parent even made a comment praising me. I was never sure if he had any qualifications or experience of judging a teacher, but I am sure his heart was in the right place when he said,

'You're a good teacher, Miss! Have you ever thought of getting a promotion to a secondary school?'

I took great pleasure in informing him that primary and high school teachers were on a level footing in the education world for the most part; people's perceptions of secondary school being a grander place to teach made me smile. It wasn't the last time that this idea was put to me by a parent!

✓✓✓✓✓

I should have known not to be an eager and enthusiastic probationary teacher agreeing to anything. When I was asked by Pete to accompany him to take a party of junior children to a residential centre, owned by the local authority, I thought it would be a good experience for me. Maggie and the other teachers had seemed rather reluctant to attend, making excuses immediately which I had not understood at the time.

We set off three weeks before Christmas, on a freezing cold December day. I was glad I had put extra jumpers and socks in my suitcase once we had set off on the journey. The forecast for the week ahead was for cold, frosty days and possible snow. On arriving at the centre, the children were shown around the grounds after eating lunch. A fire drill was carried out so that children knew what to do should an alarm go off in the night. They should exit their dormitories, go through a fire door and down the staircase to reach an exit door right next to the assembly point.

Dormitories were on the second and third floors of a large late eighteenth century listed country house, owned by landed gentry until our local education authority bought it in the early 1950s. It had been a way in which the councillors could give children from the Black Country a residential, country experience. After the horrors of the Second World War, it had been a welcome break for generations of children, giving them a glimpse of life in the fresh air rather than the smog which often polluted their young lungs. The grounds were a mixture of cultivated lawns and flower beds and a huge field where children could run wild. Beyond the boundary lines there were woods and many country pathways to explore. The site was down a short drive, in the centre of a small village with timber framed, black and white cottages from centuries before. To the children from the Maze, this place must have seemed like somewhere from a different world.

There was an old stable block that had been converted into shower and locker rooms. At the far end of this covered quadrangle was a classroom. When the centre personnel left for the evening, apart from one member of staff who was always on duty in case of emergencies, Pete and I would take over any activities until the morning. The children would shower before bedtime, put on clean clothes and would walk the short distance into the house. They would relax in one of the downstairs rooms, next to the dining hall, with a warm drink and biscuits, watching a suitable video before going up to their dormitories where they had left pyjamas, slippers and a cuddly toy ready for night-time.

All went well for two days. The children loved the experience of being away from home with the independence it brought. The days were full of walks to the local woods for nature studies and visits to a stables and a roman villa site not far away. On the third evening they settled into their beds and fell asleep quickly, overcome by the countryside air and activities. My head hit the pillow in my bedroom, and I too dropped off to sleep easily.

It was around two o'clock in the morning when the shrill sound of the fire alarm pierced the silence of the centre. Luckily, I had decided not to bring nightwear but to have some tracksuit bottoms and a t-shirt on in case I needed to get up quickly should a child be ill. I scrambled around for my glasses, grabbed my tracksuit top, got into my trainers and headed across the short landing to the girls' dormitory. Panic filled the room. Girls were jumping out of bed and trying to find slippers. It seemed like hours before everyone had moved towards the staircase, but it probably was just a few seconds. I was last to get out of the building. Pete had managed to get the boys out just ahead of me.

Looking as if he had seen a ghost, the duty officer from the centre did a name call to ensure we were all accounted for. There was no smell of smoke, no flames but I could clearly hear a heavy vehicle in the distance, moving closer towards the centre. I guessed it must be a fire engine and just minutes after the alarm had sounded, there were five firefighters ready to move into action. After an inspection of the building, it was declared safe to enter. Everyone was relieved as the children were standing in the cold, in the middle of a December night, with just pyjamas or nighties and slippers on. We were all taken into the room where a few hours before we had sat drinking hot chocolate and eating jammy dodgers, watching *Bugs Bunny* and *Tweety Pie*.

The questions began. Who had phoned the fire brigade? How had the glass on a fire call point been smashed? A sudden realisation came over me that the fire alarm had been caused by one or more of the children sitting in front of us on the floor. Eventually, after interrogation that *Columbo* would have been proud of, and a process of elimination, the two culprits who had sneaked out of the building, down the road to a phone box were discovered. They had made the mistake of calling the fire brigade before they had returned and smashed glass on the call point. No wonder the fire engine had arrived so quickly!

At three o'clock in the morning, having put the children back to bed as best as we could, the two culprits stood, faces to the wall in the entrance hall, next to the staffroom. Their parents would be called to collect them four hours later. They were sent home in disgrace. Pete and I were hugely embarrassed by the whole event and for the rest of the week all children knew not to cross a line in any way. I was glad to get home and vowed never to return.

✓✓✓✓✓

Discussion in the staffroom in November had centred around just one topic, Christmas. It was decided, after a disaster the December before with all the main cast going down with chicken pox, that the teachers wanted an easier time and so a carol concert at the local church was planned. Pete arranged for a visit to the church as a dress rehearsal, so the children could familiarise themselves with where they would be standing or sitting before the concert the next afternoon.

When we returned to school after a successful practice that morning, each classroom became immersed in a delicious citrus perfume. Oranges were made into Christingles with four cocktail sticks full of sultanas skewered into each fruit's skin. A red ribbon was wrapped tightly around the circumference and finally a pure white candle was plunged into the orange as a reminder of Jesus, the light of the world. The Christingles were labelled and placed into wooden fruit crates to be carried down to the church the next day.

The Christmas concert afternoon arrived and after an early lunch the children were placed into pairs to walk as a long line down to the church about half a mile away. They chattered as they walked, some were singing carols, and all were excited to perform their songs to their parents. My class were to walk in last. The Christingles were hastily handed out, and I had drilled the children several times already that day, about candle safety,

'Remember to keep your candle away from your body at arm's length. Do not, under any circumstances stand too close to the person in front of you. '

My eyes were everywhere as June lit the candles. Maggie beckoned the front child to move to their position. The children moved off in a line and I looked proudly on, watching them take their places in the choir stalls. The junior choir were singing 'In the Bleak Mid-winter'. A tableau had been created at the front of the altar with some of the reception children dressed as nativity characters. It looked and sounded beautiful. A soft line of candles moved slowly down both aisles of the church. My mind went back to a similar nativity scene when I was about six years old, and I started to recall those images until a scream shattered my daydream.

There, a few rows away, in the opposite aisle to where I was standing was one of my girls with her hair on fire. A parent grabbed their coat, and the fire was out within a second. The child was not burnt thankfully, and her hair was just slightly singed. However, there was a pungent smell of burning that was more powerful than the citrus smell that had earlier filled the church.

Christmas gifts started to arrive. Whilst Park View was in one of the most deprived areas of the UK, the parents were an extremely generous bunch. Presents appeared from almost every family; a few I am sure were 'knock off' whilst most were given genuinely as a sign of thanks. There were endless boxes of chocolates, bottles of wine, trinkets, slippers and the most memorable Christmas present of all time, a toilet roll cover which consisted of a Barbie doll wearing a large, crocheted woolly dress, large enough to fit a loo roll underneath.

✓✓✓✓✓

Pete had been acting headteacher for a term. The decision to keep the school open after the next summer or to close it was to be made before the Christmas holiday. The local authority had wanted to close the school due to falling numbers but an army of parents and grandparents who were invested in the school and who had all attended it years before, fought a massive campaign, proving that the school was sustainable. A celebration disco was held when the decision was announced to keep the establishment open. I was elated that I had been given another term's contract at the school.

Pete would be acting headmaster for another term until a substantive leader was appointed to start after the Easter holidays. He did apply for the headship but his age and lack of ever applying for any other leadership jobs other than the deputy post at Park View Primary were against him. I had loved working for Pete, but if I am honest, I knew in my heart that he wouldn't have coped well. Even back then he had struggled with the paperwork and the duties of being a headteacher. He was too laid back and enjoyed his popularity and his carefree lifestyle, holidaying in Spain at every opportunity.

On the day before the interviews for the headship were held, seven candidates including Pete, toured the school. I recognised two of the visitors. Keith Wilson, the deputy headteacher on my first teaching practice and to my surprise I knew a third candidate, Stephanie Miles. She was the deputy headteacher at Northwood Primary, my old school. We had moved to a new house back in the same street as where my Nan still lived. My brother had been in her class, so I recognised her instantly.

90

Keith became the headteacher the next day. A new era would begin after the holidays.

Keith Wilson arrived on the first day, after the Easter break, like a whirlwind. Whilst he was a small man, his personality was larger than life as was his quiff. His perfectly coiffured hair sat neatly to one side of his head, and I often wanted to ask him how his hair stayed in place and mine never did! He was a man with a mission to improve the school. He raced around the building in his black Cuban heels, the steel tips warning of his advance thirty seconds or more before he burst through the classroom curtain. His brown suit was the only aspect of his appearance that seemed mundane. Within a term he had changed every single aspect of the school. He wanted to turn Park View Primary into a racing yacht. The trouble was that we were stuck in safe backwaters on a canal barge. His crew were unwilling sailors.

The arrival of Keith changed the dynamics of the school overnight. He wanted a reputation, and he didn't care how he got it. Within a month, despite reservations from the rest of the staff he was selling ice creams at the staffroom window at home time. He seized an opportunity to make a profit for the school instead of Mr Whippy who had rung his ice cream bell outside the school gates at home time for years. Keith offered a cheaper version and a '99' was his speciality. It was the end for Mr Whippy's daily visits. These were not the days of Healthy School awards or 'health and wellbeing'. His plan to increase the number of pupils on roll worked and we began to attract children and parents for the first time in years. Who could have guessed that a chocolate flake stuffed into a scoop of ice cream could change a school's future?

Within a week of being at the school he approached me one late afternoon and told me he wanted me to change classrooms. The infants department had three teaching rooms. I had been placed at the end of the area, in a classroom away from my infant colleague, June who was teaching the younger children. The middle classroom had been used by a playgroup for toddlers and parents. It had been a way for the campaigners to tempt parents to enrol their child when they were four to boost the numbers on roll. There was no nursery and Pete had taken this idea on board as soon as the parents had mentioned it to him. It was noisy on certain days and distracting to June's class and mine, but we had tolerated it to save the school. I asked him when he wanted the move to take place, expecting him to say next half term after the Whitsun holidays but he didn't.

'By Monday please.'

We joked months later about how he had watched me walk across the playground to leave school that afternoon. He said I looked like I wanted to kill him. In truth I probably did as I had spent half the holidays getting all my new displays done. The thought of taking everything down and having to make new ones filled me with horror. I should have to move all the furniture, organise the tables and a million other jobs. I was determined to show him what I was made of and immediately went to the caretaker, asking if I could go back later. After a positive response I made a plan. I left school at 5 o'clock and after having my tea and some help from Colin and my mum, I returned two hours later. That night we worked. And when the caretaker came to lock up, she was shocked at what we had achieved. I would show Keith what 'Monday' looked like. Next day when he arrived at school at 8 o'clock, I was there, in my new room ready to teach. The playgroup toys, large building blocks and slide were all in their new room too. The displays would take a few days longer......perhaps by Monday.

Whilst many of his methods riled the staff, Keith was forward in his thinking and within a month of being at the school we received our first computer, a shiny new BBC Micro with its black and red keyboard and cream body. The computer, monitor and floppy disk drive sat on a sparkling red trolley with a shelf underneath for any floppy disks. A timetable was drawn up and it was each teacher's responsibility to collect the trolley from the previous classroom after school for a morning session or at the beginning of lunch time for an afternoon session. With just five classes in the school, we were allocated the trolley twice per week. I had never been a technical child or adult, but I started to enjoy having the machine in the classroom. 'Granny's Garden' and other similar programs became popular, and the children worked hard to get their turn. Joe adored the computer. It was a way to get him to finish work. As I had shown the most interest amongst the staff, apart from Maggie, Keith encouraged me to try new programs and for the first time since leaving college he enrolled me on a two-day course to learn more. Becoming the school expert even opened doors to Mr Simmonds who, when no-one was about, would ask me the odd question about the computer in the staffroom. I was surprised he had realised I was there!

Reading resources at the school were based around the Reading 360 scheme. I had come across the reading scheme before at college but had not been enamoured by it. The books and text were boring, but I had dutifully made my reading tins up with flashcards. One of my uncles smoked a pipe and had collected tins for me. I think of how smoking is frowned upon now and the thought of placing words into tins that stunk of tobacco would be banned these days, but this was a regular practice in the mid nineteen eighties.

One day Keith announced he wanted me to trial a new reading scheme he had heard about. Our school, or rather I the youngest teacher by many years, would be trialling it. As we were to be a 'pilot' school it meant we got many books for free and a huge discount off an order should we want to extend the scheme as and when it was published. Keith, being keen to be seen as a trail blazer, was delighted at this arrangement. It meant that I had to use the new reading books, change all the flashcards to suit the new scheme and follow the teacher's manual to see if it worked. In return for taking part in the pilot, teachers would be expected to report on how the scheme was working and have staff from across the region watch reading lessons with the new resources. I moved to a world full of *Kipper, Biff, Chip and Floppy the dog*. The characters in the new scheme called 'Oxford Reading Tree' were painted on the walls, flashcards were everywhere. Games were made as instructed, the banda machine worked overtime. I had been teaching for less than a year, but people were wanting my expert opinion on a new scheme. With one fell swoop I was on my way to modelling teaching, something I would do for the rest of my teaching career.

Before I knew it, the year was ending, and it was time for report writing. I had never had to write a report before, and it was a tedious job handwriting each child's statement for the end of the year. I had, for a long time, written with a fountain pen and had to be careful not to make inky marks on the pages from my blue or black fingers. I had only eighteen to write but I shuddered at the thought of having to write more than thirty reports as colleagues in other schools had to. I determined that

I should dread every May and June for ever more because of the task ahead each year.

With the arrival of Keith, I had started to think about this third term being my final one at the school. I had now been given three temporary contracts and, as Park View had been saved from closure, a permanent position would be advertised. I began to apply for other teaching posts as I knew I could not be guaranteed the vacancy at the school.

I had also begun to worry about the observation by an education officer from the local authority, bringing the end of my probationary year to a close either successfully or unsuccessfully. Pete had observed my teaching once in two terms and seemed to have been pleased with my progress. Keith had observed me within two weeks of arriving at the school and had generally been complimentary but now the days of waiting for the letter, announcing the arrival of Miss Atkins was imminent. I knew it would be Miss Atkins. She was a specialist in nursery and infant teaching and, as I was teaching the middle and top infant class, she would be my observer. One observation to seal my fate. There were no mentors or set release time for probationary teachers in the early 1980s, just a one hundred percent teaching timetable and a couple of observations from the headteacher. The letter duly arrived, and the date was fixed. I looked at the day and time and my heart sank … it was P.E.

A week quickly passed, and the day of the observation arrived. Staff had been told by Keith that under no circumstances was anyone to send a child through the hall when my lesson had started. He wanted no interruptions by any child or member of staff whilst Miss Atkins was observing. She arrived punctually and went into Keith's room for him to brief her on my progress. Although Keith had only been the headteacher for a few short weeks he had many experiences of working with students and probationers. I heard the Cuban heels as he brought the visitor into the hall. I had managed to get out all the apparatus at the end of lunch with help from Maggie and Pete. Even June had wished me good luck, but Mr Simmonds had shown no interest in the proceedings.

I prayed Joe had a good lunch break and that he had not argued with anyone. He seemed calm when changing for PE. but had no kit. I made a pact with myself that no child would ever have to do sports in their underwear, like I'd witnessed in my own infant class, so I purchased lots of spare shorts and t-shirts which I took home and washed each week.

There were pairs of spare black pumps, so he was given a full kit. This always pleased Joe.

In came my observer. Well into her sixties, Miss Atkins was a tall, slender woman with short curly grey hair. Her already pale pallor, together with the cream suit she was wearing, gave her a ghostly appearance as she floated into the room. Her sharp features and the lack of expression scared me. This was her job, and she was intent on delivering a verdict on my teaching. Her views would mean the difference between me passing my probationary year or having to be closely supervised for a longer length of time. If I failed, my teaching record would be tarnished before it had properly begun. I might never get a permanent job. My body trembled as I began. My throat went dry. The next forty-five minutes would seal my fate.

The lesson began. To warm up, the children walked around the apparatus and mats. I blew my whistle, the one I had been given by my mother on my first day at college almost four years before. They stopped and started again on a second whistle. This activity went on for a few minutes until I instructed them to sit down. They were placed into groups and asked to move along the apparatus using different body parts. When I blew my next whistle, they stopped and sat down. For months they had been trained, with the help of my whistle, to move with their group to the next piece of apparatus and to sit when commanded. On my final whistle they began their routines. For the first time all year the class had no reminders, no warnings and no crying that someone had stepped on a toe or was bumped in the face. It was amazing how five small little sticky, coloured stars, promised to every child who worked hard and followed all instructions in the PE lesson, could be so motivational that week. Miss Atkins wrote reams. She rarely looked up, but her ears were alert to every sound. After forty minutes she rose from her chair, nodded to me and left the hall. Her face gave away nothing. My fate was in her hands.

A few days later a letter arrived informing me that I had successfully passed my probationary year. I was elated but I had to get a permanent job. Finally, I was able to apply for a permanent post at Park View when it was advertised. After the interview I came out of the room shellshocked. The questions had been much harder than I expected. Perhaps I wasn't meant to stay at the school. Feelings of doubt crept in. Tears started to fall at the thought of leaving. I loved the challenge of teaching in this area. It wasn't easy and the families had some real hardships, but the people were genuinely salt of the earth and at that moment I wanted to teach their children more than anything in the world. Ten minutes later I was crying with happiness. I could stay.

✓✓✓✓✓

I started my second year in teaching with a much larger class. Numbers were now rising rapidly just a term after Keith had taken over the headship at the school. My class size had risen from eighteen to thirty. More tables and chairs had to be found from around school. Oxford Reading Tree continued to be introduced in all classes now that more levels had been published. Visitors came to see the new books and there were many model lessons as the scheme gathered momentum in the primary world.

Joe had now moved to Mr Simmonds' class, and I was fearful he would befriend the teacher's walking stick. I had Joe's little sister who was very well behaved compared to her older brother. She had made friends with another child from an African Caribbean background who had moved schools, probably because of Keith's ice cream sales. It was good that the school was moving forwards and there was now a glimmer of diversity emerging. Unfortunately, this hope was short lived. A beautiful Pakistani child called Shireen arrived in the area with her mother, brothers and sisters. Social Services moved the family to a council house on the Maze after Shireen's mother had fled her violent husband. The child had the most gorgeous brown eyes and golden-brown skin. Her tiny arms were covered in colourful bangles and her bright salwar kameez attracted the attention of all the little girls in the class. She loved school and was very bright, her English improving by the day. The room was lit up by her wide smile. She disappeared after just two weeks. A violent mob chanting obscenities and racist slurs stoned the windows and the family disappeared, with the protection of several police officers in a riot van. Shireen's face haunted my thoughts. I begged that she and her family found peace elsewhere. The phrase '*You can't teach an old dog new tricks*' comes to mind sadly.

✓✓✓✓✓

I settled into a rhythm with my new class and the pupils seemed to follow. From being my least favourite subject to teach, P.E. became some of the lessons I most enjoyed. The children thrived at sports and would rush to get changed for P.E. as soon as they had returned from lunch.

One afternoon, in the mayhem of jumpers, tops and shoes seemingly everywhere in their rush to get changed, I noticed one small child, new to the school, sitting crying. Joy was a poor little mite. She was painfully shy and rarely spoke beyond a whisper, even when I called her to read. Keith had shared no background about her or her older sister, but it had been noted by me and Maggie that both children were very quiet. It would be easy to hide in a class of thirty children if teachers paid no heed to them. Maggie had already spoken of her concerns about the older girl. Her reading and writing were poor, and she had no confidence. Joy's sad face worried me. She had the features of a china doll, but her red lips were chapped by biting them. The child had no colour in her cheeks except when she felt embarrassed. She was also shorter than most of her peers. She rarely smiled in case she drew attention to herself. I was puzzled that this child's sad demeanour was so visible. On her first day at the school, I wanted to hug her and tell her everything would be alright, but the appropriate moment had not yet arrived, and I was waiting for her to become more settled.

I approached Joy and was about to speak to her when I saw a puddle on the carpet, emanating from her chair. Remembering my own accident years before, I managed to get her out of class to the toilets. I noticed some marks on her thighs as she stood up. A new classroom assistant, Lyn, had just started at the school. Now that the roll of pupils had risen rapidly Keith had seen the urgent need for someone to help June and me in our classes. I called Lyn to support Joy in the toilets, whispering that I had seen some unusual marks on her thighs.

It was an hour later when Lyn returned and motioned to me to come outside of the classroom curtain to speak. I had assumed Joy had been too distressed to return to class and had stayed with her. Lyn's eyes were red, and she wiped a tear as she started to explain to me what had happened. As she had begun to help the little girl to change, she too had noticed the marks I had mentioned to her, on her inner thighs, imprints of finger marks, purple and black. A few were yellowing.

Neither of us had received training about abuse. We lived in a world before the cases of Victoria Climbié or Baby P. There was no guidance on abuse or documents such as 'Every Child Matters' which years later

97

recommended education, social services and police working together to keep children safe from harm. Instinctively Lyn had sought Keith, pretending to Joy she had gone to find some dry socks. Keith had not entered the toilets but had instructed Lyn to stay with the child whilst he phoned Social Services for guidance. When Lyn had delicately asked how she had got the marks on her legs the poor child had spilled her story. Not only had she been physically abused but also sexually.

My only thoughts were of that small child of five; her innocence gone. My stomach lurched. I had not expected this story as the reason why Joy was such a sad little girl. The horror hit me as I realised the consequences of the afternoon's events. I tried to wipe away my tears before I returned to the class. When a child asked where Joy was, I replied that she had left because she was poorly. The reality of a five-year-old and her sister three years older, being taken into care and never returning home was too much for young ears, too much for me to contemplate. It was the last day I ever saw Joy but there have been countless days since when I have thought about her or visualised her in my dreams. The perpetrator of the children's suffering should have been a man they could trust. He should have cherished the girls but instead he abused them. I had grown up without a grandfather and had missed out on the relationship with him. Joy and her sister had suffered at their grandfather's filthy urges, and I wished that he would suffer in prison when other inmates found out his crimes. Life really had its ups and downs at the school from the bleakest of moments to the happiest of teaching memories. Sadly, it would not be the last dark time in my teaching career …

✓✓✓✓✓

It was time to decide on a Christmas performance and the staff chose a nativity play. My first Christmas had been the disastrous carol concert, but this performance was to have a cast of a thousand, (well a hundred and twenty-five), costumes and a script. None of the staff seemed nervous about the show as they were all well versed in everything that could possibly go wrong, or so they thought. This was my first ever performance and I was nervous! The rehearsals had gone remarkably smoothly. The words were all learned, the carols sung sweetly and the movements on and off stage seemed to go well. Keith had purchased a portable stage with some of his ice cream profits. It was collapsible and the parts could fit on a large trolley kept at one corner of the hall. With a

98

couple of days of practices, the stage had earned its money and was being well used. The dress rehearsal went without a hitch, but Maggie started to worry.

'Something will go wrong. It's going far too well.'

She sounded like the guy in *Dad's Army*, the one who cries in an anguished voice,

'We're all doomed!'

June started to pray even more fervently. Mr Simmonds was void of any emotion, but Pete had gone pale. I started to panic. It seemed we were doomed.

The next afternoon the children were ready, dressed, excited and full of chatter about whose parents were coming to watch the play. The show had been called *The Journey of the Star*. The story took you on the adventures of the Christmas star as it travelled around the world to Bethlehem. It had been put together by Maggie, Pete and June. Mr Simmonds had some appointment to attend and had not contributed to the planning meeting. I had just sat there, agog at these three geniuses who wrote a play in thirty minutes and in sixty minutes had a character list, assigned the parts and had hunted out suitable music.

The opening number began with 'Twinkle, Twinkle Little Star' played on the piano by June who turned out to be a fine pianist. Little reception children came on dressed as stars, or at Park View, in what clothes their parents and the school could find that matched the colours needed. Large star shapes, covered in silver tinsel, were strapped to their chests. The main star came onto the stage, wearing a black leotard and tights with an enormous gold star on her chest and a golden tinsel crown on her head. She saw her heavily pregnant mother who was crying at the sight of her daughter looking so angelic. The star cried so much she had to be taken off stage. Hastily Maggie signalled to a 'bright' star to take over the lead role which he did to the delight of his family.

The next few minutes went smoothly and finally the story reached Bethlehem. Onto the stage came a 'donkey' dressed in grey trousers and a matching top with a pinned-on, grey woollen plait for a tail. Then came Joseph and Mary, a junior boy and one of the girls who had been in my class last year. Joseph had an old brown curtain wrapped around him. A tea towel was on his head, kept in place by a thin piece of brown cord.

Mary wore a blue t-shirt together with a head scarf made from a white tea towel with a blue cord to secure it. Joseph had his fingertips on her shoulder as he was unwilling to wrap his arm around her. He led the girl around the stage towards the upturned P.E. box that was doubling as a manger, full of hay. Baby Jesus, a doll from June's class was ready for its big moment, having already been placed in the box. It was a lovely scene as the choir children, sitting on P.E. benches to the left and right of the stage, sang 'Silent Night' softly. Just as they had reached the words '*All is calm....*' Mary let gush the most enormous pee ever seen. The stage was flooded. Joseph stared at his soaking wet black pumps in disgust. Mary began to cry as someone from the audience shouted,

'That will be her waters breaking!'

The rest of the play continued without the precious new stage and without actors. All the children joined the choir, and the rest of the story was told in songs and carols. At the first staff meeting of the spring term in January it was hastily decided that it would be a carol concert in the school hall that year, to allow the stage to dry out thoroughly after a deep clean. Keith had no choice but to agree.

✓✓✓✓✓

Almost a year after he had become headmaster, Keith was proving to be a good mentor to me, although to other members of staff he could be moody and unpleasant. He was actively encouraging me to learn more about the computers. We now had two trolleys, one blue one for the infants and one red one for the junior classes. I enjoyed showing the staff new programs and even Mr Simmonds seemed to listen when I was asked to speak to everyone in a staff meeting for the first time about a new writing pad that we had purchased to assist weaker writers.

Lyn, the classroom assistant and I quickly became friends. She was a couple of years younger than me, but we had more in common than any of the older members of staff. Even though Lyn was twenty she still suffered terribly from spots and wore thick makeup to hide her scars and any new outbreaks. She styled her hair like Farah Fawcett, using copious amounts of time and hairspray to keep her flicks in place. Compared to the rest of the staff, her clothes were bold and bright. She would wear red trousers and stripy blue and white sailor top or white trousers and a multicoloured, gypsy top. She was small in height. The older junior children towered over her so she decided to wear wedged heels whenever she could to make herself taller.

Lyn was a great artist and the artwork she produced with the children was sensational. It made the displays look vibrant and inviting. The atmosphere changed with two younger members of staff. The place, which had been stuck in the fifties and sixties, seemed to be moving full speed ahead to the mid1980s. She would give me lifts home in her little red Mini and we would chat about the day. Sometimes she would turn the radio up loud and we would sing a Simply Red or Madonna tune in unison. There were occasions when we remained quiet if Social Services had been involved. We both needed silence on these days.

When we were both least expecting it, June announced one morning that God had won. She was resigning to concentrate on becoming a full-time minister. Although she had been a quiet member of staff, and of little use to a probationer, she had been there when needed. Her older colleagues were greatly affected by her news and even Mr Simmonds wished her good luck in her final days.

Her replacement was the opposite of June, a teacher just a few years older than me with three years more experience. For some reason, which I did not comprehend, I was jealous when Lucy arrived, dressed in a long flowing green dress, bright earrings and high heels. I thought Lucy's life was more colourful than mine. With long flowing ginger hair, I did wonder how often she might use a nit comb. She came every Monday morning as fresh as a daisy. She was always 'out' at weekends, staying at one friend or another's house or later at her boyfriend's. Gone were all the tears and praying from the classroom every morning or afternoon. The staffroom came to life with chat on love lives, television programmes and music. It felt completely comfortable for the three of us, in our own separate areas, pretending to be Cyndi Lauper as we blasted out 'Girls Just Want to Have Fun.' Lucy insisted that Mr Simmonds spoke to her each morning. After two years of hardly acknowledging my existence and having muttered the slightest of pleasantries to me in the staffroom, he saw me and said,

'Good Morning!'

When a bout of chickenpox hit the school badly, it was decided to double up so that teachers could get a few jobs done. I took first turn at having what was left of the two classes. Next day it was my time to catch up with planning, making resources and record keeping … or so I thought. Keith decided that he wanted to use me as his 'witness' when visiting a child who he suspected of playing truant. When Keith got *'a bee in his bonnet'* he was unbearable. The previous day he had telephoned the parent and had ascertained that the child did not have spots and should have been in school. The parent gave Keith her blessing, after he insisted that he would track the missing child, should he not turn up the next day.

Off we went in Keith's rather snazzy green MG. I did wonder if this was a wise move as we were heading to the edge of the Maze. Keith seemed not to be bothered as he was in a mood that morning, determined to hunt down the child. I had good, comfortable walking shoes on so if the car was pinched, I could walk back to school. We set off to a block of high-rise council flats, about half a mile from the Maze. I felt a little like *Cagney and Lacey* on a stake-out, me being *Christine Cagney* due to the blonde curly hair from another perm. Keith was *Mary Beth Lacey* as he had the same haircut and colouring, apart from the quiff.

As he parked the car in the car park, I spotted, out of the corner of my eye, a small group of unemployed ex-Woodfield lads in their late teens eyeing up the motor from a short distance away. I had thought it was a mistake to drive to the flats!

Park View flats were slowly crumbling and were badly in need of painting. There were three high rise blocks on the site, each with sixteen storeys. Graffiti covered some of the walls where the bins were stored. Even though it was not permitted to enter the area around the rubbish chutes at the bottom of each block, the padlocks on each metal gate had been broken years before and never replaced. Local drug addicts would hang about hoping for a fix if a dealer turned up to peddle his little plastic packets or a few ounces of weed. On numerous occasions, the council had tried to paint over some swastika signs. The different coloured patches on the walls gave away the many failed attempts.

Keith looked at the numbers on each block and strode confidently towards the furthest from the car. In we went, no keypad for security. As he stopped at the lift, I noticed an 'out of order' sign taped to one of the doors. We began to climb up thirteen flights of stairs. The lower landings smelt of urine but as we went higher, there was an overriding smell of weed on some floors. When we reached the thirteenth floor, I was quietly cursing Keith for wasting my time out of class on this mission. Why did he need me, a young, inexperienced teacher when he could have managed perfectly well himself? I could hardly be his bodyguard!

We found the flat easily and knocked on the door. A level of panic could be heard coming from within the flat with voices raised initially until silence fell. Two knocks later Keith decided to act like *The Bill* as he shouted that he was going nowhere. Eventually a familiar face opened the door slightly. Keith put his Cuban heeled shoe in the doorway just like *Mary Beth* would have done. There was a thirteen-year-old boy who was also absent from school due to chickenpox by the look of the blisters on his face.

'Is Micky in here?' demanded Keith.

The youth could see it was futile to lie and blabbed straight away.

'Yes, he wants to catch chickenpox, so he keeps coming back home when our mum's out.'

We entered the flat and found Micky hiding under the bunk beds in a bedroom. He wasn't alone in the room as there was an unusual pet who became a little unsettled as Keith opened the door. He marched Micky out of the flat with me following behind speechless at what I had just seen. Keith called to the teenager with the chickenpox,

'Billy, you need to get the dustpan and brush. There's manure in your bedroom.'

Even Keith laughed as we walked back towards the carpark. Had we both dreamed we had seen a piebald cob, fourteen hands high on the thirteenth floor of a block of flats? Anything was possible, it seemed. It was a common occurrence to see a 'trotter' in the area. A horse attached to a harness would pull a sulky cart. These contraptions were lightweight, without a main carriage body and often had just two wheels. A seat for the driver was attached to the shafts. 'Trotter' racing was commonplace. During playtimes children would often run to the fence to watch the horses trotting past the school gates, practising for races. Locals would clear the streets of cars on race days, money passing hands as to which driver would win. All bets were off if the police heard of the event. I was

103

not surprised I had seen the cob. I had heard the stories so many times of horses in the flats. After all I had attended the local high school!

It had been an eventful day, a truant trying to catch chickenpox, a 'trotter' horse on the thirteenth floor of a block of flats and an MG on bricks, four wheels missing!

✓✓✓✓✓

At the beginning of the next term Keith announced we were to have some work experience pupils from the rival secondary school to Woodfield for a week. I was pleased to think I would have some help in the classroom for a few days.

On Monday morning a young girl of about fifteen was shown into my class. I took the register quickly and rushed the children into the assembly, paying little attention to the girl until we sat down waiting for all the classes to enter the hall and settle. As I glanced at the teenager I thought she looked familiar. Perhaps she was related to someone in the Maze I thought. I asked her name.

'My name is Jill, Miss. Jill Slater.'

' That's easy to remember. We have the same surname.'

Suddenly the smile on my face became hard to maintain. Panic engulfed me. I struggled to breathe. My cheeks warmed and I stuttered as I asked her what she was going to do at lunchtime.

'I'll go home. It's not far. I live in Kelsey Avenue.'

I knew already where she lived. My worst fear had come true. Sitting next to me, oblivious to our connection, our blood, was my half-sister. She was the child my father and his second wife had produced. I knew from my mother that I had half siblings, a brother and a sister, but never in my wildest nightmares did I think I should ever meet either of them. I held myself together somehow until break when she went off with her friends to chat about their morning so far.

I spotted Lyn and grabbed her arm, pushing her into the ladies toilets. Looking confused she stared at me, surprised at my behaviour.

'Have you seen that work experience girl in my classroom?'

'Yes. I keep thinking I know her from somewhere. Her face is so familiar.'

'Her name is Jill Slater. I think she is my sister.'

Lyn gasped. She knew about my background.

'Oh, my goodness! She looks just like you. That's it. She has your face.'

The rest of the morning was a blur. At lunchtime I sat in the staffroom, stunned and in shock. My appetite had vanished. Keith entered the room and made an announcement that the students would be moving classes in the afternoon to give them experience of working with all ages of children. Lyn came into the room, made a cup of tea and sat down with her packed lunch. I noted that she seemed to have applied a little too much blusher earlier in the day but thought no more of it.

I'll never know if she had a chat with Keith or if he had planned to move the work experience students around. All I do know is that my sister was never put back into my class for the rest of the week.

I had taught at Park View for just over three years and began to feel unsettled. Keith had become more and more unpleasant in his demands for change. He began to explode at children and staff if anyone did anything wrong or didn't exactly follow his rules. His moods increased and when talking to him, I often felt as if I was walking on eggshells. He did not share with anyone that his marriage was in difficulty and that he and his wife were on the point of separating. One day in the corridor by his office, I saw Keith snarling at an older boy for arguing on the playground, his voice full of sarcasm and hostility. Perhaps the boy had done something stupid but the verbal battering he received was unwarranted.

When I saw an advertisement in the local newspaper that my old school Northwood was looking to employ a new nursery teacher, I plucked up the courage to speak to Keith.

'Hi Keith. Could I have a quick word please?'

Keith nodded.

'I was wondering if I could put your name down as a referee for a job application. I've spotted a teaching job nearer to home in a nursery and thought I'd try for it.'

'If you think the grass is greener somewhere else, then apply.'

His answer had been unexpectedly sharp, his tone unnecessary. The post at Northwood wasn't a promotion; in fact, it was the same salary that I was being paid at Park View. I was determined to give the application my very best shot. A couple of weeks later, I attended an interview and recognised the headteacher instantly; she had been my brother Paul's teacher when he had attended Northwood. I had also spotted her when she toured Park View as a prospective candidate for the headship along with Keith and Pete two years before. If I was successful at interview I should be going home. When I informed him that I was handing in my notice, Keith offered more sarcasm.

'Good luck if you think working for Stephanie Miles will be a bed of roses.'

I was relieved to be finishing at Park View as the Easter holidays approached. Keith had become more hostile to me, barely speaking. I had no ill feelings towards him, but his explosions of temper had become worse. He could not suppress his venom to staff, nor hide his hostility to children. His barbed comments to me in staff meetings were painful and embarrassing. When I had spoken to Lucy about his mood, she had explained that his plans to make me an IT coordinator, in the next school year, had been destroyed. It was not to be. I didn't want a promotion. I wanted a headteacher who was kind. I left the school and never saw Keith and his Cuban heels again.

Chapter 6
Back Home

When I walked into Northwood on my first day as a nursery teacher, my feelings were a mixture of nervousness and pure excitement. I belonged there and had secretly dreamed of returning since the first embryonic thoughts of becoming a teacher years before. I knew instantly it had been the right decision to come home. It felt like putting on an old pair of comfortable slippers.

Although almost all staff had retired or moved on since I had been a pupil, a few familiar figures greeted me within minutes of my arrival. There were two classroom assistants who I recognised from my childhood; then came Liz Wootton, who had known me all my life. Other unfamiliar staff popped their head in to greet me. The atmosphere was so different to Park View. There was a feeling of life and energy in the place that had been lacking in my first school.

Now the headmistress after a promotion a year before, Stephanie Miles, was very attractive with a decent figure, and she knew it. Her shiny, black high heels clattered around school, replacing the sound of the Cuban ones that I had grown accustomed to. Her skirts were always short but not tacky and in summer her bare, sun-tanned limbs seemed to make her even taller than her five feet, seven inches when she walked into a room. If she had not chosen a career in teaching, she could have been a model. Her face would have made her a fortune, with just the right amount of make-up, looking fresh faced rather than overdone. Her blonde locks were perfectly placed, framing her face and draping carefully down her back. Stephanie presented her perfection to the world but unfortunately one aspect of her life was by no means perfect.

Stephanie was a woman with a history that was famous around the area but nothing to do with anything educational. Her reputation was that of a 'man eater' and there were legendary stories of her being married three or four times. When my brother had been a pupil at the school, parents were full of stories about her school camp exploits with a male colleague, sex in cupboards after school and many extra curricula activities, too many to mention. Although these stories were almost certainly untrue, now she was in her late forties she was thought of as a cougar. She had apparently married her third husband and had two boys and a girl with this man. How she managed to look so perfect and so polished after having three babies was a miracle.

With a charismatic personality, Stephanie could charm ducks off a pond. She could tame an aggrieved parent into submission within a couple of minutes. She would captivate governors with her plans. I wanted to hate this perfect woman, but I could not. I liked her. Perhaps her charm had worked on me, but she was funny and bubbly. She knew the school well and the work atmosphere was relaxed and happy.

Northwood was in an area I knew well, more affluent than Park View, but certainly wasn't at all posh. The houses were an evenly balanced mixture of council and owned properties, and most people had jobs of some description. Traditionally the dads would work, and the mums would stay at home or work part time. The children wore uniforms, unlike when I had been a child at the school. To an untrained eye all the children looked the same. The reality was different. Some collars on shirts or blouses were bright white whilst others were grubby and worn. I knew the area so well, or so I thought. There was no clear distinction of the 'Haves and the Have Nots'. Some families living on benefits appeared to have more than households with both parents working.

✓✓✓✓✓

There were two nursery nurses, Laura and Dawn, in the class who had been in nursery since it had been set up four years before. They had qualified with their N.N.E.B. qualification and each was highly talented and experienced in working with young pre-school children. It took a few weeks for me to get used to not being a solo teacher anymore. I decided not to change any routines. The children and staff would feel more secure without change. Why break a record when it clearly was playing well?

Laura was taller and of slimmer build than me or Dawn. Over the years that I worked with her, she had a range of hair styles varying in shape and length. When she tired of having short hair, her locks would be grown longer until she was ready to have a perm. On one occasion her looks were spotted by a film crew visiting the school to make a training video about teaching traveller children. She had to pretend to walk into school to speak to staff as no real gypsy mother would be filmed. Her deep brown eyes, dark hair and a suntan from her last holiday in Turkey made Laura a perfect actress for the part. The irony was that back in her family history there had been gypsy blood.

Her conversation in the staffroom was always lively. She would chat about her family and the banter they gave each other. One year Laura and her brother began a joke around an extremely large pair of knickers one of them had come across on their holidays. The game was to pass the article to the sibling without them realising they had received it. Sometimes it would take months of preparation. Laura would share her hilarious plans in the staffroom. Weeks later the knickers would be returned by her brother when she least expected. The stories she told got wilder as the tricks they played on each other grew bolder.

The other stories Laura would tell involved travelling abroad with her family or boyfriend. Sometimes, near Christmas, she and her friends and relations would hire a coach to visit France for the weekend on the booze run. On the Monday after this annual event, she would come to school absolutely knackered as the party had travelled through the night to reach the Midlands in time for work. She swore by a product called Bright Eyes which was a glue-like gel that stuck to her eyelashes to keep her eyes open. You could always tell when she used this substance as she looked like a rabbit stuck in the headlights when she walked into school. At lunch time she would sit in the staffroom, eyes wide open but an occasional snore would remind you she was having forty winks.

Laura was hilarious. However, if she was ever riled about an unfair decision made by Stephanie, Laura would air her views to her publicly, pulling no punches. I think she secretly liked being called into the office for one of her 'Mr Kipling's French Fancy' talks to appease her. Laura wouldn't change her mind, but she liked rattling Stephane's cage occasionally when it was necessary, and the cake made it more enjoyable!

Dawn was a more serious character than her colleague, but she still could be funny when she wanted. I always felt comfortable talking to her. She had great faith and did a lot of work for her local church. She had a great empathy with parents. Ever practical, she liked to solve problems. Having started her nurse training a few years before, she was naturally the first aider when any accident occurred in nursery. She would look at a child's arm if they had fallen awkwardly and always had an instinct for fractures.

One of Dawn's many talents was an ability to hold a straight face when a parent told her something which we found funny. We were not being cruel, and we did not mean any offence by laughing at people but sometimes they would say ridiculous things which we howled at when nursery children had gone home. Dawn would always be the straight guy, managing to hold a conversation as Laura and I were bursting to laugh.

'Oh Mrs Donaldson. I am sorry to hear about your husband's piles. Have you tried a rubber ring?'

'Good afternoon, Mr O'Connor. Are you all well after having upset tummies? That's very kind of you to bring in some home-made biscuits for the teachers. We're all on diets so it's best you take them home.'

One day she surpassed herself with a parental conversation.

'Good morning, Mrs Hobs. It's lovely to see you back on your feet. How are you? How's the baby?'

The mother showed Dawn the new baby and the nursery nurse dug a little deeper.

'So, what did you call her?'

'Simone.'

'That's lovely. Did you give her a middle name?'

'Yes! Simone Madonna California Vienna Hobs'

Even Dawn's face twitched slightly. Her eyes looked like saucers as she composed herself. Laura went behind a curtain and bit hard on her hand to stop any sound she might have made. I just stood there next to Dawn, hoping my professionalism would see me through, but I could feel a wave of hysteria pressurising my cheeks.

'Oh! That's a nice name? Why did you call her that?'

That was it. I had to move away from the conversation. My cheeks could take no more. I felt them burn and my smile became more strained as my lips began to crumble.

'I have to go to the office.'

Dawn and Mrs Hobs stared at me as I rushed out of the room. I made it as far as Laura and the curtain. I began to bite my hand as I reached her. My teeth sank further into my skin as Mrs Hobs replied.

'Well, we liked the name Simone. Madonna is our favourite singer. California was a holiday we went on three years ago that we loved and Vienna … well Vienna is where she was conceived.'

110

'Ahh! That's … interesting.'

Even Dawn struggled to hold herself as the woman moved away and left the room. The laughter was uncontrollable for the next few minutes. The nursery children stared at us but carried on playing. What silly games the adults in this nursery played!

There was a good rapport between the three of us and it was a joy to go to work. Every third week each of us would be 'on art'. This meant that one member of staff would organise the art activities we had all planned, normally around a theme. On Wednesdays it would be a cookery activity. If it was Hallowe'en the biscuits would be shaped like cobwebs with icing to decorate, at Christmas it would be Christmas trees, Easter would be Rice Krispie nests with mini chocolate eggs. There would also be opportunities for lots of healthy eating which never seemed as popular with the children … or staff!

Working in nursery was always funny. The children, because of their age, were always doing things that were unexpected. One day I was calling the register in the quiet room that was just off the main classroom. It was a small space but just perfect for register or storytelling. I was in a rush to get the register called quickly so we could get on with all the activities we had planned. The register started as normal.

'Anna?'

'Yes Miss.'

'Billy?'

'Yes Miss.'

'Benjamin?'

Benjamin was an extremely quiet member of the class, one of the youngest and it had become clear from the first weeks of being in nursery that he wasn't the brightest of children in class.

There came the most enormous rip-roaring fart ever heard to man or woman, let alone a child! It was totally unexpected but had been perfectly timed to answer the register. The laughter started from behind the curtain as both Dawn and Laura had heard the noise. The sound came into the quiet room, and I thought it best to start singing some nursery rhymes to stifle the sobs and laughter. I had to sing for a good ten minutes that day!

✓✓✓✓✓

One of my favourite parents at Northwood was a woman who had problems naming her children, unlike Mrs Hobs. I met her when her first child was to start nursery. She came in to register the child and filled in the forms. The first space of the form stated 'name'. After establishing the fact that she had to write her child's name, and not her own, she filled in the form and put down her pen.

'I have to tell you that his name is Jonathan, but he is to be known as Johnny.'

I explained that he could be known as Johnny but on all official records he would be Jonathan. He would be taught to spell the longer version of his name to prepare him for life as an adult. The mother nodded and picked up the pen again to continue her task. A few minutes later she finished and sat back in the chair.

'Would you mind if I fill a form in for my second son?'

I found a second form from my folder, and she lifted her pen ready to fill it in. Again, after ten seconds she looked at me and said,

'Now this one is called Derek, but he is to be known as Dekky.'

I could see a pattern emerging and leaning forwards towards her, offered some advice. I pointed to her tummy. It was clear she was six or seven months pregnant.

'Mrs Coleman, you do know that you can actually register a child's name at birth to be whatever you wish? '

'Really Miss Slater? I thought you had to have proper names. That's why Johnny is Jonathan and Dekky is Derek.'

I took a breath.

'Yes Mrs Coleman. Probably proper names are best, but you could have registered Johnny as Johnny.'

A few months later, after Johnny was settled in nursery and not long before Dekky was to start in nursery, Mrs Coleman came into school with the new-born baby, a few days old, in her arms. It was another boy. The usual new baby talk commenced with asking how she was and how the baby was doing. Without thinking I asked her what she had called son 'number three.'

'Well, a few months ago you said I could call the baby what I wanted so I did. '

112

I leaned forwards in anticipation, hoping that the name she called her third son was what she wanted to name him.

'Meet Mike Mohammed Ali Sylvester Stallone Coleman,' she cooed as she looked fondly at her new baby.

I wanted the floor to open and swallow me. All I had said was to register her baby with the name she wanted to call him. Now Mike Mohammed Ali Sylvester Stallone Coleman had a burden for life, and it was all my fault. I wondered if he was destined to marry Simone Madonna California Venice.

It was at the sports day at the end of my first term that led to the biggest surprise a parent has ever given me; in fact, the surprise came in threes! The weather had been good for the last couple of weeks and the forecast for race day on the school field was hot and sunny. A letter went home to ask parents to make sure children had sunhats and sun cream as it was going to be a scorcher of an afternoon. Before lunch we got the children to carry chairs out onto the field for parents to sit on and some of the older children carried mats to place on the opposite side of the racetrack for the children.

After lunch Stephanie appeared wearing a pair of tight white shorts, and a white t-shirt which exaggerated her tanned limbs. White trainers finished the look, making her less tall than usual. I had never seen her without the high heels before. Off she jogged onto the field, all eyes on her, especially the fathers in the crowd.

The afternoon went smoothly, and the races were almost completed when Stephanie had the bright idea to encourage parent participation. She must have been on a course about community engagement. Grabbing the loudspeaker, she asked for volunteers to take a place at the start line. The fathers went up first, basically to ogle the headteacher's legs at closer range. The race was amusing. All the macho men stroll up, adjusting the waist of their trousers and flexing their biceps. A couple attempting a quick stretching exercise or two, completely forgetting they were not running an Olympic sprint. It was just a short run, on a school playing field in the Midlands, on a baking hot day. There was no prize, but all seven volunteers looked determined to win as they set off for the finish line. The children screamed and shouted until the race was done a few seconds later. The victorious father lapped up the praise from the crowd and grabbed his two delighted children for a hug.

Next it was the mothers' turn to answer the call. Up came a few older mums for the laugh and several younger ones who were more competitive. The race started but within the first ten metres a huge roar went up from the crowd, followed by an almighty chorus of laughter. There was one of the older mothers, who had been wearing a bright pink boob tube, with no straps and a mini skirt. The garment had slipped down to her waist and there were two enormous breasts bouncing up and down as she raced to the finish line. When she reached the end, she leapt into the air. Her skirt had risen to where her boob tube had ended, at her waist, and on show now were the afore mentioned two double Ds and a backside that had been forced into a pink G-string. She had certainly coordinated her clothes that day. Stephanie never had a parent race again whilst I was at the school …

✓✓✓✓✓

Nursery days were bliss. The children were delightful. It really was a lovely environment to work in. If the weather was good the children could play in the nursery garden with Laura volunteering as she loved to get a suntan ready for exotic holidays. Dawn liked baking cakes. We would spend the days which were always busy, working well as a team, each playing a part in this well-oiled machine. Every day we laughed until we cried at some of the funny things that happened.

When new children were about to start nursery, they would come with their parents for a visit beforehand. When Janice appeared in her best frilly dress with long red ribbons hanging from her hair, she looked like an angelic china doll until she opened her mouth. She was a proper little madam. Having been in nursery for about ten minutes she took it upon herself to pee in the home corner, proudly announcing to her parents and me,

'I needed a piss!'

Her doting parents never flinched or expressed any horror or embarrassment at their daughter's behaviour. As I sat open mouthed looking between the pair of them and Janice, I waited for some sort of apology. Instead came the mother's response,

'Don't worry our Jan. You can't hold it in if it needs to come out. Love you!'

Once she commenced in nursery, Janice demanded her own way and tried to boss adults as well as children. She would argue about any toy as she had no concept of sharing. The main concern was that Janice swore frequent. At the end of my tether, after a particularly exasperating day when the 'f word' had been used many times, enough was enough. I decided to speak to her mother. The threat had made Janice cry, but I wasn't sure why. I was only certain that she would be greeted with a bag of sweets.

I called Janice's mother to one side, discreetly explaining that I was concerned about the language that Janice was using and asked if she could have a chat with her daughter. The mother had a booming voice, rather like her child. Every time I told her what Janice had said she would use a loud expletive, in shock at her daughter's language. Her friends, standing a distance away, could hear her and they started to chuckle at her loud responses. In her poshest voice she replied,

'I am so sorry Miss. I really don't know where the bloody little cow gets it from. She's such a little bastard.'

The laughter got louder and louder from the other parents. Janice's mother turned around.

'What? What the bloody hell are you lot laughing at?'

As I went back into school, I could still hear the women teasing her as she continued to protest her innocence.

Just after two years spent in nursery, everything changed when Miss Atkins made a visit to the school. She was still a school advisor. I had been chosen to be observed and, after a session in nursery, I was asked to go to the head's office. There was Stephanie and Miss Atkins having a chat. They spoke about other matters and then, as if suddenly aware of my presence, they both looked towards me. Stephanie spoke.

'Miss Atkins has persuaded me to move you to one of the infant classes in September. It would be good to have your steady influence in main school.'

There was no point in arguing, I knew. Miss Atkins had much more power and persuasion that a young teacher barely five years out of college. I was desperate to stay in nursery. I had loved working with the children, the banter amongst the three staff but it was not to be.

When September came, I was placed in a reception class and never returned to nursery. Years later when a nursery teacher was off ill, I would secretly adore covering the sessions myself as I cherished my time in nursery so much. For the rest of my teaching days at Northwood I would be moved between reception, year one, year two or year three classes. Stephanie would haul staff into her office each June to tell them where she was placing them for the next academic year. I always felt like a puppet, at her mercy, when I stepped into her room.

I moved into reception class and along came Laura too. I was delighted to continue to work with her. Into the world of Letterland we went with *Annie Apple*, *Clever Cat* and *Fireman Fred*, to teach phonics but I found myself also in *The Village with Three Corners* with *Roger Red-Hat*. I should have been a millionaire if I received a pound for every time a child read the name *Johniffer Yellow-Hat* for the twins *Johnny and Jennifer*. For maths we used individual SPMG Infant Mathematics booklets. I was glad of Laura's company. Her cheery nature kept me going but we soon needed to support each other just days after we began the new school year in our new classroom.

Some of the children who had just left nursery were also in the class, the rest had moved into another reception room. In addition, there was a new boy, the third of five children in a family to move into the area and into school. His name was Barry and perhaps he is the child I most think about of all the children I have ever taught. In the first few weeks after the summer holiday all the children were getting back into the swing of things. Barry hadn't been to nursery so me and Laura expected him to be unsure and not so confident as the other children.

Barry was tiny compared to some of the other four-year-olds. He always looked smart, and his uniform was spotless. His short dark hair was immaculate. Outwardly he was a well-turned-out little boy but the world inside his head was burdensome for such a young child. He always seemed to carry his worries on his shoulders. Although he could smile and had an infectious laugh, his mood swings were wild and tempestuous.

One day Barry came into school refusing to speak, even to answer his name when register was called. He had no snack money and when I asked if he had had breakfast, he shook his head and looked away from me, burying his face with his elbow and arm. There was nothing to do but find a snack for him. Perhaps it might put him in a better mood after morning break.

When I collected him from the playground with the rest of the class, he followed everyone in, and I thought he seemed more like his usual self. As soon as his name was called to come to do some work, he flatly refused to leave the box of Lego he had been playing with. Laura tried to cajole him, but he seemed to build a defensive wall around himself. In the end I asked him to go with her to the art area to cool down and talk about what was the matter. He again refused but this time he started throwing anything he could reach, Lego at first, then the box, then items on a nearby table. Laura took him by the hand and marched him out of the room when he hit a couple of children with the building bricks.

No door had been built between the classroom and art room. The open plan building, which I had grown up with, remained and there was just a curtain in the space, where normally there would be a door. As I poked my head through the curtain Laura was touching her eye where Barry had just head butted her. He ran towards an area where items like paint pots were stored and grabbing a paint brush by its head, he attempted to stab both Laura and me. Barry was out of control, but I had to gain some semblance of calm back to the proceedings. I stepped back through the curtain where the rest of reception were happily playing or working and asked a child who I knew could cope with a message to take a note to the office. Within a minute Stephanie came racing into the area. Barry was frogmarched to Stephanie's office where he continued to cause mayhem until his parents were sent for. The boy was suspended from school for a few days, but we all feared for him.

On a 'home visit' before another child in the family was admitted to nursery, the two staff had come back to report a strange atmosphere and had noted a baseball bat in the living room. Dad was an enormous guy with lots of muscles on display which we had seen on the odd occasions when he stood at the school gate in a vest top and tracksuit bottoms. The mother was cautious with her answers to anyone in authority, always avoiding eye contact. Despite the way the children were dressed for school, she seemed better dressed by far. There could have been some domestic violence, but we had no evidence to make any allegations.

117

Stephanie had already contacted Social Services as she had been worried about Barry, the entire set up of the family, the nursery staff observations and some of the other things the older children had said in school. The final straw came when the school community were buzzing with tales of armed police and a siege in the street, at little Barry's house. The stories of ten police officers to hold the dad down to make an arrest sounded plausible. He was a huge man who clearly worked out often and looked very capable of handling himself in any eventuality. Many rumours circulated about drug dealing and gun running and after a court case, most tales were found to be true. He went to prison, but Barry had no real respite, despite his father being locked up.

A few days after his arrest, when Barry's father had been placed on remand awaiting trial, we had a training day in school. Sessions were held in the spacious nursery room Extra seating was brought in from around school, some from the staffroom and a couple from the entrance area, by the school office where visitors and parents sat waiting to see Stephanie. One of the teachers carried in a chair and sat down. As he got comfortable, he felt something hard against his lower back so without thinking he placed his hands behind him to feel what was wrong with the chair. What he found made him jump up. He had luckily found the handle end of a large carving knife. Just a few short days before, Barry's father had been sitting on this very chair, awaiting a Social Services meeting.

Barry returned to school. His eyes looked dull, yet his school uniform was perfect, the white of his shirt gleaming. There were imperfections when you looked more closely. He chewed the cuffs on his jumpers, his shoes were always scuffed and there was often a wet patch on his trousers although he would never admit he had had an accident.

Laura, who was less threatening to some parents than a teacher, would try to get into conversation with Barry's mother and it quickly became apparent that as the third child of five, he was treated differently to the other siblings. The mother would greet Barry with a stare and cross words but when the older two children came to find her, after the school bell had gone, she gave them cream cakes or sweets. She would give Barry's sister, barely a year younger a cake and one to the toddler she had strapped into his pushchair. Barry … he got nothing.

We were told to document everything that happened in class and so I began to dread going to work. Note taking was useless in a reception class

118

with thirty or more four-and-five-year-olds demanding attention. I came up with a plan to quickly grab a second or two in the store cupboard, situated within the room, to make a few voice recordings into a Dictaphone. Hours were spent writing notes at night.

Stephanie, sensing that Laura and I were on the point of breakdown with the boy, suspended him again after another violent attack on the nursery nurse. Enough was enough. All kinds of professionals attended meetings and one day, without warning Barry was gone. His siblings remained, but he was placed in a residential school, in the countryside, miles away from home at the tender age of five. I look back in horror at that story now but there were no other options for a boy who was emotionally, mentally and physically abused, whose home was unsafe and whose behaviour was so violent he could have killed a child or member of staff. When I see news headlines about child abuse, I always think of Barry and wonder what happened to him. My heart still aches for news that he did not end up like Joe at Park View Primary. My fear is a darker future for him.

In 1988 the National Curriculum was introduced into English schools, bringing many changes. Along came white folders for every subject. Each classroom had a new shelf built to house a set of documents for each teacher. Although we all wanted to battle against the new way of working, it was an educational strategy that we could not ignore. Endless planning meetings were timetabled at lunchtimes, after school, whenever staff could meet in teams.

Teachers complained about the workload and 'Baker Days' became a new phrase in every staffroom. Every academic year there should now be five days laid aside for all teachers to receive training. They were so named because the education minister at the time was Kenneth Baker. Initially these five non-teaching days were spent in schools to prepare for the National Curriculum to be taught in every class.

Gone would be an infant group or a junior group. We quickly took on the labels of 'Key Stages 1 and 2'. Nursery would be called 'Early Years' when their curriculum was brought in. Statutory Assessment Tasks, usually referred to as SATs, would take place each summer for year two and year six children, We were no longer able to develop our own schemes of work or topics. Titles of units of study were given to us, with

119

topics that did not interest the children. A straitjacket had been placed around the teaching profession.

In the year I had left secondary school, Pink Floyd released *The Wall* album. The title track, 'Another Brick in the Wall', had reached the dizzy heights of number one in the UK music chart, selling over a million copies in the five weeks it held the top position. The dawn of the National Curriculum reminded me of the video which accompanied the single's release featuring pupils marching towards a meat mincing machine in a dystopian world. Although the new curriculum brought many positive developments over the years, in 1988 it felt that the very heart of teaching, had been ripped from me, and replaced by a government monster.

Pressures began to be felt when league tables were introduced with the results of SATs being published. It was impossible to make comparisons between schools. Consideration began to be placed on the number of children receiving free school meals. This was to show how much deprivation there was in an area. Mini league tables with similar schools were created. Data became powerful. 'Accountability' was the buzzword. The joy of teaching became tarnished.

The next couple of years saw steady changes also to the staffing at Northwood. From being an older, more settled staff, probationers were placed at the school by the local authority when someone retired. The staff I worked with seemed to change each year. Laura went back into nursery and Dawn came out. Just when the school seemed settled something devastating was to happen in my personal life.

✓✓✓✓✓

On a late November evening in 1991 I stayed up late until two o'clock watching the annual *Children in Need* show on the BBC. I knew it was a mistake as I should need to get up and be in school for a Christmas Fair at ten o'clock on the Saturday morning. I would be tired. I had been placed on the bottle stall which I knew was always busy so there would be no chance to have a snooze in a quiet corner of the building. In the late afternoon I left school shattered and decided to go to bed early. After a quiet evening watching telly, half dozing at times, I thought about going to bed. Mum had already gone up for the night and my brother had been in his room for hours like a typical teenager, avoiding adult company. Colin was still watching a film.

Earlier in the week I had hurt my neck and shoulder when a child had slipped on some ropes in front of me whilst I had been teaching a P.E. lesson. My instinct was to step forward to save her from falling onto her face as she had attempted to do a somersault in the air between the two ropes. In the process I twisted awkwardly, and my neck and shoulder had been painful all week. Colin gave excellent massages and had used 'Tiger Balm' on the site of my pain for the last couple of evenings which had brought some relief. I asked him if he would do a quick massage on my neck before I went to bed. He nodded and I sat down in front of him on the living room floor. The jar of Tiger balm had been opened and he began to massage my shoulder.

Within a couple of seconds, I felt no pressure and asked him to press harder, but his fingers did not change; they had stopped completely. I turned around and saw Colin's contorted face. He was staring at his hands and his lips had drooped on the left side. He could not speak. I jumped up and ran to the stairs, calling for my mum. As soon as she saw him, my mother took control and asked me to telephone for an ambulance. Within six hours Colin died in hospital of a massive intracerebral bleed. Had he survived we were informed he would have been blind, deaf and paralysed. For an active man, still climbing telegraph poles to install telephones for BT, he would not have wanted that ending to his life. The comfort in his death was that he did not suffer. The pain came from the shock of his departure from us.

Colin had been a fantastic stepfather. My list of guilt grew at never telling him so many things … he had rescued us all those years ago. He had given me and my mother a wonderful life. He had given me a brother. He had given me lifts to and from discos and friends' houses, playing taxi driver without complaining. His homebrew had given me a taste for wine but not beer. He was gone and I should never again be able to ask him about his adventures in the RAF.

Most of all, I could not tell him that he had been far more of a dad to me than my invisible birth father. I had been so stubborn in never taking his surname. Now I could not apologise for the stupid notion that my birth father would not be able to find me if my surname was changed.

Finally, I could not remember ever telling him that I loved him very much. This broke my heart more than anything else. I lay on my bed, numb to everything that had happened. Our lives would never be the

121

same. Heartbroken is not a strong enough word to express how we all felt … how we still feel.

✓✓✓✓✓

Around this time a new deputy headteacher was appointed to the school. No one could ignore his presence and power. When Gerald walked into a room everyone stopped to stare. His sharp shrew like features made him look ill-tempered and he carried an anger within him which did nothing to dispel myths about having fiery red hair. He had come with a reputation of being unpopular in other schools he had worked at. I wanted to judge him on his merits at Northwood. He certainly made tongues wag as soon as he arrived.

Gerald was a small man, trim from a diet he was permanently using to keep tabs on his weight. He would check his appearance in the staffroom mirror at every opportunity, making sure his hair was perfect. He only wore clothes from a rather expensive tailors and looked like a mannequin. He often wore white suits and I always wondered how he could possibly manage not to get paint or snot on his clothes. I realised that much of his success in keeping clean was because he rarely went near children.

With an obsession for perfection, he disliked anyone who was even slightly overweight and would offend them, suggesting they follow his diet, if he caught them eating a biscuit in the staffroom. His opening gambit would be sharp and to the point,

'Those biscuits aren't good for people who are chubby.'

When he spoke about teaching, he expected perfection but avoided sharing any classroom practice if he criticised a member of staff.

'The way you managed that lesson was dreadful. The noise was horrific.'

Gerald had a passion for noise. If he felt a class was noisy, he would enter the room and tell the teacher off in front of the children, humiliating staff. He would criticise any teacher who raised their voice but when he chastised a class, he became nasty and unfair, blaming every child for one stray loud voice in the room. Worse still, his cheeks would glow red, and he would shake with rage when he began to speak if something or someone annoyed him.

'For your punishment class two you will all stay in and sit in silence with no snack.'

He mainly left me alone apart from one spiteful occasion when he took me to one side at the end of an assembly. As the classes began to leave the hall he whispered to me,

'You sat very provocatively in assembly this morning. The older boys made comments about your legs and underwear.'

As usual, I never commented. The children asked me why my face was so red when we returned to class. I lied that I had been hot in assembly. I felt humiliated and sure I had not sat in the way he had described. My tights and underwear were black that day. The children would have seen nothing. I had made a sarcastic comment in the staff meeting, the afternoon before, about a new planning sheet Gerald had designed with no consultation. He disliked any criticism and had not waited twenty-four hours to punish me.

Gerald loved controlling people and making them uncomfortable. His target was initially women, especially Liz Wootton and kept referring to her as an older lady coming towards the end of her career. Liz was still as sharp as a pin and her class management was excellent. She had complied with all the changes that had been made over the years and when National Curriculum had been brought in, she accepted it and began to work to the new systems put in place. Gerald didn't like Liz's teaching. He felt it was old fashioned and that Liz needed to retire before her time came to do so.

Liz was off ill with a bad chest for a week, so Gerald moved all her tables around in her room and arranged all her furniture differently. When she came back on the Monday morning, she was shocked to find the changes. As she started to move the tables back, Gerald stopped her and criticised her entire classroom management which had always been superb. It was horrendous to watch my old teacher and much-loved colleague be bullied by this man. If anyone complained about him, Stephanie seemed to turn a blind eye to his behaviour.

Liz did not complain about the deputy, she stuck to her guns, did not get the union involved but calmly got on with teaching as she had done for years. When she did finally retire, she took great pleasure in leaving Gerald without a thanks or goodbye. His insincere best wishes would have stung, and Liz was not prepared to listen to any falsehoods.

123

Later Gerald would target anyone. He believed people were fools to remain in the same school for longer than six years. He also had a habit of throwing out resources claiming they were tacky or outdated, when they were perfectly fit for use. Once he was caught attempting to throw out registers that went back to the days of the Broomhill schools, historic documents for the area.

The result of Gerald's nastiness was that the staff were united in disliking him. For *Children in Need* one year everyone, except for Stephanie and Gerald, dressed in disposable, white hooded overalls. Nursery staff had been given the task of getting children to print large dots all over each outfit with black paint. On the day, we all had face paint applied so that we were dalmatian puppies. We roared with laughter as we stood in the staffroom. When Gerald walked into the room, he had no idea that he was the main character *Cruell(a) De Vil*. Perhaps we were cruel, but the joke felt appropriate. We did it for all the colleagues who had been humiliated and lost to the school by the bully we all hated.

✓✓✓✓✓

Stephanie's love life had seemed to be stable for several years. She was married with three children with a kind and respectable husband, but she had grown itchy feet. One Christmas, when we created an extravaganza of a Christmas production for the parents, it was decided that it would be such a popular concert we should put on three shows. One performance was scheduled for an afternoon and there would be a show on two consecutive evenings.

On the first evening Stephanie came around the classrooms as the staff were busy preparing the children for the show. There was a guest with her, a man of around the same age who was very well dressed in a smart navy suit with a pale blue tie and white shirt. He was extremely suntanned, probably from a sunbed, unless he had just travelled from a sunnier climate. She introduced the man as Alistair and from the formal introduction I thought he was an official from the education office. On the following evening Stephanie's husband and family attended the performance as they normally did. The party included her parents whom I had met on numerous occasions. Not long after Christmas we heard rumours that the third marriage had broken down and less than a year later her male friend at the Christmas concert became husband number four!

124

With this knowledge Gerald seemed to do as he liked in the school and had a power over Stephanie that no-one could understand. I often wondered if he blackmailed her in some way, given the history of the headmistress's love life, but I'll never know the answer to that question.

As a staff we gained small victories over the situation, such as the dalmatian event. Another was when we had Christmas lunch. Every year we would sit at a decorated table in the staffroom, all soft chairs moved out for the event. We always looked forward to the banter. The meal was cooked well by the kitchen staff who would bake a few extra treats. One particular year, the second year Gerald had been at the school, he had organised the staffroom in a similar manner. Crackers, cutlery and napkins were placed ready for everyone. We all entered the staffroom and found a place to sit. Stephanie did her usual speech, and the meal began to be served. Gerald got up from his place next to an electric socket where he had placed a tape recorder. Instead of Slade, Wizard or the usual Christmas tracks, the most depressing music ever created spluttered out of the speaker. Laura, never one to mince her words, without hesitation shouted,

'What the bloody hell is this? It sounds like funeral music. For God's sake put Christmas music on. This is like a dirge.'

We all burst out laughing. Everyone had felt the same but had been too polite to complain. Gerald spoke,

'This is Leonard Cohen. He is a wonderful poet. It's beautiful music.'

Laura was in full charge,

'It might be wonderful to you, but no one wants this for a Christmas meal. Put on something jolly.'

Gerald had no move to make. For once it had been checkmate. Laura had a 'Mr Kipling's French Fancy' talk with Stephanie afterwards, but Gerald was not invited into her office.

Just after Christmas, the school got notification that we were to have our first ever Ofsted inspection in six weeks' time. Every single night, in the run up to the event, I slept badly. Each time I closed my eyes, I had a dream. A few years later, I realised that this dream must have been a premonition but at that time it meant I was panic-stricken.

Ofsted inspectors and authority advisors, 'Men in Grey Suits' were chasing me. They were faceless, all identically dressed in grey suits, wearing black bowler hats. No matter where I ran, they would hunt me, carrying knives. I was on a promenade at a seaside town I did not recognise. Everywhere I ran they followed. I was outnumbered, as more and more came after me. I would run until I could no longer keep up the pace. Then I would enter an unfamiliar 'Bed and Breakfast' and run upstairs to a room, locking the door behind as I got to safety. I should try to hide in a wardrobe as they broke the door down. Just as they were about to catch me, I would escape their clutches by jumping out of a window. I would limp towards the esplanade. The chase went on and on.

I would wake exhausted and soaking with sweat each morning for the next six weeks. I did not want to go to sleep as the dreams became more vivid and violent. I dreaded evenings when it was near bedtime.

After six long weeks, on Monday 11th March 1996, the inspection began. All lessons overseen by Gerald and Stephanie were approved before we could prepare resources. Lesson plans were written in long hand; no one had yet thought about typing lessons on a computer. If you made a mistake, the whole page had to be started again. Everyone was exhausted before we had even begun to teach. The scrutiny lasted for the whole week, with inspectors finally leaving on the Friday afternoon. Feedback to Stephanie, Gerald and the governing body was that the school had scraped through the inspection but had 'a serious weakness in English.'

The week had been a significant one for the school but for more than just the inspection. On Wednesday 13th March 1996, a wicked man had walked into a school in Dunblane, killing sixteen children, one teacher and injuring fifteen others who had just started a P.E. lesson. I saw the news that day. My guilt will always be enormous at the fact I could not acknowledge this tragedy because of the Ofsted visit. There had been no time to take in the terrible events. It wasn't until the Friday morning's assembly that we prayed for all those lost souls. The inspectors also sat in assembly. The hall was silent as a candle was lit. I cried and I am pretty sure most other adults in the room did too. This moment would be the end of parents and visitors walking into schools freely. It was the beginning of keypads, security gates and six-foot fencing in every school in the United Kingdom, or so I thought.

Gerald went into overdrive with his plans for improvement once the Ofsted report had been published and an action plan drawn up to support school development. Out went anything Gerald did not like. He blamed all the staff for being lazy which was not true. We all worked hard. Clearly, we had to improve the teaching of English, so I know some of the changes were necessary but often Gerald was brutal, so we felt resentful of anything new. In came mini whiteboards for every child to write on. Blackboards began to be removed. 'Interactive learning' became a buzz word. No one knew exactly what it meant but it made Gerald happy. Stephanie rarely commented and went along with everything her deputy suggested. The changes were painful at times but in all fairness to the man, the school did begin to see an improvement in all aspects of English.

Just four years after he had arrived at the school, it was announced one day that Gerald had gained a promotion to run a school of his own. We were all elated at this news, and I felt like putting flags up in my classroom on the day he left.

His replacement, a man called James, could not take up his position as our new deputy headteacher until he had served his notice at his current school. Before his departure, Gerald had approached me one day for 'a quiet chat'. These chats usually meant you were in trouble for some misdemeanour but occasionally it meant he wanted something.

'I'll come straight to the point, Emma. Stephanie has asked me to approach you to see if you would apply to be acting deputy for a term until James arrives.'

I was shocked. I had slowly gained promotions over the last few years, initially being given a responsibility point, as they were called in those days, for information technology and sex education. I didn't want to be a leader but when an opportunity had emerged years after moving to Northwood, I took it. With this second promotion I had become a member of the senior leadership team, in charge of the infant and nursery classes. Promotions had happened mainly because of circumstances and had not been planned as a career path I wished to take. I had not expected this topic of conversation and had just assumed Stephanie would run the school without a deputy until the new man arrived. Responsibility was something I wasn't looking for. I loved being on the leadership team but, due to my lack of confidence and the shyness that I still had, even after teaching for fourteen years, I had no notion to be a deputy and there was no way I could ever be a headteacher.

Gerald was persuasive, telling me it would only be for a few weeks and that it would be good experience for me to see if I ever did want to be a deputy headteacher. Despite trying to avoid giving an answer, he was relentless until I agreed to think about it. Perhaps it would be a good idea to dip my toe further into the murky pool of leadership. My letter of application had to be written. In the back of my mind, I thought that I might fail when it came to an interview and was banking on this idea to get me out of the situation in which I had been placed. Of course, I was wrong. The interview, when it came, went well.

That day I learned something about myself that I didn't know existed. Once I was in the room with Stephanie and some of the governors, it struck me that my reputation was important and that I needed to do well even though I did not want this temporary position. When I was offered the post, I wanted to run, screaming out of the room. I accepted and regretted it immediately.

On Gerald's last day, the staff were in high spirits. We were breaking up for a holiday but more importantly, Gerald was finally leaving. Even Stephanie, who had never criticised any of her deputy's actions or behaviour towards staff, was in a good mood. I could have sworn I heard her say, under her breath as we all watched Gerald walk towards his car,

'Good riddance!'

✓✓✓✓✓

After the holidays I arrived early on the Monday morning for my first day as deputy headteacher at Northwood Primary. It was my little school, where I had danced and sang as a child with Mr and Mrs Burton vacuuming in the background. I knew every inch of the place and my love for it had grown even deeper as a teacher for the past ten years. This was my moment, and I knew it. That careers teacher, all those years before had said I should never be a teacher. I wished I could have told her in that moment what I had achieved since she had written me off.

Walking into the office and sitting at my own desk felt strange. This had been Gerald's desk and although it would only be mine for a term until James arrived, this would be an opportunity I should never get again. I sat there for a minute or so, in silence, thinking of all the moments I'd had in this building when Stephanie rushed into the room to burst my bubble.

'Get your coat and come and see what's happened!'

We walked quickly through the hall, along a corridor towards one of the junior classrooms. I could feel a coldness as we neared that part of the building. When I saw the mess in front of me 'imposter syndrome' kicked in straight away. How could I support Stephanie with this? I wasn't a deputy. I didn't know what to do or say. Over the weekend, after the caretaker had last checked the building, at least one person, probably more, had smashed every single windowpane and the door in the exterior wall that was comprised totally of glass. It was the same in three other classrooms. A mobile classroom, across the playground, was the worst hit. The door had been smashed in and paint had been thrown around the room. The carpet was wrecked. In total, fifty-eight windows in the school had been smashed. Stephanie looked at me, shaking her head,

'Welcome to senior leadership!'

The rest of my day was spent comforting parents who had heard the news, speaking to the press and meeting several members of the governing body. I learned an important lesson on that first day which would stay with me forever more. Be prepared to change your plans at short notice as you never know what might happen! Many more days in leadership led to those same thoughts over the years. It had indeed been a baptism of fire, or more accurately, glass and paint.

Over the next few weeks, I found myself preparing weekly diary sheets for staff, sanctioning orders, allocating and managing curriculum leader budgets. I became an accountant, a secretary, an organiser … and I was surprised to be enjoying the job more than I had expected. I missed the contact with children and the relationship a teacher builds with his or her class, but I did not miss the planning, the assessments or marking.

There were no more major issues during the term. The days slipped into weeks. When James made a visit to the school for me to hand over my work to him just before the holidays, I felt an emotion I had not expected. Why did I feel jealous of this man?

✓✓✓✓✓

James Macintosh became the new deputy head at the beginning of the summer term and as much as Gerald had been hated, James was instantly a hit with children, parents and staff. Everyone loved his funny jokes and his booming voice as he strode around the school. His predecessor had been small, but James was a giant of a man in comparison. His six feet, six inches frame filled any room he walked into, as did his personality. He was made for the job and the school deserved him after the years of misery we had endured with the previous incumbent of the position. Jamie, as he liked to be called, was a musician and, when he taught us all to sing silly songs in assemblies, everyone in the hall laughed until we cried at lyrics such as. 'Johnny had a head like a ping pong ball' and 'Ye cannae shove yer granny aff a bus.' Jamie made the school happy, and we were all grateful.

The new deputy also had other talents. He knew how to teach and how to improve a school. He had been placed in charge of maths and straight away started year six booster classes for children to prepare for SATs. He also made sure that English booster classes were begun with me leading the charge for this operation. He concentrated on the four rules of number, and I taught sentence structures for just five weeks before the assessments took place. When the results came out later in the term, the school had improved from the previous year's statistic by almost twenty five percent in each subject. Jamie was a massive asset to the school and Stephanie knew it.

Whether Jamie's success made Stephanie feel redundant or less popular I'll never know. The result was for her to seek solace away from number four husband and into the arms of a younger male teacher who had been at the school for a few years less than myself. Off came the wedding ring and on came the flirting. When Jamie broached the matter of an inappropriate romantic relationship, between her and the male teacher, it was categorically denied. When parents saw them shopping at a local supermarket together or a member of staff saw them at a rugby match sharing a cup of hot chocolate it was denied. No explanation was offered. If anyone raised the matter, they were swiftly threatened with a solicitor. It was no one's business. It was, indeed, a private friendship between about two people. Stephanie could not see the consequences of her being constantly in the man's classroom. She was flirting in front of children aged eight and nine years of age and stopping the teacher from doing his job. Both adults were limiting the learning going on in class.

Jamie would calm everyone down when staff became irate. When Stephanie and the man were away on a course for the day, he organised a long playtime so staff could air their views. It was decided we should all join the same union for strength in numbers. Jamie was not shy to tackle difficult conversations, but he could not get Stephanie to see sense. Why did this attractive headteacher need to constantly seek new relationships? Was it the thrill of the chase? Did she enjoy the secrecy behind an affair? I'll never know. It was Stephanie's one flaw which made working for her a poisoned chalice.

In my own relationships I had begun to see a carpenter/joiner called Mark. We shared a great love of music and animals and got on instantly. We started to spend weekends out, going to pop concerts or walking in the countryside. I decided that there was more to life than planning schoolwork on Sundays. I made sure I did all my tasks during the evenings after school so that I remained organised and well prepared. My personal life was changing but school life stayed the same.

✓✓✓✓✓

Ofsted visited in the second year of Jamie's time as deputy. With his guidance and the staff confidence in him, the school was graded as 'Good' and was much improved from the inspection a few years before. My dreams had seemed less frightening this time but there had been a re-visit by the *'Men in Grey Suits'* for a few nights. Results in Key Stage 1 and 2 were rising and targets were being met and surpassed in some cases. As the inspectors and chair of governors drove away after giving Stephanie, Jamie and me the result of the inspection, the three of us hugged each other and congratulated ourselves on surviving. As I looked at Stephanie who was adoring the news, for a moment she was back to herself as a lovely, charming person who cared about the school community. Five minutes later she left me and Jamie. We knew which classroom she would be heading towards.

Jamie had made a great name for himself in the local authority. He was extremely ambitious. When he was approached to become an acting headteacher of a school that needed strong improvement, Jamie faced a huge challenge, but he truly was the man for the job. His personality was huge, and he had the commitment and determination. Just as Gerald had approached me three years before, Jamie talked to me about being acting deputy once again. This time I gave in quickly. His time as a deputy was coming to an end. He wanted to be a headteacher and to make the ultimate decisions. Sometimes he had shown his frustration with the way Stephanie was behaving. Her mind was no longer on school. She was constantly away from her desk and in my colleague's class. These days no one spoke to the man and, despite us all venting our opinions to Jamie, he was powerless to do anything and so was everyone else.

So, I became acting deputy headteacher for a second time and luckily there was no broken glass on the first day. I knew most of the systems and was familiar with the work Jamie was doing. I had been at Northwood for almost thirteen years. Jamie would soon be leaving permanently, and I considered what I should do when the deputy head post came up. The profound connections I had with the school from my childhood days meant that there would have to be an extraordinary catalyst for me to ever contemplate leaving the establishment. I saw myself being there until I retired. Perhaps I could be the permanent deputy if I applied for the job.

A few weeks later there was an important meeting about a computer suite being built. The funding for such a huge undertaking was to come from a grant application from a local community project which was, and remains, a massive amount of money. The sixty thousand pounds would be spent on an extension to an area of the original building, the furnishment of the room as a computer suite and all the new hardware. The layout looked stunning on paper, and I was excited to be taking on the project that Jamie had begun.

The day of the meeting arrived. I had put on my best suit for the occasion and made sure we had plenty of refreshments ready for the big consultation. This would be the final session for all those involved in the project from the grant funders, clerk of works overseeing the plan, architect, computer consultant and me and Stephanie. Everyone started to arrive just before the designated time and, after pleasantries were done, the meeting got under way.

We were about ten minutes into the session when Stephanie rose from her chair and gave a lame excuse that she just had to pop to a classroom to check on something. I guessed immediately where she had gone. I was literally lost for words. I knew little of the plans for the computer suite and had only just seen some documents for the first time after the meeting had commenced. To my immense surprise not one visitor asked where the headteacher was. At the end of the session, which had gone on for

132

around an hour and a half, there was just one comment amongst the visitors. The architect joked that Stephanie must have been kept busy by the children. I knew the truth. After bidding the visitors farewell, I went off in the direction of the junior classroom where she always was. As expected, she was sitting on a table, laughing and flirting with her colleague. He was supposed to be teaching but the children were being ignored. I could not continue. I decided at that moment I could not be the deputy headteacher at Northwood. I could not be a teacher there either. To accept Stephanie's poisoned chalice would kill me.

The deputy headteacher role at the school was advertised when Jamie returned from the secondment. He had secured a permanent headteacher post at the school in which he had been working. He had already handed his notice in and had just six weeks until he left. Pressure began for me to apply for the post, first from Jamie and then from my friends in school. Stephanie sent Jamie four times to ask me to apply. I had always been someone who said, 'Yes' to please people but I said 'No' for my sanity, for what was right for me.

Northwood was my school. I had danced around every inch of the building. I carried some of the older furniture into this place. I should have been elated that the deputy's job was within my grasp, but I was devastated. I could not work for Stephanie any longer. I had lost all respect and trust in her. How could I work for someone that lied and seemed to forget her responsibilities to the children, the parents and her staff? I did not have the power to change anything.

Instead of applying for the deputy headship at my beloved Northwood, I applied for another post, heartbroken to leave. The advertised job was for an assistant headteacher. Did I want this path to leadership? No, but I knew I had come this far and there was no turning back. Being *just* a classroom teacher was no longer enough. Often the chains and burdens of being in senior leadership were overbearing and uncomfortable, but I could no longer remove them. Teaching was my life, leadership my anchor.

Chapter 7
Walking Into An Abyss

The job at Larkshill Primary had been advertised at just the point when I had finally had enough of Stephanie's shenanigans. This post was for an assistant headteacher for the infant classes to work closely with the assistant headteacher for the junior department. The school was enormous, more than twice the size of Northwood.

It was a Victorian building which reminded me of my own school days, back at the two schools I had attended with my mother, all those years ago in the sixties. The similarities ended at this point. There was an impressive staircase in the middle of the building for staff and visitors. On a half landing between the two storeys was an enormous staffroom. Two further sets of stairs, one at each end of the school, were less noteworthy and purely functional for children to use. There were around three hundred and eighty children and well over seventy members of staff. This would be an enormous challenge, to secure the post and to leave Northwood after thirteen years.

I visited Larkshill before I applied for the post and liked the headmaster, a man called Gary Weaver, instantly. He was a gentleman in every sense of the word. He spoke quietly, calmly and seemed a man to trust, although I did not know him. He had a good reputation in the area, that was all I knew. More importantly, when I slipped in a sly question about how long he had been married, at an appropriate moment on the tour of the school, his answer was reassuring. To small children he would have appeared enormous, as he was well over six foot. He always bent down to a child's eye level when speaking to them, not afraid to approach little ones as some headteachers are. I had worked with Jamie who had filled a room with his personality and charism. Gary filled a room with his humility.

There were several remarkable omens about me joining Larkshill Primary. The first one came on the day of interview. I had arrived at the school ten minutes before my allotted time, my presentation in hand and more Rescue Remedy than I should have probably dropped onto my tongue. I was taken to the staffroom and asked to wait to be called into the interview room. I waited and waited. Any staff that came in asked me if I wanted a drink, but I was scared to take up the offer in case I needed the toilet in the middle of the interview. I sat for almost an hour. When Gary eventually came to fetch me, he apologised immediately. He did not explain why my interview had been delayed but asked if I needed a drink or a toilet break. I gratefully took up the toilet offer. As I looked in the mirror, I slipped a few more drops of Rescue Remedy onto my tongue for good luck before setting off to the interview room.

Gary opened the door and there sat a group of men and one woman. Blinds had been drawn, making the room dark. The only light came from an overhead projector switched on ready. My presentation, about making use of data, began. It went well. I sat down, when offered a chair, for questions and the rest of the interview.

It was only now that I had a chance to see the faces of the interviewers. Although no one turned on a light even when the overhead projector was switched off, I now noticed that sunshine also filtered into the room through a few slits of a broken blind. I was sure I knew a face from the past, but I said nothing even when everyone was introduced to me. I waited for a name. A man who looked in his forties to fifties, with short greying hair and a small moustache, sat smiling at me. He was overweight and the seams of his short-sleeved shirt looked to be bursting. This was the biggest surprise in years. A face from the past, the school heart throb, the boy who had a fit in French all those years ago was the chair of governors. It was Kenny Middleton, the John Travolta of Woodfield High School!

The interview went well and ended with the usual question,

'Now you have completed the interview, would you still like to be considered for the job.'

I smiled and nodded,

'Yes!'

The whole group of interviewers spontaneously burst into laughter and cheered. The noise and behaviour shocked me, sending me off guard. Why were they all laughing? Had I said something wrong? What had I done? Gary explained when the group had composed themselves.

'I am so sorry Emma. The reason for our little outburst is that the previous candidate, when asked that question, answered that she did not want to be considered. It took us all by surprise. That is why your interview was held up.'

The group all laughed again at the joke. I laughed with them. The interview finished and I was told not to leave the building. I was led back to the staffroom and offered a drink, which I readily accepted this time. Less than five minutes later the school advisor opened the door and asked me to accompany him back to the interview room. I was offered the job and when I gave a positive response everyone laughed again. The omen of following a candidate who said, 'No' haunts me still. Did she know? Did she get a vibe that I missed? Perhaps I had missed something important in my visit, talking to Gary, looking at all the information about the school. Why had she said, 'No' but I had said, 'Yes'?

The second, yet most awful and shocking omen came exactly eleven days after commencing at Larkshill Primary. The Twin Towers, in New York, were decimated in terror attacks. No one could see light in the world that day. Humanity seemed lost except for the exceptional acts of bravery witnessed as televisions across the globe displayed images of devastation and the stories of escape or death.

Such was the disbelief and grief around the world after the atrocities that I can barely remember any of that first half term except for just one incident exactly nine days after 9/11. We had an authority inspection. Several of the local education advisors visited the school, observed lessons and created a report. The inspection was a preparation for a real Ofsted visit that was looming on the horizon. My lesson observation went well, I felt. The advisor, in giving me feedback rated it 'Good'. The discussion lasted a lot longer than the two minutes in which he gave me a verbal critique on my lesson. His main purpose for the meeting was to extract from me my thoughts of the school, the teaching and the standards. When I was hesitant to answer him, he insisted that I did.

'Well...err...'

'I want your thoughts. You must have formed an opinion by now?'

I had an opinion, but I was too reluctant to speak my mind. I could not tell this rather abrupt, unpleasant man that I thought the school was poor. The standards of learning were very poor, much lower than Northwood. The brightest children in my class lacked confidence to try anything new and were working at levels more like middle ability groups at my previous school. The vast majority of the class were at least two years behind what they should have been in reading, writing and number work. Some children, around a quarter of the class had no sight vocabulary, could not hold a pencil, recognise any numbers or count to five consistently. The standards were frankly shocking for five- and six-year-olds.

'Come on. You are an assistant headteacher now. You know the school enough to speak. What is your opinion?'

There was no hiding place. I sat in my classroom, face to face with a man who demanded an answer. When I did start to speak, my thoughts poured out, telling him everything, except the part where I regretted moving to the school. When I stopped, he had just one thing to say.

'Have you told Gary Weaver your thoughts?'

As I started to shake my head, he rose from his chair.

'Well, there is no time like the present. Come!'

Off we went, up the stairs to the headteacher's office. Already sitting there was Gary and another advisor. The poor man in front of me, who had employed me a few short weeks before, listened to my feedback. He never flinched nor spoke and when I was done, he smiled and thanked me for my honesty. Later, on our own when the visitors had left, I apologised profusely but he shook his head and told me it was all in the game that these advisors played. I regretted speaking to him in such a way but, in doing so, we did share a moment in time that was highly significant in the fate of the school.

Gary was a decent man. His gentle nature with these children was calming; the pupils and staff adored him for his kindness. He went out of his way to give children experiences that they did not often get at home such as residential visits and outings to the seaside. Over the years, he built a fabulous rapport with members of the local community who would help with gardening sessions, sewing and cookery. These were important skills to develop in an area that was bleak for employment. Gary saw that teaching children how to manage their money on a tight budget was essential.

The area was almost all council owned properties and only a few parents had jobs. The number of children on free school meals was higher than most parts of the UK. Managing on a tight budget, learning to grow and cook your own food were important to these children, and in turn, their families. Aspirations in the area were limited. If a grandparent had found employment in a factory, office or shop then the parent was likely to have also worked. However, the local manufacturing industries, famous since the start of the Industrial Revolution, had been hard hit. Factory after factory had closed over the years, meaning fewer skilled and unskilled jobs available. In families where unemployment had been the norm for generations there was likely to be a child who saw no need for a job. In fact, there would be children who openly said they did not need to work as they could get the 'dole'. Breaking this cycle of hopelessness was important. By gaining confidence to cook, sew, garden or try other life skills, personalities started to sparkle and there was a way into communicating with these children and their families.

Just one year before, Larkshill's separate infant and junior schools had merged. Gary, being originally the junior school headmaster, had different standards upstairs to the downstairs headteacher. Upstairs the junior school was colourful and, for the most part, had enthusiastic younger staff. Downstairs the infant staff were older and stuck in the past. Their low expectations and aspirations for the children were shocking. Teaching was poor. Children would sit listening to a lesson introduction for an hour, hardly having time to put pencil to paper by the time the bell went. The staff could see no wrong in their views nor could they see a child's right to be taught by teachers who cared.

'Oh, he'll never be any good at reading. His mother and grandmother were illiterate.'

'*You can't make a silk purse out of a sow's ear*. It's the gene pool you see.'

'Don't expect much from her. She's as thick as wood. Even thicker than her father was.'

Less than six weeks after being forced to speak to Gary, as if by magic, Ofsted inspectors came. They only saw a small number of lessons which were 'Satisfactory', with a tiny percentage that were 'Good'. The infant classes, with the exception of my own, all had 'Unsatisfactory' teaching. The school was immediately placed into 'Special Measures'.

There was only one thing I could do, turn up the music in my room before and after school, sing and dance to all my old favourite songs. It cheered me up for a few minutes at least each day.

The *'Men in Grey Suits'* came after the verdict from Ofsted was officially announced. They were sometimes from the local authority, including the unpleasant one who had forced me to speak to Gary. Sometimes they were Her Majesty's Inspectorate (H.M.I.) who visited termly to report on progress. When I heard their footsteps and caught sight of their grey suits my heart would sink. They were never satisfied; they wanted the speed of progress to be more rapid than anyone could manage.

After my first Christmas at the school, the following two terms saw all the enthusiastic, young teachers from upstairs leave, along with the junior assistant headteacher. From the group of seven leadership team members, four got new jobs. Rats from a sinking ship, abandoning us to the stormy waters we were in. There were just three of us left, me, Gary and an older man, Trevor who was near retirement and refused to leave until he had done his allotted years for his teacher's pension.

Eventually three of the infant teachers were moved to a system in education called 'capability procedures' which is a process to support failing teachers. As staff move through the system it becomes more serious if they cannot show progress in the work they do in class. Ultimately, they could be dismissed. Two teachers went off on long term sick with stress, the third dug her heels in and refused to leave until she was forced to quit. I have no knowledge of the exact details of each teacher's case. I was asked to support them individually which I did. I faced the other infant teachers as their leader. I was the youngest of all of them by twenty years, in most cases. This was an uphill battle that I needed to win. Gary and the advisors wanted me to be a model teacher, showing the failing ones how to organise their lessons to be effective. I tried and failed, week in, week out.

In cases such as these, it was often the practice when failing staff reached a crucial phase in the capability procedures, they were placed on *'gardening duty'* This was a polite term with several meanings. It meant that staff had agreed to leave and, in negotiation with the union, they would be given their full pay until their leaving date, although not at work and a one-off payment to get rid of them. Imagine this ... on a building site, if your work is shoddy, you are sacked on the spot and may not even get money owed for work you have already completed. In teaching if you are crap, you get your salary but don't have to go to work for weeks until your contract is ended. You get a pay-out of thousands of pounds, and you can teach in a different authority a few days later. Inadequate teaching is not placed on record, if the teacher jumps before being pushed …

There are teachers who protest against capability procedures and the grading of lessons. They feel judgements are subjective. People who make them haven't taught in years and cannot teach themselves. I have heard all the excuses to get rid of the system. My views are two-fold. As a leader placing someone in capabilities was one of the hardest aspects of my job. I have wasted many tears and lost endless nights of sleep caring about an individual who just could not teach properly. Hours and hours of support, talking, trying to tweak changes in practice to make a difference; I tried them all. My second, most important view is for a child. He or she gets one chance at primary education. The damage a child can suffer at having poor teaching is irreparable. Life chances lost for that five- or six-year-old, but also for their own offspring, later.

✓✓✓✓✓

Long before Ofsted or the advisors had visited, Gary had booked a short residential session for a party of infant children. In the spring term. We were to go deep into the Shropshire countryside to a centre owned by the local authority. It was the one I had visited years before with Pete, on that infamous visit, so I was familiar with the layout of the building and the routines expected and knew the fire drill well! I had vowed never to return after the fire alarm incident but there was something about the children at Larkshill. I realised such an experience would be brilliant for them. Some had never seen the countryside before. This would be a precious event.

We were to take forty children, most being on free school meals and went for no cost. On the day we were due to leave, the children and their parents appeared bright and early. For some, it was the first time they had been on time for school ever. In came all the children with their new suitcases on wheels. A few had rucksacks that had been packed for an adult to carry and one child had a plastic bag with a pair of pyjamas, one pair of pants, a pair of socks, a spare t-shirt and pair of shell suit bottoms. A wet towel was at the very top of the bag.

The boy with the bag was Daz, a lively character from my class who had a wicked sense of humour and was popular with everyone. He wasn't

140

particularly bright, but he tried his best in lessons and had not yet developed the negative feelings about school which he would find in later years; the sarcasm about education that his family and friends expected him to have.

Daz was a small chap with light mousey coloured hair. He was forever pushing up his thick black rimmed National Health spectacles that needed adjusting for tightness. He had a cheery, cheeky grin that melted my heart, the instant I met him. He would drive me crazy with his constant chatter and playfulness, but he was such a likeable child that I ignored his silliness. Other children might have thought he was confident as his hand would shoot up to answer every question. The chewed cuffs on his jumpers told a different story. He was nervous and unsure of himself, but he liked to play the class joker.

Just a few weeks after I had become his teacher the children had been sitting on the carpet. We had been having a conversation about dreams and aspirations. What did the children want to be when they grew up? There was the obligatory firefighter, police officer, spaceman, helicopter pilot and hairdresser. A child had bragged they wanted to be in the army like their uncle who had been sent to Afghanistan. Another child went off track of the conversation telling us she had been to Spain. I reminded the children that we were talking about what they wanted to do when they grew up. Daz loved to outshine the others and had a real competitive streak in him. He would cheat at any game, with a twinkle in his eye. Up shot his hand to speak next.

'Yes Daz. What would you like to be when you grow up?' I asked naïvely.

'No Miss, I want to tell you somewhere I've been that no one else has!'

'Okay, make it quick so we can get back to what we were talking about and get some work done,' I replied, tersely.

His face beamed. His eyes twinkled and he pushed his glasses up from his nose for the thousandth time that morning.

'I have been to prison.'

The class groaned. I didn't know how to handle this topic. Should I stop it dead or let it go a little further?

'So have I!' said several children together.

141

My eyes widened further. Daz began again,

'Well, you haven't lived there, have you? I've lived there.'

Everyone groaned again. One child told him he was lying. I just wanted the floor to swallow me.

'I have, so there! I lived in prison because I was in my mum's stomach.'

Twenty-five children and I nodded our heads in acceptance of his story. That made sense. No one said another word. We completed our writing and drawings of dreams and aspirations. Daz wanted to be a policeman. I could envisage his life with the police force but not perhaps as he did at the age of five and a half. Every day was turning out to be a surprise at Larkshill and this day had been no different.

Back to the residential visit, Daz was excited to see the countryside. Besides prison this would be the biggest adventure of his life. I sat down on the seat beside him when he beckoned me to do so.

The coach started off and for a while he chattered excitedly about his new clothes. By now his things had been transferred to a suitcase with wheels. His case was filled with spare clothes the school had acquired over the years that would go home with him afterwards. He now had a toothbrush, toothpaste, flannel and soap in a soap box. It seemed Gary and the staff had ever aspect covered for the *'plastic bag children.'*

As we came off the motorway, Daz's eyes widened, and his voice went into a high pitched shrill. His questions came thick and fast.

'What's that?'

'It's a sheep, Daz.'

He squealed with excitement.

'What's that?'

'It is a cow, Daz.'

His squeals became louder. He could no longer sit still, trying to jump up and down but luckily the seatbelt stopped him from moving too far. Then he started again.

'Are we nearly there yet?'

'Not long now Daz!'

He asked the same question every thirty seconds, I swear, for the last ten miles. When the coach stopped, he went silent.

'Are you excited Daz?'

'Miss, this is a long way from our house. I'm a bit scared of those cows.

Daz had a fabulous time, running around the large playing field at the centre in his free time, finding things in the woods, charging up the hills, and dancing in the puddles in the wellingtons he had been given by the centre. The colour came into his pasty, ghost like cheeks and he laughed from the moment he woke to the moment he fell asleep. He loved his big adventure and so did I, watching him and the other thirty-nine children thrive and push themselves to achieve things they had never experienced before.

Of course, there were a few learning curves along the way. Daz seemingly, never ate at home with a knife and fork and no lunch time supervisor had ever mentioned this to me. The staff had a dining table in the centre of the room, placed where we could see each of the children's tables. Our job was to call groups of children up to be served and at the end of the meal choose the best-behaved table to encourage good manners when eating. Our first meal, cooked by kitchen staff at the centre, was spaghetti. The children ate it because they were hungry after their adventures in the session and because it was familiar food for most children. Daz had eaten spaghetti before he informed us, shouting from his table a metre or so from ours. He had been placed there, along with a few others so we could keep a particular eye on them because of behaviour or specific needs.

After telling him to lower his voice, my eyes went back to other groups and my own meal. It was then that one of staff from school, a classroom assistant called Libby, touched my arm and nodded towards Daz's table. There he was, plate to his face, licking the tomato sauce. As he looked around, when his name was called, his lips, nose, glasses and most of his face were covered in the sticky, orange mess. His hands were also covered as he had not used any implement to eat the meal. His fingers had been his tools for picking his food up. Off he went to be washed, after a second helping was given to him by the understanding kitchen staff.

The days at the centre went quickly and when it was time to return home, no one wanted to go, not even me. I understood Gary's purpose for organising the trips and what it meant to everyone, staff included. The bonds made on a residential really paid off back in school. Children gained confidence in both themselves and staff which helped them with their learning.

We arrived back at school at around two o'clock, on time for a rendezvous with parents for an early home time that Friday afternoon. Thirty-nine parents were there, waiting for the coach to arrive and within a couple of minutes they had all left, leaving just one child, Daz. We waited for fifteen minutes. Someone went to phone his mother but there was no reply. After half an hour and no contact, all staff who had been on the trip went off home to have a lie down and a G & T. I told Libby to go but she insisted on staying. Daz had a special place in her heart. We decided to walk him and his new suitcase on wheels home.

We had almost reached the end of his road when we caught sight of his mother and her friend strolling along, both pushing their younger children in pushchairs. Then we heard his mother shout,

'Oh Christ! I forgot our fuckin' Daz. Hello Daz! Are you alright babby?'

There was no apology for us or, more importantly, for Daz. She rubbed the top of his head, and he gave her a smile. Off he went, pulling his case of 'new' clothes behind him, trying to tell her all about his adventures, whilst she carried on her conversation with her friend, oblivious to his chatter.

✓✓✓✓✓

A few weeks later Daz's aunty came into school asking to see me urgently. I managed to get someone to cover my class whilst I took her into a small meeting room downstairs. The area wasn't much bigger than the size of an average shed. There was barely space for a desk and two chairs, but the room was occasionally used when a parent wanted to speak to a member of staff and was conveniently situated near the main entrance.

Her tattooed hands trembled as she started to speak and at first words came out of her mouth that made little sense. Realising she was struggling, I put my hand on her arm.

'It's okay. Take your time. Slow down. Would you like a cup of tea?'

A cup of tea soothed most things and usually any offers of a brew were taken up but today this gibbering wreck of a lady refused one. I knew her desire to talk to me must be a serious one. The dark roots in her dyed

144

blonde hair were all the more visible as she placed her head in her hands. Her black bra, underneath her white vest top, could be seen. She wore blue denim jeans cut off at the thighs to act as shorts. Pink flip flops were on her feet. This tiny slip of a mother, barely into her twenties, shook from head to foot.

'It's okay. I don't like school. I hated it as a kid.'

This was not a shocking statement as many parents had disliked school. Times were different now, teaching was different but persuading people who had had negative experiences of education, to trust teaching staff could be an uphill battle.

'I need some help with our Julie, Miss. I don't want her turning out like me.'

Julie was also in my class, alongside her cousin Daz. She too had been on the residential trip and had loved the whole adventure, just like all the children had. She had a lot of potential, a bright girl but her behaviour often got in the way of her moving forwards with progress. She loved to chatter, disturbing herself and others.

As I looked at her mother's troubled face, I could see a massive resemblance between the two. I wondered if this mother had also liked to talk. What had ruined her chances in life? Was it the low value the generation before had placed on school? Was it the crowd she had mixed with, who dodged school and played truant as often as they could or was it the fact at fourteen years old, like so many other girls in the area, she had found herself pregnant? The school was just a mile and a half from the high school I had attended. Five of my own classmates had found themselves in the same 'family way'.

'Our Julie's behaviour is worrying me. I can't get her to do a thing at home and I know she was in trouble yesterday at school because our Daz told me.'

I reassured her, concerned she was making a mountain out of a mole hill. Julie liked to talk. She was never in trouble for anything else.

'I don't want our Julie in bother. I want her to make something of herself. I don't want her to turn out like me. I was up on a charge of murder at the age of seventeen. 'Cos I was underage I didn't get too long as it was dropped to manslaughter. '

145

Here I was, in a small room with no panic button, with a woman who had killed someone. I tried to carry on the conversation as normal. I remembered Daz's story of living in prison. This meant his mum *and* aunty, two sisters, had been 'inside'. We sorted out a reporting system so she knew how Julie was doing each day, a simple system with stars and ticks as she told me she could not read. Sometimes I just wanted to hug these parents. They had been through so much and could do so little. If they had been born into a different family, their futures would, almost certainly, have been less difficult.

✓✓✓✓✓

Supply teachers came and went as more teachers left or went off sick. I have a great respect for replacement staff in general as they have a hard job to do, filling in whilst a substantive class teacher is absent. Children sense a supply teacher at a hundred paces and even children who have exemplary behaviour normally, can be tempted into silliness in class. There were a few supply characters in that first year who are memorable but not for their great teaching skills.

'Trolley Dolly' arrived with a large shopping trolley full of resources which must have acted like a comfort blanket to her. I knew she would struggle as soon as I saw her. She had to get up and down a large flight of stairs with her black and white patterned contraption. Not only did she wear a large, oversized raincoat in class, in summer when it was over sixty degrees, but she also had a shoulder-length black wig. Her true age was unknown, but my guess was that she was well into her seventies. The children in her class ripped her to pieces so she only lasted two days before a halt was called to her services.

On another occasion *'Uncle Fester'* appeared. He looked like the living dead, with a strange skin condition and no bodily hair. His lack of eyebrows or eye lashes and ghost like features were unsettling. Clearly, he had medical issues. He was unable to control a class and decided at lunch time that he felt unwell to continue for the afternoon of his first day. That was the end of *'Uncle Fester'*.

When a bubbly young lady in her late twenties appeared, I was hopeful that this might be a supply teacher we could keep for long term cover. She didn't even make it into class as she promptly threw up in the toilets, two minutes after arriving. She announced it was morning sickness, left a few minutes later and never returned.

When we telephoned for supply the only supply teacher available was often *'Trolley Dolly'*. Sometimes we were desperate but never tempted. Juggling staff became a daily occurrence. When H.M.I. visited on one occasion, I was the only teacher in the infant department, when teachers had called in sick that morning. I had to hurriedly plan for two other supply teachers, half an hour before the inspectors were due to arrive. Naturally there was no continuity, the standards in school fell even further and the children suffered greatly, emotionally as well as academically. Working in a school in 'Special Measures' meant that every single child or member of staff was affected by this label of shame. The downwards spiral had been rapid and a darkness appeared in every corner of the place despite the summer having arrived.

✓✓✓✓✓

The end of the final term loomed. The weather had turned warmer, and everyone was in break up mode. I was just about to leave school on the last Friday afternoon before the holiday. I thought I would go home early so I grabbed my bag about half an hour after the school bell had gone and was heading for the front door when one of the secretarial staff called me into the office, explaining there was a call for whoever was in charge. Gary had been on a course all day and the junior assistant headteacher had already moved on to another school. I was the most senior member of staff, so I took the call.

A father was on the phone. At first, I thought he was complaining, then I realised he was in fact concerned about what his son had been up to during the school day. The boy, a junior child, had brought home a small canister which contained a liquid. On the canister was a danger sign and a warning about being explosive. The man told me that his son had the canister from a friend at school and that lots of canisters had been handed out. My heart went into my mouth. I asked for the names of any other people involved. The child was put onto the phone. I could hear his father threatening him that he should tell the teacher or get the belt. The boy blabbed straight away, giving everyone's name that he knew who were involved and who had given out the canisters.

I put the phone down after telling the father I would go to the house and collect the canister as soon as I could. The secretary found the names and addresses of all the children involved and with the list in my pocket, I set off. I had just reached the school gates when a hand was placed on my shoulder. It was Trevor from upstairs, a member of the senior leadership team. He had just been heading off too, but the secretary had caught him, getting him up to speed quickly on what had happened. I was glad of Trevor's company and support. We turned back, got into his car and set off. He knew all the roads and addresses well. In less than an hour, we had all the canisters back, and had witnessed a lot of children been told off by their parents. The main culprit had what was left of his brand-new chemistry set, given to him that day as a birthday present, handed over to Trevor. His teacher promised to show he and his classmates how to use the chemicals and do some experiments safely. After that we headed for the pub. I stopped shaking after my second pint of cider. A song by Beck played in the background, 'Lost Cause'. An urge came over me to cry, for the school and myself.

The year was over. It had been a baptism of fire. I loved Larkshill and hated it with equal measure. The school I had joined eleven months before had changed so much. Excellent teachers had left; some staff were off on long term sick. Gary looked haunted always. He remained calm. I had never seen him lose his temper, raise his voice or seem rattled by the situation we faced. The *'Men in Grey Suits'* kept coming. Meetings were held in secret, sometimes even without Gary present. I had, through no fault of my own, walked into an abyss. It was a living hell.

✓✓✓✓✓

The new school year in September 2002 commenced with five supply teachers in place, a couple of new appointments on temporary contracts, two teachers on long term sick, me, Trevor and Gary. The staffing problems of the school did not stop the visits by the *'Men in Grey Suits.'* They revelled in the fact the school was struggling and maintained the push to see Gary resign. They were adamant they wanted him out. His quiet, purposeful nature was too soft for them. He had done everything asked of him, having a headteacher consultant to mentor and guide him, given me a leading role in raising standards in reading, writing and spelling. He had written endless action plans, achieved milestones with progress shown in data I was now producing for him, but it just was not enough. The progress was too slow. The *'Men in Grey Suits'* wanted Gary's resignation. They had wanted it for a year but for those twelve months he had stuck at it, improving the school, moving things forward. They were not satisfied.

One morning in December, a few days before we were about to break up for the holidays Gary called me into his office, sat me down and told me he was done. I cried. The *'Men in Grey Suits'* had snared him finally. His energy and enthusiasm had gone. He was broken. He asked me not to tell anyone and that he would announce his news the next day in a staff meeting. It was the blackest of days.

The staffroom filled up slowly the next afternoon, after school. People were chatting about holiday plans, Christmas shopping, what games would be played at the Christmas party in two days' time. Gary walked in, quietly handed out a folded, personally addressed note to each member of staff and slipped out of the room just as everyone unfolded their papers. The room went silent. Then came the sounds of sobbing. As the most senior person, they began to ask me questions, but I had no answers.

'Who will be the head?'

'What will Gary do?'

'How can we get out of the mess we are in?'

'How is Gary's leaving helping the school?'

The only question I could answer was that I should not be the acting headteacher. When making a staffing structure with the governors, Gary had had the forethought to suggest his second in command were assistant headteachers and not deputies. The subtle difference was that assistants could never be asked to be the headteacher or deputise for him.

For the next couple of days Gary spent his time comforting staff. Some wanted to start a petition to stop this nonsense, but he quietened everyone who was irate, he calmed all the staff who were crying, and he spoke honestly of his relief, after being under so much pressure. For the first time he relaxed and let his guard down. He had held it all until now with a quiet dignity. He told me to get another job as quickly as I could. I nodded in agreement. I wasn't sure how I would find the energy or the emotional capacity to apply for other jobs or to go through an interview. The experience of the last four terms had been exhausting and I felt that I would be trapped in a snare until the *'Men in Grey Suits'* caught me too. My nightmare from 1996 was coming true.

The last afternoon was traumatic. The staff had planned a few nibbles after school as a farewell to Gary. He had other plans. The children's Christmas parties upstairs and downstairs were in full flow. Staff were handing out sausage rolls and cakes when I glanced through the windows between the hall and the long corridor outside it. Gary was walking along, eyes fixed straight ahead, carrying a cardboard box and his jacket. He had no intention of attending the nibbles session after school. When everyone ran up the stairs to the staffroom at the end of the day, they were left with a present each and a message on the noticeboard saying, *'Sorry!'*

We ate the mince pies, crisps and nibbles that everyone had planned. Someone had brought in a Christmas hits CD, and it blared out in the background. Instead of crying, those who were left drank fizzy pop to his good health and happiness now his burden had been removed.

✓✓✓✓✓

On the first day back in January 2003, I walked across the icy carpark with no cars in sight. I had no idea who would be running the school. All I knew was it was not me. About half an hour later a lady appeared and announced she was the acting headteacher for the term. Her name was Georgina, and we could call her George. I instantly liked her energy and determination to help the school, but she made it clear she would probably only be there for a term. She was, in fact, a deputy headteacher at a local school who had been seconded for a term. I shuddered when she told me this news and was shocked that the *'Men in Grey Suits'* had not put in place an experienced, successful headteacher. I found out within a couple of days that the authority had a plan to merge two schools, one being Larkshill with another local school which had gone into Special Measures. The plan, all along, was to close two failing schools and merge them under new leadership.

George fought a good fight, rather like her namesake when he tackled the dragon. Her approach was more powerful than Gary's gentle ways of doing things. She had been given a headteacher mentor who supported her and attended some of the meetings. As usual I was excluded from most, as the *'Men in Grey Suits'* had ignored me for a long time now. I was doing a good job, getting great lesson grades, when they turned up, and my English data was continuing to show massive improvements for a good percentage of the pupils.

One thing that the *'Men in Grey Suits'* had not considered was the impact of Gary's departure on the children. He had been a wonderful, steadying influence on the whole school. The behaviour of many children began to decline rapidly on the playground at break times as they too

150

could sense a tension in the air. Some of the supply and temporary staff struggled to keep control in their classes. The school descended to a new depth. Behaviour policies were quickly rewritten, handed to all parents and displayed in all classrooms but it made no difference.

Trevor had been a staunch defender of Gary. As the spring term concluded Trevor announced he too was leaving. He could no longer cope with the *'Men in Grey Suits'* nor the changes taking place to the school. He was tired of dealing with behaviour issues in the junior classrooms. The supply teachers could not control their classes and he was forever having to leave his own class to sort out problems. His departure was the final blow. Trevor had been at the school for years, but his methods and behaviour management were excellent. He commanded attention if he walked into a room. Children and staff admired him. His leaving meant that I should be the last member of the original senior leadership team. Gary had loyalty from everyone, but team spirit was now gone. The governors had all resigned after Gary's departure. We sank further into the abyss, and I was in despair.

George's short time in charge also came to an end, not before she hosted union and parent meetings about the planned merger of the schools. Her term was hard and unpleasant. She openly admitted that the authority had asked her to stay on, but she refused, not wishing her career to be tarnished any further with the name of Larkshill on her CV. I had spotted two deputy headteacher jobs and applied for them both within an hour of reading the adverts. I awaited any news, in desperation. Easter came and went as did George.

✓✓✓✓✓

For the second time in the space of four months the carpark was empty when I faced the first day of the summer term, my second summer at the school. A phone call came at half past eight from one of the advisors to tell me that a headteacher was on the way, and would I hold the fort until he arrived. I told him I would look after the school until the new headteacher arrived but if he had not appeared by lunch time I should refuse to be in charge. Surprisingly he agreed.

Just after nine o'clock a gentleman appeared, requesting a meeting with me. He informed me that he was the headteacher. Both myself and George had prepared for the day by organising for me to have a day out of class to support a new head. Tim, a rotund man in his late sixties,

151

possibly early seventies was a pragmatist. I liked his style immediately. He told me I looked ill and gave me some advice.

'Get another job as soon as you can. Even if it is not in teaching. Get out!'

He went on to criticise the way he had been asked to cover a school in Special Measures late on the evening before a new term. He had been approached about the possibility of taking the school a few weeks before the Easter holiday and had said he would do so if needed. He had asked the advisor for good, advanced notice should he be required to lead Larkshill. He had only received a call at half past ten, less than twelve hours before he sat with me. This was weeks after George had announced she was not returning. Why the *'Men in Grey Suits'* had left it until the night before the new term started, I'll never know.

The rest of the day was spent in a meeting with Tim telling him the whole sordid story of Larkshill, the motivations of the authority in wanting to merge two schools, Gary, everything just spilled out of me like Mount Etna erupting. He came up with a plan to survive. We could not win but he and I needed to survive for the children's sakes. He said he would not leave for the term, but we should both leave in July. I trusted him completely. I had no option. He was the supply acting headteacher. I had never known there was such a thing but clearly there was, and he was my saviour.

When the *'Men in Grey Suits'* turned up the next day he was prepared. He knew everything I knew already, and he insisted that I attended all meetings with him as I was his assistant. They consented to my attendance for the first time since I had been made to let Gary know my feeling eighteen months or so before.

Within a couple of weeks Tim had reluctantly agreed to also lead the other school. It was extra money, and I didn't blame him for turning this disaster to his advantage. The headteacher had resigned, and the authority saw a quick way to merge the schools with an 'acting executive headteacher.' We each did what we needed to survive. I started to pack up my possessions. I was leaving. I had already made my mind up that I should resign. My letter was written, ready to hand in to an interim governing body that had been put into place a few months after Gary and the old governors, including Kenny Middleton, had resigned. Just four days before I needed to hand in my notice, I secured a job at another school as a deputy headteacher. It was just half a mile from my old secondary school.

I shook Tim's hand as we both stepped out of the door on the final day of term. Our plan to survive had worked. We were both leaving and not looking back. We left what had been described by an H.M.I. inspector, a few days before, as '*Probably the worst performing primary school in the country.*' I breathed a sigh of relief.

I hated to leave the children. They were amazing and needed good teachers and a good leadership team to give them the best possible start in life, but I could no longer be one of those teachers for my own sanity. The last two years had been the most stressful of my whole career to date and I needed to move on before it broke me like it had broken Gary. My boyfriend, Mark, told me afterwards that he thought the school would end me, end him and end our relationship. It hadn't but I was broken and needed mending. It would take time, but I would mend.

On the day after breaking up and leaving Larkshill, Mark was late arriving for a date we had planned. I paced backwards and forwards worried that he might have been in a car crash or had, after all, decided that enough was enough because of my life in teaching. When he finally arrived and rang the bell, I ran to the door only to be faced by a stranger, or so I thought. There, dressed in full costume from head to toe, like something out of the eighteenth century, complete with a tall top hat, was Mark dressed as Mr Darcy holding chocolates and a bottle of champagne. When I stopped laughing and he had changed, off we went to plan a break away to Scotland. It was just what I needed.

Chapter 8
My Salvation

John Hutchins wanted a change in direction when appointing a new deputy headteacher. He was looking to build a senior leadership team in his desire to turn the school into an 'outstanding' one. At my lowest ebb, I had been fortunate enough to secure the position at Hawthorn Street. I loved the school instantly. Maybe it was the euphoria of being away from the hell of working in a failing school. I prefer to think it was because I had stepped into another world, full of colour and warmth. Being a mere one and a half miles away from Larkshill, the school felt like I had travelled to another universe. The headteacher, however, was on another planet to everyone else.

John had been headmaster at Hawthorn Street for about eighteen months. Although he was only in his early fifties, his white hair made him look older. His style of clothing for work was always safe and predictable, never wearing ties that were too bold or suits that were too new. He rarely polished his shoes which I found odd. Despite his best efforts to have posh vowels, he had not quite achieved his goal to lose his Midlands accent. He would talk about shopping at Waitrose without any awareness that parents and staff would all shop at the Asda or Lidl.

It only took days for me to realise that John had obsessive compulsions. Firstly, he was a penny pincher. He hated any kind of waste and would measure stock to exacting amounts. A teacher would be given thirty pencils and no spares. He calculated the lowest number of crayons that a class would need for the year. When I asked for a ream of paper, I was given thirty sheets. His obsession with waste almost ended in disaster in my first Christmas at the school. He thought he had excelled himself in the amount of ice cream purchased for the party. He insisted that a block of ice cream, advertised for twelve servings, would be suitable for a class of thirty pupils. It was impossible to cut melting ice cream into such small pieces. Most children had a few drips of vanilla liquid on their jelly. Staff were left sticky and frustrated by his miserly ways.

One of his other obsessions was to label every possible piece of equipment with instructions in how to operate them. Whether it was the microwave, the laminator, the guillotine or the dishwasher; they all had labels. There was no point to his notes, but he thought staff were wasteful and broke things through lack of care. If he caught anyone putting too much dishwasher powder into the machine, there would be a public chastisement for being wasteful and not reading instructions.

John also loved regulations. He would quote some local council rule at the least appropriate moment and lacked empathy for anyone who needed flexibility. On one occasion a member of staff asked for time off to attend a funeral. Both her father and mother-in-law had recently passed away and now her uncle had died too. John granted her the funeral time but could not help himself in quoting council rules. The woman came back into the staffroom and sat crying. When someone asked her what was wrong, she repeated what John had said.

'He said "Yes, Melissa, You can have time for the funeral, but I wish it had been someone closer." What does he mean?'

I took no pleasure in explaining that John had been quoting the council policy on attendance at funerals. The guidelines stated that time off for funerals should only be for close family members like parents, husband or wife or children. So that day John had wished this poor woman's husband, mother, father-in-law or her two children had died instead of a beloved uncle so that she could attend the funeral within the council's policy. John alienated himself from everyone because of his lack of understanding of the real world.

The staff told me they dreaded Christmas party day as he would produce a precise itinerary that even the most organised staff would find puzzling. It went something like this: -

1.15 p.m. Collect children from playground
1.22 p.m. Begin party games in classrooms
1.49 p.m. Children should visit toilet and wash hands
1.58 p.m. Children to enter hall for party food (see seating plan)
2.13 p.m. Children to return to rooms
2.15 p.m. Santa to commence visits to classrooms
2.45 p.m. Santa to leave school
2.49 p.m. Classrooms to be tided. Rubbish in plastic bag provided.
2.54 p.m. Children to collect reading packs
2.55 p.m. Children to get coats and jackets

155

2.58 p.m. Children to be lined up by classroom door
3.00 p.m. Bell for home time

Despite him talking of wanting to build a senior leadership team, John preferred to work solo. He would not delegate tasks other than curriculum development and it would take much persuasion, over many weeks, for him to come around to an idea that I could help. He compartmentalised roles and his inflexibility to change systems made me wonder if this man, with so many obsessions, was perhaps on the autistic spectrum.

Apart from John's annoying ways and his own lack of team spirit, the staff at Hawthorn Street were a great bunch of people. Everyone loved working with the children who came from very mixed backgrounds. Some lived in mortgaged houses on the abandoned land near my old high school. Thirty years before it had been flooded and full of mine shafts. Now it was an estate full of detached and semi-detached houses. Less than a mile away was a council estate where other pupils lived. It was very familiar with its rows of terraced, red brick houses. For fifteen years I had not taught Maze children, but I was back where I felt comfortable.

The school had an excellent reputation locally and there were waiting lists for children to be enrolled each year. Everyone wanted their child to attend Hawthorn Street. Built in 1970, the building had low ceilings, small classroom spaces and curtains where doors should be. Plans were in place for interior doors which appealed to me. For the time being, when I played music in my room, I turned the volume down. I did not think the headteacher would approve of Debbie Harry or Mark Knopfler playing at full blast before or after school.

There was a mixture of older, established teachers who had worked in the school for over twenty-five years and some younger staff who had been there less than ten. Claire was a member of the leadership team with just a year or two less experience than me. She had a wicked sense of humour and a laugh that was naughty. She would never do anything mean or underhand to John, but the thought would cross her mind. We began to work in earnest together on a project with other local schools. I found out, just days into the job that she had applied for the deputy's position and had been unsuccessful when I was selected. Whilst I am sure Claire was disappointed at not gaining promotion, she seemed willing to work with

156

me and we went on to form a good partnership. Perhaps John had planned our collaborations, but we seized the opportunities to develop the teaching programmes, assessments and planning as we were like minded and wanted to make the best school we could for the children.

Often, Claire was too hard working, and I feared her health would suffer as schoolwork consumed her life. Her complexion was always pale, and she never had time to apply make-up to disguise her tiredness. She was a great worrier. It did not matter what her worries were about; it could be school, her family, friends or just the weather. She never relaxed, except when she watched replays of *Midsomer Murders* at night in bed, falling asleep after fifteen minutes. I saw much of myself in her. We were like peas in a pod. Years later she would become my deputy headteacher and she gave me tremendous support in difficult times. If I needed to cry, which I did occasionally, I would seek Claire out and we would stroll around the roads surrounding Hawthorn Street, chewing over the problems and trying to find solutions. Sometimes we would come up with master plans whilst during other walks we fell into despair, and both cried at the sadness of situations we faced as leaders. I'll be indebted to her for ever for those tough days.

✓✓✓✓✓

John had organised for me to observe all teachers during the first term Having come from a leadership team that had been fully drilled in observations this was second nature to me, but I did worry about being younger than half of the teachers and having to make judgements on their classroom practice. It felt as though John had given the new deputy headteacher an initiation assignment, to irritate and annoy the teaching staff as a jobsworth and upstart!

Rachael was the first teacher I observed. I was relieved that she was the youngest teacher on the staff. However, when I observed her, she was wise beyond her years, destined to go far in her teaching career. She was a charismatic member of staff, popular with everyone. Her tales of family and holidays abroad reminded me of Laura at Northwood. Her voice was lively, her body animated, and her heart was full of passionate for her job. After the dreary lesson observations at Larkshill, it was a pleasure to see a teacher who was advanced in her craft.

One lunch time, not long after I had commenced at Hawthorn Street, Rachael burst into the staffroom accompanied by Susan, the classroom assistant for year two. At first neither of them could breathe let alone speak. Their entrance had been dramatic, and all eyes now looked towards the pair for an explanation. As they glanced towards each other tears rolled down their cheeks. Clutching her chest, Susan shook her head in surrender. We gazed at Rachael in bewilderment. She attempted to wipe her eyes and took a deep breath. Her explanation gushed out for fear she wouldn't be able to control herself for long. She explained that she had been teaching a phonics lesson on the digraph 'oi' and that the children were asked to give examples of words containing the 'oi' sound and to put the word into a sentence. She had chosen Tara.

'What word can you think of Tara? She replied … '

Rachael started to shake. She couldn't finish the sentence for laughing. Tears started to fall uncontrollably again. It took a few seconds to gather her composure.

'Sometimes my dad says to my mum "*Oi*, give us a shag!" I started to shake. I couldn't stop shaking …'

Staff who had been taking a sip of tea or coffee spat it out; people choked on their ham and cheese sandwiches. Soup went flying and Weight Watchers meals were splattered all over the carpet and seats. Everyone roared.

'It was unprofessional of me, but I had to go into the quiet room. I couldn't stop laughing. Susan had to take over!'

Rachael was the ultimate professional, calm in all situations so this image triggered our laughter again. A couple of women ran to the toilet in case they wet themselves. Just as the joke was finally dying down John walked into the room to use the microwave. Rachael repeated the story to him. In his usual unperturbed manner, he gave a smile and said,

'Well, at least she got the correct digraph.'

Only he could have commented on Tara's phonics knowledge!

✓✓✓✓✓

Mae was a no-nonsense northern lass who was within ten years of retiring. Despite having lived in the area since attending the same teacher training college ten years before me, she had not lost her Geordie accent. I sensed she toned it down for Midlands folk. When she talked about her homeland, the accent got stronger. I would often tease her by mentioning Sunderland. Mae would take a deep breath; her mouth would pucker, and she would suck her lips until they had almost disappeared. Every time she would say the same phrase.

'Eee … they eat the babies there!'

She was a force to be reckoned with despite her outwardly calm persona. To the world she was a middle-aged teacher with short curly hair and an ordinary appearance. What people soon found out was that Mae was an activist. She would never raise her voice. It was her sarcasm that was her weapon which John could not handle. There was nothing more that Mae liked than to tease a response from him. She took great pleasure in doing so to bring John down to earth with a bang. Her best moments were in staff meetings when he had spent an hour going through some new initiative which he had created and was going to implement. John liked rules so Mae's answer to his silliness was to follow union directives to the letter. The teaching organisation had ordered members should only attend staff meetings for one hour per week. When John had been new to the school, he had stupidly tried to continue his meetings after the allotted time.

At exactly 4.28 p.m. each Thursday Mae would look at her watch, give a sigh, and shuffle slightly. At 4.29 p.m. Mae put the lid on her pen and would gather the forest of paperwork that the headteacher had given out that week. She would straighten the papers into a smarter pile by tapping them on her knees. At 4.30 p.m. Mae would put her diary and paperwork into her bag, stand up and put her jacket on. By 4.31 p.m. Mae would have said her usual farewell,

'That's me off then. The hour is up!'

John Hutchins would sit there, in dismay each week, never quite understanding why Mae chose to leave at 4.31 p.m. He could not grasp the concept that staff meetings should only last for sixty minutes. His expression never changed, but it was plain that her weekly actions annoyed him. John's tone would sound a fraction sharper and, despite his politeness towards her, he was irritated by Mae. His voice would betray his calmness. Staff appreciated the hint to finish and within five minutes the meeting would be over.

At every opportunity Mae would wind up Hutchins in devilment rather than for any real cause. His superior voice, full of nonsense and educational theories grated on everyone's nerves. John's attempts be posh, despite his working-class background, vexed Mae. She was proud of her own upbringing and disliked his pretence at being something he wasn't. John would come into the staff at lunchtime and attempt a conversation about school improvement. Everyone was eating their lunch or chatting about the latest episode of *The X Factor*.

'Remember staff, make sure to hand in six exercise books for scrutiny tomorrow. Of course, we are pushing to raise standards in writing this term as we strive to be 'outstanding.'

We always looked in Mae's direction for sanctuary. She knew the signal. One line stopped him in his tracks and annoyed him into a silent rage. It was evident that he held his tongue. Despite his determination to show no reaction to her quips, only a glint in the eyes gave away the torment he held inside.

'Well John. I'm just striving for mediocrity.'

Conveniently the microwave would ping at precisely three seconds after Mae had burst his bubble. He would open the door, place his Waitrose meal for one on a plate and set off for the few lonely paces back to his office.

✓✓✓✓✓

One person with a huge personality was Susan, a highly experienced N.N.E.B., more recently known as a learning support practitioner. She should have been a primary school teacher, but her life had led her down a different path. She was a jolly lady in her early forties when I first met her. She was precisely three hundred and sixty-four days older than me which I often quoted to tease her. With golden highlights in her mousey short hair, Susan always looked sunny. Being a lady of a slightly larger size, when she gave a cuddle to a child or member of staff, it made everyone feel warm and safe. Despite being five feet, or shorter if the truth was known, no one could ignore Susan. She was a larger-than-life character. Her voice often preceded her as she entered a room. The children loved her banter with staff, and they found her comfortable and funny. She would make the same entrance every morning. Just as I settled my class and they were all working quietly, in she would come.

'Morning Miss S! Morning kids!'

Immediately there would be giggles. The *'Eager Beavers'* would look up, laugh and get back to work. The *'Desperados'* would put their pencils down and milk every moment that they could get out of not doing work.

'Thank you, Mrs Postlethwaite, for disturbing all of us!'

The banter would begin.

'My pleasure Miss S! What are we learning about today?'

Hands would shoot up. Susan would always choose a *'Struggler'* to answer and would give a knowing smile when the child was correct.

'We are learning about halves and quarters.'

'Oh, I love that topic in maths. Is Miss Slater awake this morning?'

The children loved to make up stories about their teacher to another member of staff, as Susan knew well, and she encouraged them every day.

'No Miss! She keeps falling asleep and snoring!'

Everyone would laugh at the fib someone had told. At this point loud snoring noises would come from around the room.

'Okay kids, back to work before the teacher shouts at me for disturbing you. Love you Miss S!'

Susan would give a cheesy grin, wave to the class and disappear into her little room next to mine. Ten minutes later the class would finally settle again. They loved the banter … and so did both adults.

After more studying and assessment, Susan became a higher-level teaching assistant which meant she could take a class of children on her own. She didn't have to plan for lessons as that was not in her job description, but Susan always went above and beyond what was required. She could conjure up a lesson, with a few minutes notice, in an emergency. She was the ultimate professional but also hysterically funny in the staffroom where she would command attention with her witty observations of children.

Although she was very easy going, Susan would march into John's office if something upset her. She was a powerful character despite her diminutive stature and would nearly pull the door off its hinges if an injustice had been done to someone. I think the head was secretly scared of her popularity and resented her for being outspoken. He did not like people who rocked the boat. The irony was that John needed people like Susan who worked tirelessly for the school, but he would never admit this. She was always busy giving first aid if someone was injured or

161

chatting when someone was upset. She was the *'Mother Hen'* of the school for children and staff.

Never shirking a task given to her, Susan excelled when she accompanied a six-year-old on a residential trip to the outdoor learning centre, I had visited before with Park View and Larkshill. Martin had some significant physical and emotional issues. Whilst sitting on the carpet listening to staff, he would lick the soles of his shoes or the flooring. He also had a compulsion to lick any fall out of snot from his palms after he had sneezed. There was always slime oozing from his nostrils which, every now and again, he would rub onto his hands for a feast. Other children tended to avoid him because of his strange habits. His diagnosis was still unclear. He struggled with every aspect of learning but was always a happy polite little chap, without a care in the world. Late one afternoon, whilst he was waiting to be collected by his parent from an after-school club, he was curious about a stranger at the school door.

'Who is this man?'

'This is my boyfriend, Martin.'

'Hello Geezer, please to meet you.'

Martin stretched out his arm to shake Mark's hand, but I was too late to stop the greeting. After the boy had left, Mark was sent to the toilets to wash his hands immediately.

When his parent wanted him to attend the residential, it was decided that the educational psychologist should perform a risk assessment on how Martin would cope with being away from home. He was well known to his mother for running away from her on the journey to and from school. He had no sense of danger and, as Mark could testify, he accepted all strangers, good or bad. He came out on the risk assessment as a *'probable death.'*

Susan and I were determined he would go. His mother begged us to take him as I think she was looking forward to a rest for a few days. I explained to John that we needed to alter a few things so that he was able to attend. It was agreed that we adapted everything we could to ensure his safety, with Susan being assigned to him as his one-to-one support. His mother readily agreed to him wearing a toddler's wrist lead, to ensure he didn't run away.

We travelled to the residential centre and unpacked. Martin was on fine form and was coping exceptionally well to all the changes in his routine and environment. He was excited but listened to instructions. The first real activity began in the afternoon with a treasure hunt. Off we went with the residential instructor into the woods that were adjacent to the centre. Children were placed into pairs and Martin never noticed that he had conveniently been placed with Susan. The instructor got the first pair of children to read out number one clue to finding the treasure and off we all set, following the pair on the task to find the next clue. When their mission was accomplished, they chose another pair to read the second clue. Then the second pair would decide where to move to next. The game was going well, and we had gone to several places in the woods, along a fence and into a field until we got to the last clue. The wonderful sunshine we had experience all day was starting to fade. There was only one pair left to read the clue and finally find the treasure ... Martin and Susan. The lad was over excited and tired now. He wasn't used to country air nor so much exercise.

Susan helped him to read the clue. The boy's eyes twinkled as he realised where he needed to go. Without warning Martin took off up a hill, crossing a field full of cows and cow pats, in totally the wrong direction. The instructor, the class and I all burst out laughing as we saw the silhouettes of two figures reaching the crest of the hill. There was a small figure a short distance ahead of another larger one who was trying to keep up. In the distance Susan could be heard screaming and Martin's laughter. The wrist lead had worked. So had Susan's legs that afternoon!

That evening the children settled quickly, exhausted by the country air. The staff were also tired, so we all went to bed earlier than expected. In the night I heard Susan moving about in the room we shared. She stumbled about in the dark.

'Sugar! Where are my slippers?'

'Are you okay, Susan?'

'Sorry to wake you Emma. I just need a pee.'

She must have found her slippers and her glasses as she set off for the toilet moments later. I felt warm so moved the duvet a little to cool down and drifted back to sleep. I never heard Susan return. I was probably snoring. When I went down to breakfast the next morning, Susan was animated and loud as I walked into the centre's staffroom.

'Well, well, well! Have I got an exclusive to tell you all!'

Me and the rest of the staff looked at her in anticipation of some juicy gossip.

'I might have to tell John. I have been sexual harassed!'

Now she had caught our attention. Mae's mouth dropped and I held my breath, fearing the worst.

'In the night I woke up for a pee. When I went back into the bedroom the landing light was still on. I was greeted by the sight of two boobs! I can tell you Miss S …it was more like Miss Double G! I am happily married. Thanks, but no thanks!'

She burst into laughter. Confused for a moment, I wondered what she was talking about. Then it dawned on me. My top must have risen a little too much whilst I was asleep. When I pushed the duvet back, I had exposed myself to my roommate. After that, on many occasions, Susan took great pleasure in reminding me that she had seen the deputy's naked boobs.

Back at school Martin seemed to settle after his first adventures in the countryside. His behaviour calmed but he continued to lick his shoes and the carpet when no-one was watching. He also had a bad habit of farting at any given opportunity and the smell would fill the classroom. His classmates would giggle and then they would start coughing when the full effect of the flatulence hit them.

One morning John had given me some leadership time to monitor learning and teaching standards. It was Susan's turn to be observed. She would take Martin and four other children to her room adjacent to my classroom for extra support. The session was going well. The group of five children started to concentrate on their individual writing tasks. Susan had a great rapport with these pupils, and they listened well to her instructions. She was explaining something to a child when a rip-roaring fart exploded. Without batting an eyelid, and knowing exactly from whom the sound had originated, Susan yelled,

'Clench boy! Clench!'

Martin looked at her.

'Please accept my apologies madam. It wasn't me. It was my baked beans.'

The smell was horrendous, far worse than rotten eggs. Everyone, apart from Martin, frowned at the awful odour. It had certainly been a potent blast! He grimaced as he attempted to follow Susan's instruction, squashing his eyes, nose and mouth until he went purple. I muttered that I had to make a telephone call and rushed out of the room without completing the observation. I roared helplessly for the next ten minutes.

✓✓✓✓✓

I had never met anyone like Heather before. Having worked at Hawthorn Street for almost forty years, she was at the heart of the school, well respected by children, parents and staff. She was the first teacher parents met when their child started in nursery. Although she was now approaching retirement, her teaching methods were modern and forward thinking. She had never wanted promotion and loved her work too much to leave her class to become a headteacher. Being the school's elder stateswoman, she was knowledgeable about all aspect of teaching and life, in general. She had a reason for everything she did. I was in awe of her professionalism and her down to earth attitude.

No one ever came close to Heather's class and style. She would light up any room she entered. She was around sixty but had the body of a trim thirty-year-old. Her hair was carefully coloured to compliment her complexion. If she wore make-up you could not tell as her face always looked fresh and natural. Her outfits were always elegant but not over the top for working in nursery.

She would tell stories about her life growing up as a house keeper's daughter in a fancy hotel in the local area. She would also talk about elderly aunt in Greece and her family croft in Ireland which she visited every Easter, just in time for lambing. Her stories were always rich and colourful. Most of all she would proudly talk about her daughter. Despite being a single parent, after her marriage had failed, she had managed to support her daughter, both financially and emotionally through university. Heather saw this as her greatest achievement. We loved listening to her tales and shared her delight when she finally announced she was the mother of a doctor.

Over many years she built amazing relationships with mothers and fathers. When children she taught became parents themselves, she knew three or four generations of families. With this wealth of knowledge, Heather's steady manner made difficult situations manageable, even when there were child protection issues. Most of all, her common-sense always provided a solution. I adored the calmness and wisdom she brought.

Heather, being of a similar age to John, had the knack of calming him down when he began a new campaign of some kind. She would not be drawn into his fads. If she felt something was not appropriate for her pupils she would say so. John always listened to her. Occasionally he made some condescending comment but ultimately, he would listen and act on Heather's advice. She was the voice of reason, the mother of the school. She spoke with a soft Midlands accent but occasionally a few Irish tones would be heard, inherited from her mother.

'Don't judge John too harshly. His heart is in the right place. He just has a funny way of showing it sometimes.'

I always nodded and accepted what she said. She was correct in her observations. John did what was best for the children. He did not have a massive ego like Keith at Park View. He was happily married, unlike Stephanie. He did not have the empathy that Gary had for children, but he did want them to do well. He wanted the school to be 'outstanding'.

John's strength was his penny pinching. By making savings he brought the school back from the brink of financial ruin he had found in the finances when he started at Hawthorn Street. By spending money wisely, he finally was able to install interactive whiteboards in all rooms which transformed learning. It meant giant screens were in each class and demonstrations using computer technology came alive. Money was also spent around the school, kitting out minicomputer suites and improving outdoor play. He had a library built which was designed around story characters. The man did have a heart; it was just sometimes hard to find it. Heather could see this, when others couldn't. She was a wise lady.

✓✓✓✓✓

Just over three years after I had moved to the school, John received the Ofsted call. We had expected it for some time and tried to be as prepared as we could. The call always came as a shock even after so many internal

166

lesson observations, Ofsted and Her Majesty's Inspectorate visits over the years. People outside of education do not understand the scrutiny that schools and teachers experience. It is always intense. There are book trawls to ensure teachers set and mark work appropriately every few weeks. There are regular checks on records and assessment judgements.

By far the worst are lesson observations. They begin when you start training and end when you retire. If a teacher says they are not affected by someone watching their lesson, they are lying. Everyone cares and everyone gets into a state of panic before each observation. Every session is expected to be of a high teaching standard but when you are observed, you move to another level. All resources are perfected, and triple checked beforehand. An individual lesson plan is as detailed as it can be. Rescue Remedy is much needed to steady the nerves. When you wake up on the day of an observation, there are knots in your stomach and your hands shake. Nothing can distract you from the fear of failing. You don't want to let the class down, your school down, and most of all, you don't want to let yourself down.

Less than three weeks after John had received the call, in came the team of Ofsted inspectors. Somehow, I escaped any observations on the first day of the inspection and I knew on the second day I would be under close scrutiny. Just ten minutes after the school bell had run, in walked the one inspector I had dreaded. So, I began.

'Good morning, everyone! Are you ready for your literacy lesson this morning? I hope you have your thinking cap on as you'll need it to write your story.'

Thirty pairs of eyes looked at me as I pretended to put on a 'thinking cap'. I already knew those children who were listening to me, copying my actions, who were compliant and would try hard to write their stories without a battle royale. I heard the few expected groans and my stomach churned as the battle began. I looked towards the usual suspects of the class who had shuffled on their bottoms to the back of the group. The little devils had moved, right under my nose. How could I get this small group of 'Desperados' to write at least two lines again? Should I threaten their playtimes, their lunch time? I needed to be careful with my approach. I couldn't make a mistake today, of all days. I gritted my teeth and continued with my questioning about what a good story should have. The answers flowed and proved that some children in the class had been listening over the last few months. I was delighted with the responses and recapped the answers the children had given me.

'Every good story should have a beginning. It should have some action in the middle and a great ending. There should be some interesting characters and some different settings.'

With the introduction completed, I felt that this part of the lesson had gone well despite having to move the gang back to the front of the carpet so I could keep my beady eye on them. I felt something touch my leg. I looked down and there was a small hand on my tights, pulling at a snag. My eyes widened and I gave a quick shake of the head to inform the child not to continue. The hand moved back to its owner, but I spotted a leaving present in the form of slimy green snot smeared on my black tights.

I sneaked a peek at our visitor. He hopefully hadn't noticed the snot incident. Yesterday I gave the class a full list of rules for behaviour in case of any visitors to the room. I promised the children extra Golden Time if they worked hard. I had omitted to mention green bogeys on tights.

The staff had been told not to look at the visitor, but I couldn't help myself. I glanced again to check if he was still writing. He had a similarity to the Child Catcher from *Chitty, Chitty, Bang, Bang*. The irony was not lost on me. He looked pleasant enough, but I'd heard he had been the most critical of the inspectors in school. He seemed to have written reams, since nodding to me on entering the room. He had sat down on the only adult sized chair and placed his briefcase horizontally across his legs to act as a writing surface. He was still writing, his head leaning gently to the left.

I gulped. I was ready to send everyone back to their desks to write their story. A few bright sparks, the '*Eager Beavers*' would write novels with paragraphs, full punctuation and have character speech flying off their pencils. '*Snotty*' would get green slime all over his book … again. The '*Strugglers*' would forget finger spaces and mix capitals and lower case in the twenty letters they wrote. The '*Desperados*' would stretch out three words on each line to make it look like they had written a whole book. I felt a quiver in my voice as I sent them off to their fate and mine.

The Child Catcher's ears must have been pricked by the noise as they moved. Should I bring them back to the carpet or let it go? I froze for a millisecond then cleared my throat.

'I expect you to work quietly in 20 seconds from now.'

I slowly whispered the countdown to zero. The room fell silent. Perhaps I did know what I was doing after all, but I would wait for my lesson grade from the inspector. I heard he only gave out 'Satisfactory' or 'Unsatisfactory' so there was no chance of a 'Good' or 'Outstanding.'

To my surprise everyone was working, the room was silent apart from the slight sound of pencils touching paper. I circulated to check on progress and to ensure that everyone kept going. As I approached David, his hand shot up, nearly hitting me on the nose as I went to lean down. My heart sunk and I wondered how I could quieten him without the inspector hearing. I was too late. He started to bellow as normal,

'Miss!'

'Yes, David? Remember your 'classroom voice' please,' I reminded him despairingly.

'Miss? You have forgotten something!'

What the hell had I forgotten? My neatly organised lesson plans, resources, worksheets etc, etc had all been placed in colour coded document wallets days before. I had checked and checked all contents already a dozen times, five at least that morning before school.

'Miss, you forgot to put the music on! The music we have for studying that helps our brains to concentrate. I also have a question.'

I glared at the child in front of me. He never took any heed of the classical music I played, in fact the first three times I had played the CD he had talked incessantly over the whole set of tracks, despite numerous warnings.

'Thank you, David. I'll pop the CD on when you have asked your question.'

'Well, I want my writing to be perfect today, so I want to check on punctuation for this sentence please.'

I really wasn't sure what had got into the child. Had an alien abducted him and replaced him with a genius? I needed to demonstrate the punctuation '*Boy Wonder*' had just asked for. From the corner of my eye, I could see the inspector had looked up and was watching me intently.

I copied the sentence which he had miraculously written in his book onto the white board and without thinking I stopped the class. Encouraging the children to solve David's problem, I received two suggestions to punctuate it and recapped on the answers. He could use simple sentences and make his long sentence into two shorter ones. The second choice would be to use a conjunction which we had talked about before. The final suggestion, which I offered, involved a semi colon which I had not taught the class yet. By now I was convinced the lesson was going to be 'Unsatisfactory.' I had nothing to lose. I put the whiteboard pen down after explaining the new punctuation mark. The class had remained silent and without being told to do so they began to write again. David gave me a cheesy grin. He glanced quickly at the inspector who now had begun to write his notes again. David looked back at me and, for a brief second. I was convinced he gave me a wink. I shook as I turned the CD player on and pressed the play button.

The class wrote, the inspector wrote, and the minutes ticked by. The 'Desperados' had completed seven lines which was a record for each of them. David had written a mini essay and everyone else had turned the pages of their exercise books several times. How David had written so much will remain a mystery, but he did, from that day, write more than a couple of lines. In fact, he went on to obtain a Level 3 in his writing SAT later that year.

As for me, 'Boy Wonder' had pulled an 'Outstanding' lesson out of the Child Catcher's bag. It just shows that bribery does work if you promise Double Golden Time!

The phrase 'outstanding' is a glory statement, something to brag about, a badge of honour. I questioned what it meant. Were the children 'outstanding'? Was I 'outstanding'? I had seen so many judgements at Larkshill and how they affected our world. I smiled sweetly when told my grading. John shook my hand. He was disappointed that the school had been judged as 'Good' but complimented me on my lesson grading. I should have been delighted but somehow the grade left me empty. Music played in my head, a theme tune from the film *Donnie Darko,* a couple of years before. It certainly was a '*very, very mad world*' in which I worked.

✓✓✓✓✓

Out of the blue, John called me into his office and asked me to have a probationary teacher in my class. I had supervised several student teachers over the years, but this would be a different situation. The lady had failed her probationary year, which was highly unusual. John thought this opportunity could offer me some time out of class to complete some of my duties as English coordinator. He also suggested this could be a good time to enrol on the National Professional Qualification for Headship (N.P.Q.H.) course. Anyone wishing to be a headteacher needed this qualification. I had no plan whatsoever to be a head but felt it was my one chance to study without too much pressure as a class teacher. It turned out that the probationer was useless. I never really got much time out of class. She failed, left teaching and ended up in the local Spar.

I continued with the N.P.Q.H. and got through to the final assessment day. I set off wearing a new woollen suit ready for a day of written and practical tasks. I had to sign a document to say I would never divulge any assessments, or indeed, the structure of the evaluations. I shall not break that promise but I can say that it was realistic and as challenging as any day as a headteacher. A few weeks later, a letter arrived informing me that I had been successful. I had met the standard for headship, but did I ever want that responsibility?

✓✓✓✓✓

Just a few days before receiving my result, I got married. Mark and I had decided we wanted a quiet wedding, so we told hardly anyone, family or friends of our arrangements. At school I told John as I felt I should mention it and so that I could have an entitled afternoon off school for personal reasons. The only other person who knew was Susan. I think the secret nearly killed her, but she managed to keep the news to herself until the day before the wedding. At lunchtime I had organised a buffet under the guise of celebrating the maternity leave of a teaching assistant. Everyone kept offering me money towards the do, but I was vague, pretending to say I would collect the money later. At the point of the buffet when baby gifts had been given to the expectant mum, Susan and John could wait no longer. Susan explained the real reason for the special lunch and John offered good wishes. Everyone sat open mouthed, their reactions were priceless. About half an hour later, I left school early, for much-needed time to make sure all final arrangements were in place.

The next day we were married in a castle dating back over a thousand years, me wearing a Saxon styled wedding dress made to measure off eBay and Mark wearing a tunic, drawstring shirt, and trousers. The only suitable boots we could find were from a rather unusual shop in the middle of Birmingham which sold alternative clothing, footwear and accessories. It sounds chaos and in bad taste but worked well. Clannad's ballad from *The Last of the Mohicans*, 'I will find you' played through the Great Hall as we signed the register. When a tourist from Canada saw us after the ceremony, the castle representative informed her this was first Saxon wedding in over a thousand years. The week of half term was spent on honeymoon in Scotland in a cottage we had stayed in before. I returned to school as Mrs Challis, but the children still called me Miss.

After a few months we moved into a three-hundred-year-old cottage in Derbyshire. It was about forty miles from Hawthorn Street. For the first time ever, my life was all about commuting. I had moved from living in the heart of the industrial Midlands to the countryside. It was bliss.

✓✓✓✓✓

I did not think that gaining my N.P.Q.H. would be important to me. Although the process had been challenging, the learning had been minimal. I had learned more about leadership at Larkshill. What I also learned over the years was that challenges came when you least expected.

John often went to headteacher conferences but had only ever been away for one day at a time. Something always happened on these days. Unlike at my previous school, where I did not have to deputise because of being an assistant head, I always had to make decisions when John was away. In the end the staff used to joke when something went wrong or there was some catastrophe.

There was the time a child had an epileptic fit in assembly, and we had to clear the hall of children and staff so he could recover in private. Then a parent collapsed in a diabetic hypo on the way to school one morning, leaving her tiny children at the kerbside on a busy road. Following this event there was an afternoon when a young sibling of a child got run over as he dashed across the road at home time. Luckily, he was not harmed but the driver of the vehicle had to be brought into school for a sweet tea to calm their nerves. There would be arguments amongst parents, and of course, arguments amongst youngsters at school that had to be dealt with.

When John announced he would be attending a two-day residential conference I dreaded what would happen. He had given me every password, every procedure including how to close the school in an emergency. Off he went to his country hotel telling me I had his full confidence in any decision I made. After the news finished that evening, the weatherman came onto the screen full of smiles about an impending snowstorm. I looked at the television in horror. The map tracking the storm showed clearly a forecast for heavy snow in the area around the school. That night I checked the window every half hour for signs of snow. Try as hard as I could there was no relaxation. Eventually, I fell asleep for the last hour and a half of the night and woke up with a start at the alarm ringing. Racing to the window I could immediately see that the light behind the curtains looked brighter than usual. We had had three feet of snow and were going nowhere.

'*Operation Snow*' kicked in. I had joked the day before that if we needed to inform each other about a snow closure day or for any other reason we needed a sensible way to get the message across rather than me phoning everyone individually. A plan was made for me to phone several key people and they, in turn, would each phone three different members of staff. The system moved to another group who would phone their three contacts so that within a few minutes every teacher, classroom assistant or dinner lady would know of a closure. WhatsApp had not been invented nor had Facebook taken off to such an extent as it later did. I had not thought the system would be needed but had planned it because a nagging voice in my head told me to do so.

Taking responsibility to close a school, to upset parents and children in their daily school routines and to stop people from going to work, is a decision that I have always found stressful. Taking charge of such an issue for the first time was scary. Most people accept the actions but there will always be some who take exception to the inconvenience. On that occasion I made the right choice, and the school was closed for two days. John had been stuck at the country hotel. He understood my decision, but I was glad to hand back responsibility when he returned after the weekend and the snow, by then, had melted.

✓✓✓✓✓

I was delighted when John had arranged for a residential again at my beloved outdoor learning centre. It was to be just a week before we broke up for Christmas and I looked forward to it for months. After several visits over the years, I knew the centre staff well. Two weeks before the trip, both me and Mark became ill with a virus which struck us down swiftly and knocked us both off our feet. I had to take a week off school as I felt so poorly. When I returned to work the next week, I felt as weak as a kitten but did not tell anyone as we were due to leave for the residential in two days' time. When the day of the trip arrived, I felt like falling asleep, every part of me ached but I was determined to go, thinking some fresh air would shake off the virus.

We reached the centre, did all the usual unpacking, fire drill and tour of the site. In the afternoon we set off for a walk. It was bitter cold and quite a mirky, foggy day. The temperature dropped and I started to shiver. My teeth chattered but I could not stop them. By the evening meal, I just wanted to sleep but I battled on. I was the most senior member of staff. Mae, Susan and another classroom assistant, Gail, had also accompanied the group. I was sharing a room with Susan again. That evening, when I finally got into bed, I dropped off to sleep immediately.

I awoke to Susan trying to tiptoe to the bathroom. It was time to get up. Sweat was pouring out of me. Despite feeling roasted, I apparently looked like a ghost. On seeing me, Susan, who had a natural gift for nursing people and a great deal of common sense, ordered me to stay in bed. I protested but she insisted. There I stayed for the rest of the visit, sleeping, occasionally eating or drinking a little when I felt able.

Gail had taken the car rather than travelling on the coach, in case we needed to transport anyone to hospital. It had been an extra precaution that John had suggested. I must admit that I did not put up too much resistance when I was told to travel back to school by car, at the end of the residential. I had managed one day of the entire trip. My stubbornness to continue had been ridiculous. It took six more weeks to shift the virus and months later I had to have an inhaler for the first time ever. Years later, when the Covid 19 pandemic hit the world, I knew how serious viruses can be and how long the after-effects can last.

✓✓✓✓✓

John had mentioned retirement on several occasions over the years, but when he called me into the office one lunch time and told me he was finishing, it still came as a shock for some reason. After feeling so safe and secure for six years and probably the happiest I had ever been in teaching, the feeling of change hit me and made me feel sick. It wasn't the fact that he was leaving that upset me, in fact, I was delighted that

174

there would be no more labels, no more Christmas party timetables and no more penny pinching. The truth was I knew I stood at a crossroads. There I was with several different roads to take but which one would I choose? I could stay as a deputy headteacher and do nothing. I had years to go until retirement, but I could stay in that role, not having to make decisions but being at someone's beck and call always. I had no control over anything but no responsibility.

I could try to get a job as a deputy or even headteacher somewhere else. I did not want to leave. I could be jumping from the frying pan into the fire again. I had already got that t-shirt! I could apply for John's job and go for the headship. There were more doubts than positive thoughts. If I failed, what would the staff think of me? Was I good enough? Could I do the job? Above all, there was one question that I couldn't get out of my head. Did I want a job that didn't involve teaching? Teaching had been my life for so many years now and the dilemma was something that constantly played on my mind, when I had considered John's retirement over the last couple of years.

John said he would make an announcement to everyone at a staff briefing next morning. I couldn't sleep that night as I knew that everyone would bombard me with questions, and I wasn't ready to give them an answer yet. I tossed and turned as the questions went through my mind. If I applied for the headship and got it and took the school in a downwards spiral, what would happen? There were so many questions it hurt my brain to think and try to make sense of everything. When the alarm rang, I was no further forward in knowing what I would do.

I could sense John was a little nervous. Despite always seeming calm and in control, never raising his voice, his tone this morning was business like and sharp. He often annoyed me when he was in this mood at his curtness to everyone, but I forgave him this morning as he had an excuse for being tense. His announcement came, followed by polite congratulations which he liked. The bell went for the commencement of school so there was no time to chat. I had my class to teach so the rest of the morning, until break, was straightforward. Then the gossip started. Had I known? When were we doing a collection? When would the job be advertised? Then, of course, the comments and questions began as expected.

'I guess you'll be applying for the headship?'

The next few months whirled by with the governing body being told formally and John's resignation accepted. The recruitment process started, and I was still at sixes and sevens over the answer to the constant questions. Then one evening, after lots of chatter, Mark said something that made me stop and think.

'You know you can do the job. Just apply! You'll have lost nothing if you don't get it, but you'll regret it for the rest of your life if you don't fill that form in.'

He was right. I could do the job although I often doubted it. I had nothing to lose if I didn't get it. If someone else got the position, I could see how I got on with them. I would most definitely regret not going for headship of a school I had grown to love and care about so much. The form was filled. The closing date passed. I could always back out if I got cold feet, I told myself.

The interview day dawned. I found myself at the entrance to a local hotel that I knew well from conferences. I was greeted by Linda, a secretary at our school, and asked to take a seat in the reception area. The nerves, which had been bubbling away since waking that morning, suddenly took over and I began to shake. I felt nauseous and my overwhelming thought was to run out of the building to breathe. Linda must have seen these changes in me. She said,

'You know Emma, my old mum had a saying, 'I can, and I will.' Now say that to yourself. I can and I will. Come on, say it!'

'I can and I will,' I whispered.

Linda nodded.

'You can and you will.'

The words seemed to soothe me. Whether it was the words or just Linda being calm, I did feel the tension disappear a little. Looking at her watch she rose from her chair and gestured for me to follow her. She walked a short distance to a small preparation room, checking every couple of steps that I was following her and not running away. She opened the door and as I went in, she repeated,

'I can and I will.'

Linda closed the door, and I was alone. I took a seat and looked at the items on the table in front of me, a flip chart, some coloured pens and a packet of Blu-Tack. There was a piece of paper and on it was typed the title for a presentation topic. I quickly read it, took a deep breath and off I went. Somewhere in my head I decided to theme my talk around the people in school: the children, parents, staff, the wider community. It seemed to work, and I began to bullet point what I wanted to comment on. The minutes ticked away, and I glanced at my watch to find that I still had a couple of minutes before I would be collected.

When the door opened, Linda led me to another room. She knocked and I walked in with my flip chart sheets and Blu-Tack. Placing the sheets on the wall in front of the panel I began the ten minutes presentation. After it was over it was time for a series of questions. There before me sat eight people I knew well, Rachael the teacher governor included. After one question and answer, I felt a twinge in my calf muscle and from nowhere came a spasm of cramp, so painful that I couldn't hide or pretend it wasn't there. I jumped up to the astonishment of the governors and education officer.

'I've got the cramp!'

It was because of how tensely I had been holding myself. With a glass of water pushed into my hands, a few seconds of laughter and jovial comments by panel members the pain dwindled, and I sat down, praying it would not start again. All tension had left my body. Nothing more could go wrong. A mantra played over and over in my head.

'I can and I will.'

When the interview was over, I went home and took off my new grey suit. The call came through about an hour later. I picked up the phone, knowing that I would either be a deputy or a headteacher in September. As expected, it was the chair of governors.

'Well, that was a day, wasn't it?'

I wanted him to get to the point, but the pleasantries had to be done. Finally, after what felt minutes but had only been a couple of seconds, he started on the reason behind his call.

'I should like to formally offer you the post of headteacher. '

Both Mark and my mother were in the room. We didn't have a phone that could be put on loudspeaker so when I punched the air, they knew I had the job. The call ended with my acceptance, and I sat back in the chair. All the tension of that day and the realisation of what I had just accepted with one word, disappeared. I was going to be a headteacher. It felt like I had just conquered Everest. How on earth had I managed to get to this point? I had been the child who had been so shy that she had wet herself, the teenager told she would never be a teacher. I always would be a reserved, quiet individual. An introvert who somehow had become a headteacher.

✓✓✓✓✓

For a few short weeks I carried on life as a class teacher but began to contemplate 'lasts': the last half term, the last assembly for my class, the last school trip. With six days to go before my last parents evening, I woke up that morning sweating and panicking. I hadn't had *'the dream'*, the one that had plagued me for every parent's evening, the one when I was late, not prepared and not ready to face any parents. It had to be bad omen. Something would go wrong if I didn't have my lucky dream but as much as I wished it and desired it, the dream did not occur. This was to be my last parents' evening as a class teacher. Everything would go wrong but of course it didn't. It was just a sign that I was moving on. The term came to an end and with it came the end of John's headship. He spent his last few days in his room, going through files and papers to ensure his work was up to date. School broke up for the six weeks holiday and I wished him farewell.

Little did I know that six weeks late, on the day before school was due to start, there would be a problem. As I arrived at the school John's car was in the car park. I was puzzled why he was there. I had been excited to sit in the chair in *'my office'*. I walked into the office without knocking and did a double take. There he was on the first day of September, no longer headteacher, but sitting at his desk, my desk. I was stunned. Somehow, I managed a polite but begrudged greeting and then turned my back on him and walked out of school. He had ruined my big day. I had wanted everything to be perfect, but John had stolen the moment. He had been in every single day of the holidays, according to the site manager, and had been working at his computer or shredding papers. On the second day of September, I arrived at school at seven thirty in the morning, half expecting John's car in the car park. The office was empty. The school was finally mine.

✓✓✓✓✓

My first few days and weeks in charge of the school whizzed by in a blur. The glamorous side of being a headteacher was that conferences always seemed to be organised at four-star hotels with full English breakfasts and lunch with three courses. There was an air of respect given by some people I had not experienced before. Children and parents addressed me in a different manner even though I had taught some of the pupils just a few short weeks before. The unglamorous side of headship was there were thousands of emails to read and respond to, everyone wanted my time and my answers to the most mundane, sometimes stupid questions. I never said 'No' to anyone and soon found my time filled with toilet roll counts, health and safety walks with the site manager and countless meetings with finance officers, governors, school improvement officers and any parent who wanted to complain. The word 'No', such a small word in many regards, was difficult to say. A few months into the job, I accepted the word. The first few times I uttered it to staff felt like I had cut them with a knife, so sharp was its meaning to me.

I certainly had my hands full. There was never a moment to even have lunch and some of my colleagues kept telling me to sit in the staffroom to have a break, which I did occasionally but I felt different. When John had been headmaster, we had loved his absence in the staffroom. It had given staff the opportunity to vent their feelings on his latest label or decision. I felt that I needed to give staff that breathing space to do that about me. I wanted to be perfect, but I was realistic. Every headteacher I had ever known would have grumblings about them by staff and I would be no different.

During those strange days of early headship, I held a training day on expectations. I wanted to give my vision for the school and the expectations I had 'for' and 'of' the pupils, staff and parents. This would also be an opportunity for staff to share them expectations 'for' and 'of' me. John had never explored his role with staff probably because he liked to lead from the front, dragging us all along. I wanted more partnership working as I had seen the power of partnerships in many school situations including at Larkshill.

It was interesting that the staff expected just one thing of me, to know each child. I knew instantly what they meant. John was utterly embarrassing, although he hadn't realised it, in the fact he knew few children's names. In assembly he used a technique where he got each

179

child who went out to the front of the ensemble to introduce themselves to the school. Staff instantly realised he did not know the child's name when he first did his party piece and we had all been shocked. They wanted me to know each child's name and I nodded. I knew exactly what they meant.

The days seemed endless and the evenings full of meetings. Travelling home, some forty miles away, was impossible at times and I often stayed overnight at my mother's house. By getting up at half past five each day and arriving at work by seven thirty the days were long and if I did go home, it would be after six o'clock when I reach my door if I was lucky. So, with less that twelve hours at home, fitting in a few hours' sleep if I could, I quickly became exhausted. Music could only be listened to in the car. There were loud tunes in the morning from Blondie or Cyndi Lauper but, in the evenings, it was quieter music, Clannad or Mark Knopfler. It was easy to tell my mood by the music that was played.

✓✓✓✓✓

One morning, just after the end of morning break, Susan knocked gently on the office door and popped her head into the room. Her cheeks were red, but I wasn't entirely surprised as I knew she had just been on playground duty. Perhaps it was cooler than I remembered. I had not been outside since seven thirty that morning and had been stuck at my desk ever since. She said, rather sheepishly,

'Can I have a word?'

I nodded and she shut the door behind her, checking to see that it was closed properly. This interested me as she could take a door almost off its hinges when she entered a room with her normal gusto. She moved towards me and began to whisper. Now I was amused and puzzled.

'I've been on playground duty with the supply teacher John arranged to cover your special needs duties.'

I nodded again, now slightly irritated that she needed to tell me this information. A lady had been given a short contract by John, covering my old duties until someone was appointed permanently as the new coordinator.

'She smells of booze.'

I looked at her. I was not expecting that sentence.

'What do you mean? She smells of booze?'

180

It was Susan's turn to nod her head. She continued,

'It's not the first time. Gail smelt her two days ago when she sat down in the staffroom next to her but thought she was imagining it. She asked me to check out the smell. We gave her the benefit of the doubt as we couldn't be certain. I'm sorry, I should have told you then.'

I put my elbows onto the table and rested my forehead in my hands. What should I do? There was no manual for this. My N.P.Q.H. had not prepared me for such a scenario. Perhaps I could ask John. Then I remembered he had retired, and the decisions were now all mine. My brain started into gear. I telephoned the local authority HR department and asked for advice as to how to proceed. After putting down the telephone I knew what I had to say and do. I needed a witness, someone to trust so Marianne, the office manager, was quickly brought into the office and given the job to observe and make notes.

The teacher was sent for and when she knocked on my door, I knew I had to start straight away, no pleasantries as usual. I got to the point, blurting out members of staff had approached me concerned they could smell alcohol on her. Had she been drinking that morning? Of course, it was denied, just a couple of glasses of wine last night. She was shocked and appalled people thought she had been drinking. I suggested, as she was due to leave in the next hour, being on a part time contract, that she had a taxi home as I believed alcohol was still present in her system. The room stunk of booze. She was lying. I told her this must not happen again and that this meeting was being recorded on paper. She was a hopeless actress, apologetic, insistent of her innocence, slurring her words just slightly.

She phoned in sick the next day and I was relieved. I hoped she would just send a letter to resign but, if there is one thing certain about headship, there are always difficult and surprising moments, in equal measure. She turned up two days later, avoided me and other members of staff. Her friendliness seemed to have disappeared and she avoided contact with any adult. Less than an hour after the school day had begun, one of the staff banged on my door and shouted,

'You had better come quickly! She's been sick!'

No name was mentioned but I knew instantly who 'she' was. I raced down the corridor, through the hall and into the library area to where I

181

had been directed. Sick was being cleaned up by another classroom assistant, the air stank of alcohol. Red wine and what looked like bits of toast stained the blue carpet. 'She' had gone to the toilet to clean herself up.

There were no soft words and no space for lies in the next few minutes after the teacher emerged from the ladies' loo. Again, Marianne witnessed the meeting where the woman was told, in no uncertain terms, that she was to go home, the authority would be terminating her temporary contract and that she was no longer needed. She cried but there was no remorse. Out poured a sad story, indeed a personal tragedy of a woman who couldn't cope with life. She had chosen to drink to blot out her misery but had just made it worse, now having no job. I asked for her car keys to stop her driving and killing someone. Without hesitation, this time she handed over the keys, planned for someone to pick the car up that evening and asked for the number of a taxi firm. As she left the school site, staff were still scrubbing the carpet. In the end it took a couple of weeks to rid the school of the stench of red wine and vomit. A drunken teacher in my first three weeks of headship had to be a record!

✓✓✓✓✓

During December of the first year as head we had snow in Derbyshire that lay around for days. Our lane was like a skating rink and on some days, we couldn't even get the car off the drive. On one occasion we managed to reach a local railway station a few miles from home and decided to travel into work by train.

All was going well until we reached Birmingham. Having already travelled for an hour and a half my feet and hands were numb with cold, and I desperately needed the toilet before getting on the tram to school. We found toilets in one of the local shopping centres and as I came out, starting to put on my gloves, I asked Mark where my bag was. I had put my new work shoes, school diary and some important papers into a rucksack which he had gallantly offered to carry. The realisation in the next second that the bag was missing woke me with a start. He had not got the bag. He instantly remembered where he had put it on the train, on the rack above our heads. We raced back to the station, slipping and sliding in the ice but the train had gone many minutes before. Off it went on its way to Bristol and the West Country. Staff at the railway contacted

182

the train crew and a guard managed to locate the bag which was racing towards Cheltenham by now.

An embarrassing telephone call to school explaining I was on my way to Cheltenham was made to bewilderment by the office staff. There was nothing I could do but to make the train ride to collect the bag which contained every single appointment, meeting and telephone number in my professional world, never mind my new shoes. An hour later the bag was retrieved from the lost property at Cheltenham railway station and within ten minutes we were back on a train travelling north. By now lunch time was fast approaching. With the snow starting to fall heavily again, and the prospect of cancelled trains an issue, we abandoned work that day and managed to get home. We had been travelling for ten hours. The school bell had gone for the final time that day. The panic at the thought of losing the school diary resulted me creating an online version and never again did I rely on a paper one, always having a backup online.

✓✓✓✓✓

It had been a few years since our last Ofsted visit, and we had been preparing for months. The talk in senior leadership meetings were always about our 'due date' which made us sound as if we were pregnant. I had changed all kinds of procedures in my first year as head. There had been several staff issues that John had swept under the carpet and when I had found them, I had opened 'Pandora's Box'. One by one I worked through what I found but it was painful for the member of staff and certainly not easy to carry out by myself. Claire had been a massive support after being appointed late in the autumn term as my deputy headteacher. Despite much interest and several candidates, she had fought off all competition and I was glad of a familiar face to talk to when my world of staffing became bleak.

I would often discuss the issues with our school improvement officer from the local authority, but he had just one answer and made it very clear that the only way out of the issues were to lead through them or Ofsted would blame me for teaching standards being poor. I hated this aspect of the job especially when the people we talked about had been colleagues for the last few years. When he called me 'dogmatic', I had to look up the word to recheck the meaning in case I had missed what he meant but I had not. I liked to speak plainly and without hidden meanings. What's the point in waffle if something is crap?

I had pondered for months if I should feel loss at no longer teaching. I missed talking to children more than I could ever tell anyone. Days and months went by when I felt I was desperate for contact with children and to teach. Sometimes I would not try very hard to find supply if a teacher was absent as it meant I could teach. I missed music in my classroom. I was conscious of having to keep an ear out for a knock on the door, so headphones were of no use.

When it was time to sort out the staff to attend the next residential, there was no question whose name I wrote first. I knew I should miss a few days of emails and form filling, but I could catch up with them. I made sure there were no diary clashes and off I went. For those precious days away in the countryside I could be a teacher again. It was something I continued to do for years after.

My days were taken up with meetings, emails, taking and making phone calls and avoiding reps from educational suppliers who tried every tactic in the book to speak to me. Marianne was very accustomed to lying on my behalf. In fact, she managed everything in the school office and many strange situations that occurred daily. She was adept at stopping parents from entering through the security gates without a good reason and would spot any suspicious character hanging around straight away.

One afternoon she saw a youth enter through the outer gates and start to mess about with the rubbish bins placed at the entrance of the school. The bins were there to catch the discarded pieces of toast or Monster Munch packets in the mornings and for sweet papers and crisps after school. A 'Healthy Eating Award' was a far distanced dream, despite the school's best interests to promote a balanced diet and active lifestyle!

The young man was unknown to the school, so this meant Marianne was on her guard. She called me to come immediately, and I raced into the office, just as he was leaving the school grounds. She had witnessed him lifting the inner shell of the bin, something I had no idea could be done. He had placed a package underneath and then put the inner bin back in position. We both raced outside but he was gone and nowhere to be seen as we looked in the direction he had hastily walked towards. Our eyes both went towards the bin. What on earth had the lad been messing with? Something told me not to touch it, so we did not go near even though we were both curious to know what he had done.

Until the police arrived, I stared at the bin. Luckily a patrol car had been in the area and had arrived within ten minutes. It turned out that a plastic bag full of drugs had been placed under the bin which was used daily by our children and parents. The police removed the bag, took a statement from each of us but we never heard any more or saw the youth again. I could not understand why someone would make use of our school bin to hide drugs. The bin was moved behind the inner gates which required entry via a keypad or intercom. It was all I could think of to do. I felt despair that I could not protect the children from the outside world.

With her calm, yet efficient manner Marianne knocked on the door and, unusually for her, she burst in without being told to enter. It was just before ten o'clock one Monday morning about five weeks before the end of term. The first year of my headship was coming to an end. I was busy finalising some celebrations as the school was about to commemorate the fortieth year of its origins. A 1970s theme day was to be held in the final couple of weeks. I looked up, a little taken aback by her abruptness but knew instantly it was out of character and must be urgent.

'There is a call for you. It is an Ofsted Inspector,' she gasped.

I could feel myself begin to shake. My heart skipped a few beats. The room spun as I gathered my composure and nodded to her to go back to her office and put the call through. I listened to my caller and tried to stop my hand shaking as I made notes. When I placed the telephone back in its cradle my whole body went into shock. I stood up, legs wobbling and walked quietly around to Claire's room to inform her. In ten minutes, she had the whole school in the hall for a 'story' whilst I sat shaking in the staffroom. Everyone had hurried into the staffroom when the message had reached them, classes left with Claire and Susan. They stared at me, and the colour drained from all their faces as it had from mine, ten minutes before. I just managed to get the words out that Ofsted would be visiting on Wednesday morning.

I did not go home that week until Friday evening. Mark went home, put together all the clothes and items I had listed that I needed for the rest of the week, and drove back to school. No teacher left before nine o'clock that evening and many class assistants stayed to help as much as they could. Everyone wanted to do well but we were all shattered on Tuesday morning. With the clock ticking for the inspection to commence in less than twenty-four hours now, every member of staff, each a necessary cog in a well-oiled machine, moved into top gear, all parts working together in unison. After school, we set off again, making final preparations, barely stopping to eat chips that someone had fetch for us. As I left that evening, my shaking had long gone. I wanted to show the school at its best, being honest about what we needed to do and where we were travelling on our improvement journey. That night I slept soundly. I was exhausted.

Arriving the next morning, an hour before I was usually in, I wasn't the first member of staff through the school gates. The car park was almost full already. As I opened the door, I could hear the sound of a staplegun blasting staples into a wallboard, the sound of the photocopier busy in the office and in the distance, music playing in one of the classrooms. I recognised it instantly as Queen, 'We are the Champions.' I smiled. Everyone was ready and most importantly the smell of coffee was wafting from the staffroom.

Marianne informed me at one minute past eight o'clock that an inspector was parking his car in the car park, followed swiftly by another couple of unfamiliar cars. She knew the script and made sure that ID badges were checked for safeguarding purposes, that the inspectors signed in and were issued with visitor badges. I greeted them as Marianne whipped the pen away from the final inspector. In they came to my office which was to be their base for the next few days. Teas, coffees and biscuits appeared, served with a smile by Linda a few minutes later. Off they went with questions, a timetable of when they would meet the chair of governors, the local authority officer and everyone else on their list. I was questioned on every aspect of the school improvement plan, data on SATs, any issues they needed to know. I was realistic and honest. The surprising thing was that when I spoke about the school, my school, I was not afraid. The *'Men in Grey Suits'* were not going to ruin us, as they had at Larkshill.

Into classrooms they went, emerging briefly between observations, then disappearing quickly into another room. Like a giant octopus, the Ofsted tentacles reached every area of the school site, every member of staff and every child in school, feeling its way through the very fibre of the building until we were all overwhelmed at its reach and strength.

Day two went in a similar way with meetings with the school council, parent representatives and other 'stakeholders' who visited school regularly. The phrase always amused me. A caveman holding a wooden club with a sharp end comes to my mind when I hear it. As I walked into the room for the end of inspection briefing, my legs felt wobbly. The enormity of the last few days hit me as I sat listening to the outcome. In my tiredness, I struggled to take in the words. The local authority officer, the chair of governors and Claire were also present. The report would be written and published within a set time frame. Certain aspects could be shared with staff, some could not. They agreed with how we had graded the school ourselves. We were '*a good school with some outstanding features.*' 'Outstanding' would not appear in the report but it was acknowledged that we had the capacity to improve further to attain this goal.

With the burden of an Ofsted inspection over, we could concentrate on the celebrations to mark forty years of the school existing. There had been a secondary modern school on the site and there was evidence in a plaque on one of the external walls which still existed about a school being there for many years before. A couple of staff had taught there almost from the opening of the school and had some good memories to share. Although exhausted after what had been a stressful five days, and the summer holidays beckoning, everyone was looking forward to dressing up. Staff turned up in seventies flairs, platform heels and the clothes of the seventies. Music played and I made sure Blondie and the *Saturday Night Fever* soundtrack were played in my office.

The chair of governors readily agreed when asked if we could spend a little money to organise a celebration for the staff for all their hard work on the evening we broke up for the summer. A venue chosen for the party was deliberate. The evening would also be for Heather. The nursery teacher would be retiring that day and the hotel held strong family links and memories for her. It had been a place she had spent hours exploring when much younger. Her mother had been a housekeeper there many years before. She loved visiting the hotel and although she had clearly stated she wanted no fuss, I think secretly she had enjoyed being the centre of attention at the party. We all danced the night away, celebrated our successes and wished our dear friend and colleague a happy retirement. It was a perfect end to my first year as a headteacher.

187

I want to say that being in charge was all plain sailing, but it wasn't. Even years later, when someone called me 'the boss', it felt strange. Little ones quickly realised there is an order of hierarchy in school which fascinated me. I guessed they understood from conversations at home about bosses. I loved making changes for the benefit of the children, striving to give them the best possible life chances. In the years since I had been acting deputy at Northwood, I had become frustrated at some of the decisions my bosses had made. Now I was responsible for all decision making from who was employed at the school to what toilet paper was used. The remit was huge, and it wasn't until I was headteacher that I fully comprehended what it meant to be *the* decision maker.

There were names I was occasionally called that cut me to the core, shattering the small amount of confidence I had. I was shocked at the tirade of abuse I received as 'the boss'. Often the verbal insults were a way that someone let off steam, but it was still unacceptable. Several parents were reminded of the council's policy on bullying and harassment of staff.

When I was called 'a bitch' the first time by a parent, I sat in silence. The parent approached me with a set of car keys held as a weapon in her hand. She was angry because a member of staff had innocently approached her about practising some reading words with her child. She claimed the teacher had humiliated her which was untrue. Witnesses told a different story to the account she gave. As the car keys came towards my face, the woman dropped them on the floor and walked back to her seat in my office. I was accused of being too calm as she screamed obscenities at me. My calmness apparently riled her because I showed no emotion. The truth was I was rooted to the spot, unable to move, and barely speak for fear of making her angrier. When she continued to be verbally abusive towards me, she was escorted from the premises by Rachael and another member of staff.

I was slowly recovering from the incident, sipping a cup of coffee with two spoonsful of sugar, which Marianne had made me. Apparently, I needed something for the shock. The phone in the office rang and I could hear Linda's voice change.

'Oh, my goodness! Okay, I'll tell her.'

I waited for the footsteps and the knock on the door, that had been left ajar. I wondered what could possibly be next in my day. It was only ten o'clock in the morning.

'Emma, It's Susan. She's just called.'

'What's the matter? She's on a trip.'

'Claire has been taken ill. She felt faint and at one point it was thought she was going to collapse. Susan has had to take over.'

My day could not get worse. Claire, Susan, together with a small group of other adults and a party of sixty children were on a visit to a country museum twenty-five miles away.

'Does Claire need an ambulance?'

'No. She says she'll be alright if she can take a few minutes to recover.'

'Call her husband to collect her. She needs to go home.'

Rachael, who was out of class for the day, had popped back to see if I was recovering from the parent incident a few minutes before. Having overheard the conversation, she grabbed her car keys and off we went. A few minutes before I had been physically and verbally threatened for a pathetic reason. Now I was off to take a class on an educational visit for the day. Life was never dull.

Being the boss was not easy and always challenging. It brought blame when I was innocent. Headship was lonely. I built a hard shell around myself. When the days were tough, as they often were, it was a protection from a world I had never seen as a class teacher. Some days I wondered why I had ever left the classroom. The *unexpected* was a beast of many colours. Sometimes it was vicious and full of venom. Rarely was it meek and mild. It was always waiting around the corner, ready to pounce.

Chapter 9
The Big Adventure Of Two Forty Somethings

Having celebrated her 90th birthday several years before, my nan remained independent, often catching the bus into town to do some shopping. Every Saturday lunchtime, she was driven to mum's house where she stayed until Sunday afternoon. There were a few small changes that we started to notice about her but nothing which caused alarm until my mother heard her screaming upstairs in her bedroom one Sunday morning. Mum raced up the stairs and called out, opening the bedroom door. Nan was sitting on the edge of the bed in her flannelette pyjamas, holding her head.

'Where am I?'

'You are at my house. Don't worry. You must have been having a bad dream. Get yourself dressed and come down for a cup of tea. You'll feel better after that and some toast.'

Over the next few weeks, Nan became more unsure of her world, even in her own house and my mother knew that the time had come to make decisions. How could she broach the subject of moving? Nan had lived in at the same house for seventy years. Mum knew it would be a battle if she made any suggestion about Nan moving in with her or to a care home. Sadly, she did not have to have that conversation.

One Friday morning, after opened Nan's front door, my mother knew something was even more wrong. Nan was not up and about as she always was. Gingerly Mum went up the stairs, half expecting to find her mother dead. When she opened the bedroom door, she saw a sight that has haunted her ever since. There was my nan, still alive but covered in a black slime. It was all over her and her pyjamas, the bed and bed clothes; the room was filled with it. An ambulance was called immediately.

After her admission to hospital, tests soon confirmed that Nan had a mass within her bowel which was malignant. An operation to remove the cancer proved unsuccessful as it had attached itself to the wall of Nan's bowel. There it stayed. My confused ninety-three-year-old grandmother thought she was having a baby. It was a sad end for such an independent woman who had been a second mother to me. Within a few days she was gone.

After her funeral, me and Mark set off for a holiday. Visits to Scotland were becoming more frequent. It was where we both could find peace and it felt like home. Both of our maternal grandmothers were born with Scottish surnames. Mark was proud of the Macdonald link, and I was passionate about my clan Chisholm.

✓✓✓✓

A few months after my Nan's passing, something changed within me. I began to search for jobs in Scotland. I can't explain where or why this notion came into my head, but it came and tormented me until I could no longer avoid speaking to Mark. One evening after work, I slipped some comments into a conversation we were having.

'There is a job I've seen advertised. It's for a cluster headteacher, to oversee two small schools. We know both places. It's for the school at Loch Dubhglas and the other is at Tarn. So, it would be a 'big' school, well about thirty children, and a 'wee' school with about seven!'

He looked at me sternly.

'You said you wouldn't consider a move. Stop taunting me with these ideas. You won't follow them through. I know you won't!'

'My nan lived in a house for seventy years, a hair's breadth from where she was born. The furthest she ever travelled south was to London, North, it was a day in the Lake District. In a few years' time, when I'm in a similar hospital bed dying, I want to have experienced an adventure. I want to be able to say I tried something different. If it doesn't work out and we have egg on our faces, we can at least say we tried and failed.'

I was shocked at how my thoughts had spurted out of my mouth, but they were now out and had been aired in public for the first time. It felt liberating and crazy, but I knew I felt better for having shared what had been in my head for days. Mark understood completely. We knew the village of Loch Dubhglas. The school was next to the carpark where we stopped for sandwiches, or for the toilet before heading further north. We had often passed through the remote hamlet of Tarn, on a single-track road full of spectacular scenery. The application form was filled in without further discussion.

Over two months later I had lost all hope of hearing anything about the job, let alone an interview. It had been a silly dream, perhaps part of the grieving process for my grandmother. I was happy at Hawthorn Street. Why would I want to move? I was busy talking to a member of staff about their plans for the Easter holidays, which were rapidly approaching, when Marianne came into the room, breathless at having disobeyed the rule of no running in the corridors. I was at the furthest point I could be away from the offices.

'There's a man on the phone for you. He is Scottish!' she gasped.

I ran down the corridor, through a P.E. lesson in the hall and into the reception area, trying to compose myself as I got within ten metres from the phone. I heard Marianne's voice gasp again.

'I'll just put you through.'

My heart missed several beats as I politely greeted my caller. He introduced himself and his job title and quickly got down to the purpose of his call. He thanked me for my application, apologised for a delay in the recruitment process and invited me to attend for interview in four weeks' time. There would be an interview on the first day and if successful I would be invited to attend a 'panel interview' the day after. He talked about a visit to the schools beforehand. When I told him we were holidaying in the area during the Easter break, he was delighted, readily agreeing an appointment to meet. The conversation lasted probably for just a couple of minutes, and I am sure, I didn't breathe for those few seconds. We hadn't contemplated two visits to Scotland in four weeks but that is what we did. The visit went smoothly, and the holiday passed without incident apart from my stomach doing somersaults at the thought of what was to come after the next journey to Scotland.

I told a very small circle of colleagues that I would be away for three days for the interviews and travel. My cover story to the rest of the staff was that I was on a headteacher course, and as the previous incumbent of the position had been on residential conferences before, this was not out of the ordinary. We travelled up to Scotland the day before the interview and settled into the B & B I had booked. It was the closest place I could find to the building where the interview was to take place.

On interview day I awoke after a surprisingly good night's sleep. Full of Scottish breakfast, I changed into my suit and freshly polished shoes.

I was ready. I set off with fifteen minutes to go, thinking I was in good, steady time. I was two minutes away from the building and it was a bright, sunny May morning. I arrived at the reception and the lady asked me my name and who I was visiting. I replied that I was a little early and that I was there for an interview. She looked at her watch and hurriedly rushed around from behind her counter, pushing a paper into my hands as we entered a small room next to her desk.

'You might have time as they are running a wee bitty behind.'

She closed the door and left me. I didn't understand. I was early for the interview. I had checked and checked the time over the last twenty-four hours. I found out much later that headship candidates had ten minutes to see questions and prepare their answers. I had seven minutes when I looked at the large clock on the wall. There were six questions, a minute a question and one minute to read through. Panic struck. What would I write with? I knew I had no pen in my handbag. My hands frantically went to both jacket pockets. Nothing. I was wasting precious time. An inner breast pocket was my last resort. My mood was instantly raised as I felt the outline of a pencil left there from the last time, I had worn this suit.

I got to work, too busy to be angry with myself for missing arrival information contained in the interview letter. I read and wrote quickly and somehow managed to get some points down for each answer. With a minute to spare, I re-read my notes and put my pencil down just as the door opened and the education officer entered. I was led into a room where three people were already sitting: two other education officers and one primary headteacher. The questions began. Perhaps the adrenaline rush had been a good thing because the limited preparation time had made me focus. I went through each point I had scribbled down and gave illustrated examples to demonstrate my thoughts.

When the interview was over, I rushed back to the B & B and got the letter out of my laptop bag. Nowhere did it say to arrive ten minutes early. All local candidates would have known that, but I wasn't a local candidate! We packed and left the B & B. The owner knew our circumstances and said he would keep the room available until four o'clock. I did not think I would return.

The rest of the morning went slowly. We visited a couple of our favourite haunts whilst we waited, thinking we might as well get a couple

193

of sightseeing adventures in before travelling back down south. We couldn't go too far in case we lost the signal on the mobile phone that I clutched in my hand. I was willing it to ring. Finally at around quarter to three the phone began to bleep. My heart missed a beat. I pushed the answer button and put the phone on loudspeaker so that my husband could also hear our fate. The now familiar male Scottish voice spoke, and I held my breath. He thanked me for attending for interview.

'After due consideration we should like to invite you to the second interview tomorrow morning at half past ten. If I could offer you a piece of advice … it is hard to understand your accent so please can you speak slowly and clearly tomorrow?'

When the call ended, Mark burst into uncontrollable laughter.

'They can't understand your Black Country accent!'

We immediately telephoned the B & B, returning to our room after having a meal at a local restaurant. That night I did something that I'd never done before; I bottled it! My nerves got the better of me. The second day would be a full panel interview and a presentation on school improvement, the title of which had been in the letter. No matter how I tried to practise my presentation speech it kept going wrong. It was either too long, too short or I stuttered that much I made a mess of the whole thing. Try as I might, I could not get the speech to go well so I threw the papers in the air and cried in the bathroom.

We were five hundred miles from home, in a different county, a different country and we knew no-one. How could we possibly make this move? How could we leave family and friends? How could we leave long established jobs? This was a fool's errand, and I was being stupid to even try for this post. Mark panicked and told me to pull myself together. He had never seen me like this. I hadn't ever seen myself like this and it was shocking. I had no clue what I was going to do or say in the next interview. Then, for some strange reason, Doris Day popped into my head, another one of my childhood heroines. I gave a smile. Nothing was going to change our fate. Midlands or Scotland? Music was always there when I needed help, so I sang.

'Que sera, sera, whatever will be, will be!'

After reasonable sleep I awoke, feeling more positive. I set off half an hour before the interview, knowing I was very early but taking no chances

194

this time. I clutched my leather document case, a beautiful Celtic embossed dragon on the front, with a huge metal buckle as a fastening. I lifted it to my face, smelling the leather and feeling the coldness of it on my cheek. This was it. This was the day we might change our future for ever.

When I reached the reception, the same lady was on the desk and she gave me a knowing smile; I was on time, this morning. She asked me to sit as I was early. In the next seat was a man who looked perhaps a little older than me, with a greying beard. He was smartly dressed but I had made no connection until he leaned across and spoke to me with a northern English accent.

'You must be the other candidate. My name is Des.'

He was my opposition I realised. I asked where the other candidates were, and he gave a smile.

'No kid! It's only me and you. Just two of us got through although there were other local candidates like me.'

My heart sank. He knew the system. He knew the people interviewing us. The chances of an external candidate succeeding against him were slim and none. I asked him where he worked, and he told me he was the headteacher of a school on the west coast. Although he was my opponent, I liked this stranger. He appeared down to earth, chatting away about teaching, and making witty remarks. Although his accent was from northern England, he had lived in Scotland for thirty years or more.

When the education officer greeted us, I noted the friendliness and familiarity between him and Des. The local candidate had the job in the bag. Des was taken to prepare his answers. I sat silently waiting until it was my turn. When I was finally called, I had the luxury of ten whole minutes. It was wonderful and took my mind off the looming presentation that had gone so wrong the evening before. With my lucky pencil in hand, I wrote reams and had time to re-read my points, add comments and revise what I wanted to say. The additional three minutes made such a difference!

The door opened and in came the education officer. He led me through to a different room to the one where I had been interviewed the day before. I glanced at the sign on the door as we entered. It read 'Council Chambers.'

I took the seat offered and glanced around. There in front of me was a room filled with tables in the shape of a horseshoe. At each table were two people and I quickly counted eight tables, three on each side of the horseshoe and two making up the top of the configuration. Sixteen strangers stared at me. The group consisted of councillors, education officials, parent council members from both cluster schools and even a union representative. I was in a whole new, alien world as the chair of the procedure introduced each member of the interview panel. There were so many names that I was only able to note who were parents.

Invited to begin my presentation, I rose to my feet, opened my leather document wallet and began, asking everyone to close their eyes and imagine a small child wearing a pair of black plimsolls. I'd used the trick before, but I knew it worked well. My audience were focused, and it gave me a few seconds to breathe and calm down before they opened their eyes again. I started to speak slowly, remembering my Black Country accent was unusual to these people. My presentation continued smoothly. The chair told me at five minutes I was halfway through my presentation. At the warning of one minute to go, I smiled. I was on my last page with four more points to make which were a summary of the presentation. I had finished my last sentence when the chair said,

'Thank you. Your time is up.'

I sat down relived that I had not thrown my papers in the air or had a panic attack. I didn't care about the questions. I had seen them; they were easy, and I had good answers. I relaxed. The rest of the panel interview went quickly and without hitch.

I left the room, happy that I had managed to complete the interview to my best ability. I had shown I had a knowledge of the Scottish system, but my fate lay in the hands of those sixteen people who knew a local candidate. Des was familiar with how schools worked in Scotland and wouldn't cost the council any relocation fees. I was convinced that the dream, which had been a fantastic adventure for two forty somethings to embark upon, was gone. Mark sat in the car outside, ready to drive back home. He had packed up at the B&B, unaware that the bubble had burst. He would be gutted but that was our fate.

Des was in the reception area and greeted me with a smile, joking that it was all over now. We sat for an eternity. He glanced at his watch, I glanced at my watch and we both listened to the clock ticking loudly on the wall behind us. We chatted about Scotland, about the Midlands and any topic we could think of that was appropriate for two strangers who were competitors to share.

After three quarters of an hour the door opened, and the education officer came in. He led us along the corridor, passed the council chambers, and up a small flight of stairs, apologising for keeping us waiting. We were taken into a small area where there were cups, saucers and tea and coffee facilities. It was a place where normally people would take a lunch break, but the room was empty.

'I am sorry to bring you in here but it's a busy place today and there are no other rooms available. Firstly, thank you for attending interviews over the last two days. Well, I want to congratulate you, Emma. Welcome to Scotland.'

Des grabbed my hand and shook it energetically. I thought he was my nemesis when in fact I was his.

'All the panel would like to meet you both especially you, Emma. Sorry we took so long to come to a decision but some of the panel felt that you wouldn't move five hundred miles. You *will* accept? I take it you *will* move five hundred miles?'

The education officer looked at me. I nodded. The shock of what just happened had not sunk in, nor did it for days after. Back in the council chambers I shook hands with all the panel who were standing and chatting in small groups.

'When are you travelling back down south?' asked the education officer.

'As soon I have finished here,' I replied.

'I am going to ask you not do that. Could you possibly visit both schools to meet the staff and children before you travel back? There will be a lot of anxiety about an incomer getting the job.'

'Incomer?' What the hell was an 'incomer?' I could only guess at its meaning. Is that how I was going to be seen … an 'incomer?' I felt a knot in my stomach. My Chisholm breeding would count for nothing with a Midlands accent. I had just accepted a job that meant putting our half-renovated house up for sale. I was asking Mark to give up his job as well as having to resign myself. Were we going to fit in here as 'incomers?' I had been given a label which cut deep into my heart. Is this how all those bus children, in the late sixties, felt when they were referred to by labels. I recalled Joe's anger at being called names. Here was I with a label too, in the second decade of the twenty-first century. It does not seem to matter if you are black, brown or white. If you don't originate from a certain area or you are seen to be different in some way, there is a compulsion to label diversity.

Over the years I have heard the phrase 'incomer' many times since it was used by the education officer. It's a term that is often said and refers to anyone not born in a particular area. If you come from Glasgow but move to a small village on the east coast, even after thirty years, you would be classed as an 'incomer.' It is just not a label I had ever come across before. In fact, I'm pretty sure it could cause an argument if you used the word in the area where I was born, where people of many nationalities, religions and cultures live metres away from each other. It is meaningless banter, often not meant to be offensive … but it is. We haven't moved on as a society even if we kid ourselves that we have.

I want to make it very clear at this point that throughout my story I have given labels to people and groups of children. These have been for comedic effect and certainly never voiced, apart from one time in the interview to get into teacher training college, when I had referred to Miss Bagshot as '*Dragon*.' There has been staff I have met who have made cutting remarks about individuals or groups of children. I even worked in a school that labelled each ability group by colours. 'Red group' were lower ability children, 'Amber' the middle ability and 'Green' the go getters but these labels were all wrong. Every child realised their place within the class. I know I did when I was small. Any form of label is wrong. We are all individuals, somewhere along life's spectrum.

As I nodded that I could visit the schools, the education officer told me to hurry. I was half an hour from Loch Dubhglas and over an hour away from the wee school in Tarn. By now it was almost one o'clock so there was a real time constraint if I was going to travel to both schools.

I suddenly thought of Mark. He was waiting outside and had no clue that his life was about to change. I uttered my apology for leaving swiftly and walked briskly out of the building, passing the receptionist looking at her watch and through the doors towards my husband who was eating a sandwich that had hastily been prepare in the B & B before the interviews that morning. As I approached the car he looked expectantly at me,

198

wanting the news. I wondered in that second if he wanted this upheaval. I nodded to him and winked,

'How do you fancy living in Scotland? We shall have to give up our jobs, sell the house, finish the house! If you say no, I'll go back in and tell them. We both must be certain.'

He smiled and, for the first time in days, seemed to relax. The decision was made. The expression on his face said it all. I had to explain that we were not making a quick exit back to Derbyshire but had to visit both schools with a time constraint to manage. He placed the last of his sandwich in his mouth, then turned on the ignition.

'We had better get going then.'

He passed me the cheese sandwiches, half wrapped in tin foil. I suddenly became aware that I was starving and devoured one quickly. Mark Knopfler's 'Local Hero' played as we drove to Loch Dubhglas. It seemed appropriate.

✓✓✓✓✓

After arriving at the big school, I peered through the windscreen at the building. This would be my school in a few weeks' time. I spotted one of the interviewers standing on the steps at the main entrance, chatting to a small, grey-haired gentleman. I instinctively knew I was the topic of conversation. The incomer was here. They continued to chatter as I walked towards the steps, staring at me intently but never ceasing their intense discussion. The interviewer made a sharp exit after a brief greeting, and I was taken into the building by the headmaster. In the distance I could hear the odd sound, but it was a quiet school compared to my own. There were only thirty-two children on roll. I smiled at the thought that this was the *big* school, when ironically my current school had nearly two hundred and sixty pupils.

I was taken into the headteacher's office, a sad, dowdy room that was filled with furniture and bookcases. Bizarrely there was also two kitchen units with a long green work surface fitted along one wall of the room. Finding a seat was difficult. Armed with a notebook full of questions about standards, records and staff development plans, I was intent on finding all the answers to things I thought I should know about the school before this man retired. The headmaster had other plans; he had another agenda. Time was ticking and I had to get to the wee school but first I was to meet the staff who were anxious about an incomer. There was that damn word again.

We set off, a short distance down the corridor to the first room, a primary four to seven class. A young teacher shook my hand, enthusiastic to make a good impression. I glanced at her. She was so young looking that it was hard to imagine her as a teacher. She was introduced to me as Caitlin but the headteacher's introductions were not over. He quickly moved on to the children, seemingly obliged to introduce each pupil to me. He also gave a briefing on each child's family which was amusing but strange.

'This is Cameron, and he is primary seven. His mother is the village doctor. That is Shona, and her father is the postman.'

Into my head came the tune from back in the Sixties from 'Trumpton'... 'Pugh, Pugh, Barney McGrew, Cuthbert, Dibble and Grub.'

Eventually he turned towards the last child. No name was given for the pupil.

'That one comes from Sheffield, near where you're from in Englandshire.'

'That one' looked at me, and nodded, accepting her fate. She knew that I too was an 'incomer from Englandshire'.

We moved on to the wee class, where a young blonde teacher, rose from the carpet, surrounded by little ones who had been busily helping to draw around someone's body on a large piece of paper. The headteacher introduced her as Isla, telling me which local village the lass had originated from and then proceeded to introduce the pupils, one by one, in the same manner that he had done with the older children. Suddenly looking at his watch, I was rushed out of the room, down the corridor and out into the playground. We had around forty minutes to get to the wee school before the children finished for the day. With my husband driving, the headteacher relaxed and started to joke a little about the village,

'Do not, under any circumstances live in Loch Dubhglas. It won't work. Keep school and family life separate,' he advised.

The journey to Tarn seemed unreal. I could not quite believe that this would be my journey to work in the future. For almost all the way, we travelled along a single-track road with passing places. The scenery was spectacular as we drove through forests, glanced lochs in the distance and hills and mountains as far as the eye could see. In May there was no snow on the slopes or summits, but I had witnessed this on past visits to the area. The road undulated, crossing bridges over burns and through land where trees had been ripped from the earth for wood production. As we passed the sign for the hamlet of Tarn, a small cluster of houses on both sides of the road came into view, old estate cottages in need of painting, in most cases. To the right was a deer farm with a field full of red deer. I hated looking at the creatures as I knew they would never be wild. It was hard to think of these creatures as being farmed like cows or sheep. The secretary from the big school, Moira, had phoned ahead to ask the parents, children and staff to stay until we arrived. The headteacher showed me into the building and into the classroom. There stood seven children of different ages and heights all grinning at me. Several parents stood there smiling and eager to chat. Again, the head introduced each child and linked them all to a parent. I was surprised to hear that of the seven children in front of me, only one was Scottish. This was a school of different cultures, families who had moved to the area for work from around the globe. He nodded to two girls.

'All the fathers work on the local estate. Their father is the factor.'

I was introduced to the teacher, Grace, who chatted away to me, asking questions about where I lived and worked and about the move. She told me she had moved away from her village and had explored the world by gaining teaching jobs but had come back to the area eventually after her adventures. Suddenly, I became aware of the time and gave my apologises that we had to start travelling back. We returned along the single-track road and dropped the headmaster back at the school where we had been an hour and a half before. He was animated on the return journey and his guard had dropped as he talked about living in the area.

'There is an annual Scottish country dancing competition in which the big school participates. The children *must* be tutored and to be of a high standard to enter. I tell you, *a high standard*!'

He banged his right fist into the palm of his left hand as he spoke. Then later in the conversation he talked about the wee school.

'Every year I am asked to attend the Burns Night Supper. It is a *necessity* that you attend.'

I knew absolutely nothing about Scottish country dancing. I had been six when I danced 'Strip the Willow' back at infant school. The Burns Night supper filled me with additional dread. I knew it involved eating haggis and that was a serious challenge to overcoming! It was as if he spoke to me in another language. How could I be just five hundred miles from home, yet it felt like a foreign country? I tried to navigate through the conversation and make sense of everything as we drove back to the Midlands.

The next day I shook as I told the staff about the job in Scotland. I spluttered the words out, reading from a script in case I lost track or forgot to say something. I had informed the chair of governors on the way back down the motorway, so it was official. I just needed to formally write a letter of resignation for the local authority, giving the appropriate notice.

The Scottish schools had a two-week holiday in October. This was affectionately known as the 'tattie fortnight' from a past tradition when children would gather potatoes with their parents, harvesting the crops ready for winter. I planned to leave on a Friday at the end of September and commence in Scotland on the first Monday in October. Claire would be acting headteacher until a new person was appointed. A few months later she would become the permanent headmistress and Rachael would become her deputy.

So, there it was. Two forty-somethings were about to embark on an adventure of a lifetime. We were giving up our jobs, selling the house and moving ourselves and two cats to live in a different country. When we said those words, we were both petrified.

✓✓✓✓✓

Just a couple of weeks later, during the Whitsun break, we returned north to arrange viewings of properties to buy. Our first viewing was just outside the village of Loch Dubhglas. We pulled into the drive and got out of the car to be greeted by the couple who were selling their bungalow.

'Hello Mrs Challis. Welcome to you too, Mr Challis!'

I looked startled as we had given no surname when making the viewing appointment, just our first names.

'You are the new headteacher, aren't you? This house is so close to the school you could walk.'

Inwardly, I laughed at the sales pitch and that news had spread quickly. The other couple of viewings went in a similar way with everyone trying the same sales technique, knowing our names, and who I was. After the third time I had to stifle my giggles.

Our last appointment for the day was about eight miles away from the school. By now we were desperate for a drink. The weather had turned very warm and, having travelled around the area with no real break, we needed a beverage or two. This was the only viewing that did not involve an interrogation about being the new headteacher. The couple did not know the local gossip, having bought the property as a holiday home a few years before. Now, with young grandchildren down south and care duties, the need for a rural bolthole was redundant. On a burning hot day at the end of May, the couple had thought it a selling feature to light a fire in the living room. So, there we sat, roasting from the heat outside and inside as logs were burning on the open fire. We gratefully sipped coffee that had been carefully filtered in the kitchen, with the delicious smell wafting around the house to tempt us to buy the property. The only selling trick the couple had not made was to bake bread. Within half an hour a deal was struck to rent the property until our house sold, a 'try before we buy'. The bungalow was perfect. The views across Loch Dubhglas were spectacular. I had to pinch myself that this was not a dream from which I should awake. How could we be this lucky?

On returning to the Midlands the serious business of moving got underway. The house had now gone up for sale, four weeks after returning from the interviews. Boxes started to be packed and plans made for the move. My homelife was chaos but school life kept me on track and determined to ensure there was a smooth transition.

✓✓✓✓✓

In the diary was a last visit to the residential centre. After more than two decades this trip would be special. We had changed the time of the visits to summer and staff and pupils appreciated the decision. It meant no coats or lost gloves, less mud and much warmer weather. Days were spent on the treasure hunts, walking in the woods or playing on the field in front of the staffroom.

One afternoon we were split into teams and my group, accompanied by Susan, went pond dipping. Of course, there is always one child who falls in and this visit was no exception. One fat little frog called Reece was fished out of the pond, along with pond skaters and water beetles. Just after we had all laughed at his watery adventure, Susan spotted a most beautiful dragonfly. The instructor told us that the creatures have a life of just under two months, if lucky when they become an adult. I looked at Susan and she nodded her understanding. In less than two months I should be gone, as would the dragonfly. Days later Susan bought me a dragonfly broach as a leaving present, a precious reminder of that day.

The other 'present' I had from my visit was a horse fly bite. As we had walked back to the centre through the meadow, I had felt a sharp pain in my left upper arm and instantly knew I had been bitten. Within a few minutes my arm was swollen and starting to get hotter. It wasn't the first or last time a horse fly bit me. It always ended with antibiotic cream and sometimes antibiotics. I refused medical help until I got home twenty-four hours later. I managed to get an appointment at a walk-in clinic at my doctors. I was threatened with hospital if the infection got worse. Luckily the medication began to work, and I avoided any further medical care.

✓✓✓✓✓

Summer holidays dawned. There was no house sale, just a few viewings. By the new school year in September, we were virtually packed up apart from a few clothes and essential items in the kitchen and bathroom. The few short weeks when we had planned to visit our friends and family disappeared rapidly.

The last day came for both of us to leave our jobs. I felt numb. I had asked for no fuss when leaving and apart from a few home-baked cakes in the staffroom one lunch time, everyone had listened to my wishes. The final assembly was low key with a couple of speeches about Scottish or cold weather. Claire wished me good luck. Then the choir, conducted by Mae, sang and signed 'True Colors', my favourite Cyndi Lauper song and finally an old Neil Sedaka tune, 'This is our last song together'. I had heard the children sing it many times before but there was something special about this moment and I felt a lump in my throat as I looked at this lovely school before me. I had arrived at the school broken after two years of hell at Larkshill. This place and the people in it had been my salvation. I had given them up for a dream. I just hoped it would be worth the sacrifice. I didn't look back as I left. If I had, I would have wept buckets.

Chapter 10
You Mean I Must Eat Haggis?

The day was dull and grey as I walked up to the school door at Loch Dubhglas. Although I was tired from the journey north, during the weekend, my heart was racing. Excitement and nervousness made me feel lightheaded. I had no idea how I would get in. I had no keys nor numbers to enter onto the keypad on the wall. As it happened, I needed nothing. The school was unlocked and as I entered, I was greeted by the teacher I had met back in May. I remembered her name was Caitlin. She had been in charge of the school after returning from the end of the summer holiday back in August until my first day in early October.

I wondered how this young woman had coped, having to teach and be the acting head. Although she was in her late twenties and a mother already to two small children, she could easily have been mistaken for someone much younger. Her short unkempt auburn hair, and pale complexion, together with a badly creased light green top and black trousers gave the impression that she had just woken up. Caitlin pushed the keys of the school into my hand, glad to be released from the burden of headship. She told me that she had taken the liberty to organise a supply teacher for the day so she could brief me on the school and the past few weeks. I was delighted to have this support, so we got down to work in the office as soon as possible. Once she got into her stride, Caitlin's confidence grew. She clearly knew the school well and gave me a real insight to what she had done since August. Her accent was soft, and I smiled as I listened to her talking about the school and the staff, pronouncing unfamiliar words and names with her Scottish tones. I was so used to Midland voices that I had to concentrate fully to ensure I understood all that she said.

As Caitlin spoke, I cast my eyes around the small room. It had not changed since my visit on the interview day. It was crammed with furniture to the point of bursting, a room no wider than twelve feet. Although surfaces were dust free and very clean, the shelves were heaving with the weight of folders, books and papers. My eyes focused on an enormous leather book, at the bottom left of all the shelving. The ancient spine, a deep brown in colour, was well used. It was a school bible which I imagine was dated from the origins of the school building around the turn of the twentieth century.

We had been talking for ten minutes when there was a knock on the door. The other young female teacher, Isla, who I had also met before, entered the room and spoke to myself and Caitlin. She was a smartly dressed lady, compared to her colleague. Her patterned dress suited her slim figure. With a fair complexion, mid-length, light coloured hair and dark brown eyes, Isla was an attractive girl. She looked no older than her mid-twenties but had just turned thirty. She too spoke with a gentle accent.

'I'm sorry to disturb you. Are we having an assembly today and if so what time?'

'It's Isla, isn't it? Yes, let's have an assembly at quarter past nine.'

'Thanks. I'll tell everyone and write it on the whiteboard in the staffroom.'

I was acutely aware that here were the two teachers at Loch Dubhglas, but I could not remember their surnames. Gone were the days of working in a primary with fifteen or sixteen teachers. I felt optimistic that I should pick up their surnames quickly. I was conscious of the time and wanted to greet all staff before the commencement of school. Caitlin said she would introduce me. Several staff had the same surname, which I was told originated from the area. Almost all of names began with 'Mac'. I shook hands with each member of staff, hoping I should remember their name when I spoke to them again.

My next job was 'to collect the children'. An adult rang a bell, and I was shown to the backdoor of the school. Outside, all twenty-eight children were lined up in two rows, one for the big class, one for the wee one. Most had uniform on. One class at a time, in they marched in an orderly fashion to the cloak rooms where they all removed their shoes. I had never seen children change shoes before on mass, except for P.E. It just wasn't a sight I had ever seen in the Midlands. I asked one child what she was doing. She looked puzzled at my question.

'Changing into our indoor shoes, Miss. We have indoor shoes to keep the carpets clean especially when it is raining or snowy.'

Snow! This was one thing I was dreading, a winter in Scotland. Would I get to school? Would I have to close school? Would I have to wear indoor shoes? I had so many questions that I felt the urgent need for a coffee, but it was only nine o'clock.

Assembly time came quickly. In came a few nursery children and their two staff. I knew both ladies were not teachers. The authority had redeployed all the nursery teachers a few years before. Then came the wee class, eyes all on me as they walked one behind the other into the room. A few who weren't looking where they were going, bumped into the child in front of them. Isla told them to sit down. Finally, in came the big class. The older children made their way to seats that had been placed at the back of the other two groups. Caitlin came last and found her seat. Everyone stared at me as I began. I remembered to speak slow and clearly in case no one could understand my accent. I glanced around the room. There were fewer children in the whole school than some of the larger classes I had taught before class limits had been introduced years ago. The roll number had gone down to twenty-eight pupils since the start of the new school year. As for the staff, there were six adults. The contrast to my leaving assembly suddenly hit me, as did the enormity of the job ahead.

I resisted the temptation for caffeine until morning break. When I walked into the staffroom with my special mug, a present from a child at my last school, I was ready for a drink. My head was swimming with information. The room felt the same as the staffroom at Hawthorn Street but with far fewer adults. I had sat there for a while when a panic rose from within me. The whole staff were in the room so who was on playground duty? When I asked the question, I wasn't expecting the answer I got. No one was on playground duty.

When a school had less than fifty children there was no supervisor and teachers did not have playground duties in their contracts. This was a revelation to me. For the past twenty-seven years I had completed at least one, often more, playground duties per week. How could twenty-eight children play without supervision? It turned out to be a philosophical question. Children were allowed to play freely as they would at home. If they needed an adult someone would knock on the staffroom door. My eyes, in that first playtime, had been opened to just one of the differences I should find between a medium sized school in urban England and a small village school in rural Scotland.

For the next few days, I religiously went out at break times and lunch times. I could not relax or leave little ones out in a playground that had a busy village carpark in front of it, with a public toilet also in view, used by tourists and visitors to the area. The gates rarely stayed closed as we shared a site with a local community building, offering adult learning opportunities. A couple of years later, when numbers on roll went up to fifty, I must admit I was mightily relieved to employ a playground supervisor at last!

I thought back to that day in March 1996 when the tragedy at Dunblane resulted in schools having security gates, keypads and lanyards for staff and visitors at schools up and down the country. It was as if I had gone back in a time warp to 1996; this school had been left behind somehow. After I had been at Loch Dubhglas a while and ventured out to visit other local schools, I found it hard not to judge the differences between schools five hundred miles away. There was, perhaps, much more need for security in towns and cities. Often in these small rural schools, doors were left open, especially on hot days. Security fencing, if any had been installed, were of little use. Visitors strolled up to the main entrances. It was a good few years later lanyards were given to staff to wear, and visitor badges issued. I never visited any school in the area with the tight security I had left behind at Hawthorn Street. I saw the children laughing and staff relaxed. I loved the freedom everyone had but it also scared me to think what might happen, what did happen once.

Less than a hundred yards from the school, Loch Dubhglas glistened in the moonlight, as I went home that first evening, Tiny lights from the houses and cottages in the village interrupted the darkness when the small row of streetlights stopped about half a mile from the school. It was a still night. The moon cast shadows of trees on the single-track road as the journey home continued. In the distance, there was a fleeting glimpse of several pairs of eyes to the left of the track, deer on their way to drink from the fresh water in the loch. The turning for the cottage came on the right and a few seconds later the road rose up a hill. As I got out of the car, I looked down onto the loch. Its beauty astonished me. An owl hooted in the distance, defending its territory. I slept well that night, exhausted from the newness of everything and from the joy of knowing we had made a good decision to move north.

✓✓✓✓

On the second day I visited the wee school at Tarn, twenty-two miles away from the school at Loch Dubhglas, along a single-track road, up and down hills and a winding A road, that most visitors would feel was not much more than a farm track. The ride was spectacular, and I pinched myself to think that I should be travelling this road twice per week. There was also a reality that in wintertime the road would be a tough one to drive. We planned that a survival kit would be kept in the boot of the car consisting of blankets, a stove, water, snow shovel, cups and dried soup packets. I also made a mental note to always have a camera to hand as red deer were often seen.

This tiny school, which had just seven pupils, had reopened after being 'mothballed' for a few years when there were no primary children in the catchment area. From the front door of the school a Munro, a mountain over 3000 feet, could be seen. From October to April snow would appear on the mountain summit and often lower down.

The exterior of the building itself was quite poor and showed signs of damp. When inside the story was very different. It was a colourful, cheery environment that the teacher, Grace, had created. She had the craft of teaching different age groups within one class, down to a fine art. The school was well organised, and I recognised immediately someone who was passionate about teaching.

Grace was a lass in her mid-thirties. She had lived in different countries around the world before returning to settle back in Loch Dubhglas where she had grown up. Her smile was welcoming, and she had a knack of making people feel at ease with little effort. Her sapphire-coloured eyes twinkled when she greeted me. Her brown, naturally curly hair was still slightly damp after showering that morning. Her quiet, unflappable personality had a positive effect on the group of children she taught. Tarn was a calm and peaceful place.

Just as Loch Dubhglas had been, there was no playground supervision at break times. Worst still, Grace could often be on her own, miles from a doctor or the fire brigade. There was no keypad or security gates. The only way to keep the children and herself safe was to lock the front door. Did there need to be security in such a remote place? A couple of years later Grace noticed a tourist urinating in the school grounds and chose the site rather than to use one of many trees in the area. Another tourist tried to put his tent up in the grounds. Although I knew Grace was competent and so level-headed, I was always worried that she was so far away. I tried to make sure she was rarely alone in such an isolated place of work.

✓✓✓✓✓

Just five days after moving north, there was a knock at the front door one evening. A silver haired woman with a stooped back stood in front of us. With an extremely posh, old fashioned, BBC newsreader voice, she introduced herself.

'Hello, Mr and Mrs Challis. I gather. I am Angela McFarlane, a neighbour from just over the way. I'm delighted to make your acquittance. I've come to meet the new headmistress.'

We felt obliged to offer her a drink. In she came and followed us to the living room. The only piece of furniture in the whole bungalow was a blow-up settee, which looked as if it needed some more air. We had arrived with two small rucksacks of clothes, a picnic basket, one saucepan, the microwave, two pillows, two sleeping bags and a plastic couch, that converted to a double bed.

'Please take a seat but be careful when you sit down. The settee has a life of its own,' I warned.

Mrs McFarlane took one look at the couch and immediately declined the offer.

'I'll stand, thank you. I won't stay. I just wanted to introduce myself.'

At this point, the blow-up settee began to make a slow, wet farting noise. As the arms and back deflated, it collapsed completely. Like a rabbit in the headlights, our posh guest hastily departed, declining a drink as she went. We found out later that she was a local landowner with thousands of acres and that she regularly socialised with the Queen. Clearly our blow-up settee had not amused her. We rarely saw her after this introduction to *Midlanders on Tour*. She must have considered us bonkers. Worst still, we had to sleep on the floor for the rest of the week.

The schools broke up for the 'tattie fortnight' two days later. The holiday went by in a flash with journeys down and up the M74 and the M6 to collect furniture and on the final journey to collect our cats from my mother's house. My brother-in-law drove one of the vans, full of our belongings up from the Midlands, with my father-in-law in the cab for company. He made his way up the country and had a set of directions for where he had to go after arriving in Loch Dubhglas. He misjudged the

210

final turning and after realising his mistake, he stopped a passing cyclist to ask how he could correct himself to reach the address he had been given. He also had a photograph of the property, together with a set of keys. He was in the middle of nowhere, no houses for miles. The cyclist knew instantly how to direct him.

'Och! That's the new headteacher's house. You took a right turn too soon.'

When we finally arrived in our van, hours later, he related the story. It seemed my arrival was the big news to the locals in Loch Dubhglas, landed gentry and commoners alike!

For the first two weeks after we had moved the furniture, cats and ourselves north, there was torrential rain and storms. The winds seemed to whip around the house up on the hills above Loch Dubhglas. The lights kept flickering and at times we lost power. There was no mobile phone signal and no chance of having broadband, unless it was via a satellite which was very expensive. Neither of us were sure if we wanted to live in this place although it had spectacular views from the front windows. As we were renting, we could do nothing until our house in Derbyshire was sold. It was autumn time. The air was cool. There was a distinct difference between twilight in the Midlands and so far north. The afternoons became darker much earlier and on a grey, dank day car headlights would be turned on just before three.

We were now in the winter term. I settled into a routine of being at Loch Dubhglas for three days per week and two at Tarn. At all the schools in which I had worked over the years, there had always been a site manager or caretaker to look after the building. A janitor came for a couple of hours every week at Loch Dubhglas. Two cleaners cleaned the school each evening. At Tarn a janitor visited every few weeks when required and one cleaner appeared every couple of days. There was no complaining. This was the system, and no southerner could rock the boat.

Grace told me stories of travelling to work in her little Corsa with snow tyres fitted when the snow piled deep to heights over six foot. The snow worried me more than anything. When it finally came in November, I found myself clearing paths from the gates in Loch Dubhglas to the school entrances. There needed to be a path to the main entrance which was used by staff and another one to the side door which the children used. In addition to this, a path needed to be cleared for children to move from the main building to the canteen across the playground. In total I would need almost two hours every morning to clear and grit the paths before children and parents arrived. Many hours of snow clearing followed over the years.

Another major difference between managing my cluster schools and ones in England was funding. Many years before, a system had come into schools in the south to have a greater control of finances. Money from the English government was allocated to local authorities and a percentage was then passed to schools for items such as stationery and furniture. The amount of money each school was allocated was linked to how many children were on roll. After a number of years more control was given to schools which led to headteachers, with governor agreement, being able to decide their own staffing levels. At Hawthorn Street, I had been able to find funding from our allocated money to provide extra classroom support personnel. My budget at my English school had been over one million pounds. Even more freedom with school funding had begun when schools were encouraged to be turned into academies or join a trust. The latest developments meant that services, which had traditionally been paid for by the local education authority such as Child Psychology, Human Resources and even School Improvement Advisors (some of the 'Men in Grey Suits'), were to be contracted out. Gone were the days when a school had to have a local authority service. Headteachers were free to look around at a range of consultants.

Within a couple of days of being at Loch Dubhglas and Tarn I wanted to know the exact financial position of each school. I knew the freedoms in the English system had evolved enormously over the years and expected the Scottish school finance system to have developed at a similar pace. What I found was that I was transported back to a protocol of the 1990s. Schools were allocated a small amount of money entirely linked to the numbers of children on roll. I found myself the financial whizz-kid, in control of around seven thousand pounds in total across the cluster. This came as a shock. There were few choices in where stock could be purchased as there was a stringent procurement programme in place. Services were provided by the authority and there were no opportunities to purchase consultants to support matters such as curriculum design or

212

school improvement. I realised and enjoyed being free of the burdens of finance as a school manager but occasionally lack of choice was like a noose around my neck.

I taught lots of lessons at both schools to cover if staff went on courses and occasionally if someone was off ill to save money. It was the thing I loved most about my job as a cluster head. Although it was hard to juggle all the tasks I needed to do, a day or two in class put me back where I felt most comfortable, in the classroom with children. One day I might be in nursery at Loch Dubhglas: on another day I might be at the wee school teaching the whole age range from four- to twelve-year-olds. On those days I felt I had won the lottery. My dream as a child had been to emulate *Anne of Green Gables*. Her tales were always about a single teacher school. It was a romantic notion, but it was hard work to ensure all children in the tiny class made progress. The days of these tiny schools were coming to an end. Each year numbers on roll were falling and often this brought talk of closure to the small communities. Tarn was no exception and time was ticking. Three children from one year group would leave in three years' time, with one left on roll in school if no new family moved into the area. For now, I could dream of being *Anne* in my little world.

When staff and visitors asked me about the differences between my previous schools and my Scottish ones there was always one answer about learning and teaching. It was the same. The terminology in curriculum documents might differ but ultimately all the classrooms felt the same. There were children who were the '*Eager Beavers*', the '*Strugglers*' and the '*Quiet Ones*'. And yes … there was always high noon with the '*Desperados!*' There were children who were well behaved and those who were not. The usual tricks were played such as blocking toilets with toilet rolls, flicking wet paper onto toilet ceilings or losing pumps when it was a P.E. lesson. There were children who concentrated and some who tried to avoid tasks by asking for the toilet just as they should have begun work. It was the same. When I walked into a classroom to make a lesson observation there were nervous teachers and those who were ambivalent to school improvement. Some were incredibly talented and some who should never have been in teaching. Some who were prepared to go the extra mile to support a child and some who would not move a muscle. It was the same.

213

There was one character I met, early on in that first term who shocked me. I had made it my business to introduce myself to all the headteachers in the area. As I approached the school building, I noticed that the front door had been left ajar. I pushed it open and went into the reception area. There was an office sign, so I knocked. No-one answered. I knocked again but there was still no answer. As I stood pondering what to do next, a child of about ten years old appeared from nowhere. I asked where the headteacher was. She told me he was on a trip.

This information threw me as I had expected to meet Mr MacDougall at two o'clock. At this point an adult appeared and explained the head was delayed but would be returning shortly. I was asked to take a seat in the office. I looked around the room as I entered. A desk and office chair were at one end of this small room. There were also five old fashioned armchairs crammed into the space. The seats had seen better days and surely could not conform to modern day fire regulations.

There were lots of books on the bookshelf, high above my head, together with a row of Curriculum for Excellence folders, all still in cellophane and untouched. Everything had been gathering dust for years. The bookshelf seemed to sum up the whole room which was trapped in time.

A commotion could be heard in the entrance area. It was the cheery noise of children laughing and chatting. The door burst open and in came a man who looked a little dishevelled after a day on a school trip. He was a slightly plump man, probably in his early sixties with silver hair and a bushy moustache. He had been out walking with a group of children. I noticed that mud was still on his walking boots as he sat down. In a deep, husky Scottish voice, he greeted me and shook my hand.

'You must be Emma. Donald MacDougall, please to meet you. Welcome. Sorry for the delay but we gave been busy today on a trip.'

I nodded.

'Now let me ask, why on earth have you moved up here to Loch Dubhglas and Tarn?'

Without allowing me any chance to respond he continued his mission.

'Well, I can tell you, take those rose-tinted spectacles off. Life is much harder up here, far harder than a lass like you is used to … and what is your husband going to do?'

214

Again, without stopping for an answer, he proceeded to rip my dreams to shreds.

'He won't get a job here. There are no jobs for men.'

I sat in silence. The man bombarded me with reasons why I should not have moved to the area. I politely asked a few questions when I could get a word in as he continued to blitz me with his cutting remarks.

'What system is used for educational trips?' I naïvely asked.

'System? System? I don't fill in any forms. If the weather's good, off we go!'

I persisted a little. I could not work out this man at all.

'So, you don't have to fill in any health and safety forms?'

'Well, you are supposed to, but I'm having none of that utter rubbish!'

As I spoke, he reached into his jacket pocket, and brought out a cigar. At first, I did a double take. Smoking on school premises had been banned for years and Scotland had banned smoking in public places before England. Then he fumbled for some matches in his pocket. No … he wasn't going to smoke! He couldn't! He wouldn't! It was illegal!

There, in front of me, he placed the cigar between his lips and opened the box of matches. Picking one out, he struck it on the side of the box and lit up. He inhaled from the cigar, breathed deeply into his lungs and then exhaled the smoke into my face until the whole cigar was no more. I looked at him in horror. I should have said something. I should have protested at him smoking but I didn't. I was a visitor; an incomer and he loved that knowledge.

Not wanting to stay in the company of this man for a moment longer than I needed, I made an excuse to leave. He didn't get up as I stood, but begrudgingly shook my hand and I left the room and the school. Tears rolled down my face as I walked back to the car. Would all the headteachers behave like this?

I am glad to say that all the other people in leadership that I met were lovely, more like Des. They all made me very welcome and always offered support. Mr MacDougall was the exception to the rule. He retired shortly after our meeting, and I was glad that I never endure his smoke again!

215

When December came around that first year, and for all the years to come, there was just one word on everyone's lips,

'Pantomime!'

Every year a group in the local community at Loch Dubhglas would pay for a coach and tickets for children and staff to go to the pantomime at the theatre in the city. The children at Tarn would go on a separate journey, paid by school fund. Sometimes I make two visits, knowing all the corny jokes and the innuendos by the second viewing. The only problem with the pantomime trip was the journey. For some reason the Loch Dubhglas children were often fine on the journey down, but when travelling back up to the village almost fifty miles away, some had perfected great skills in projectile vomiting. One year myself and a teaching assistant were covered in sick, and I could not get rid of the vomit odour, stuck in my nose, for several days. There were the *'Vomiters'* who could throw up at any opportunity and the *'Watchers'* who would watch a friend and begin to retch themselves within seconds. The vomit game got out of hand and staff became weary of it all, so we tried an experiment. At breaktime, before setting off for one trip to the theatre, we gave the children ginger biscuits as a snack.

After the first time, when no one was sick on the journey there or back we thought it was a possible fluke. When we carried out the experiment for the second year, it worked again. After that ginger biscuits were brought for every single trip as those Loch Dubhglas children could watch lambs being born, walk fearlessly through storms to school but they could not stop being sick on coaches!

✓✓✓✓✓

I shall admit that I needed a translator for the first two years and on many occasions, staff needed a translator for my speech as they often looked at me and asked me to repeat what I had said. No one ever told me they could not understand my Midlands accent and dialect, but I was aware of being careful not to use too many unfamiliar phrases. The Auld (old) Scots' dialect took some getting used to. Sometimes when I heard a new word, I would practise pronouncing it badly with my Midlands vowels to smiles or even laughter, if it was repeated incorrectly. Other times I should digest the word and try to understand by the context of the conversation as to its meaning. My favourite words and phrases were as follows:-

216

Bahooky – bum, backside. I wasn't sure what on earth the classroom assistant was talking about until she showed me her damp bahooky, after sitting on a wet bench.

Bissim – cheeky. There can be more than one meaning of the word bissim and several different spellings of the word. In some references it can be about a woman or young girl of loose character but for use in school it always meant a wee bissim, cheeky child.

Blether - chat, gossip. A popular phrase in both schools. Everyone enjoyed a good blether, whether it was about a family, villagers or about no one in particular.

Boorach – a heaped pile, mess. One day the clerical assistant, Moira, referred to her desk being a boorach. It was a phrase I had never come across before but one I learned quickly as my desk was always a boorach.

Dreich - miserable, grey, wet. This word was learned quickly as it rained incessantly the first two weeks after the final move north of the border.

Whit's fur ye'll no go by ye – what is meant to be, will not pass you by. Anyone entering a philosophical debate seemed to include this phrase somewhere in the discussion.

✓✓✓✓✓

My predecessor had warned me about organising speakers for assemblies. The local ministers from the various church groups were enthusiastic to get involved in the life of each school. When one of the ministers approached me, I was reluctant to let him through the door, due to my colleague's warning. However, the minster was persistent, and, in the end, I gave in purely because I could not think of another excuse.

He was a quiet man, rather shy when I had met to him a few days before. He looked harmless enough, a man in his thirties, softly spoken. He was quite the gentleman with a white dog collar neatly in place, complimenting his black suit and shirt. I had given the minister a topic of friendship to talk about. It was a safe subject, I thought.

The children walked into the room where we held assemblies and sat in their usual rows, little ones from nursery at the front, on the floor, with the infant children behind them. The older children sat on chairs at the back. Staff positioned themselves in a semi-circle around the group. In came the minister as I remembered him, shy and rather quiet. He smiled

217

at the children as I introduced him. All eyes were on him as he began. Let's just say he immediately went off the expected script.

'Who fears God?

I sat up straight, shocked and now alert to every word. His character changed from being Peter Pan to Captain Hook, in the blink of an eye.

'God will punish our many sins.'

He told an obscure story from the bible, one that was bleak and hard to understand. He spoke with a passion and great fury that I had not seen within him before. There was no talk on friends or being kind. He went on and on for ten minutes, with anger in his voice, erupting every time he mentioned the word 'sin'. He spoke as if he was addressing an audience of adults. I wanted to the earth to swallow me when he began pointing to various children and staff. He was now shouting to individuals, including me,

'We are all born sinners, you're a sinner, you're a sinner, you're a sinner.'

I tried to intervene at one point, but he refused to give way. He had the attention of the room and he intended to preach with power and fear. We sat in the staffroom later that morning, long after the visitor had gone, reeling from the assembly. I had wondered if it was me who felt uncomfortable, but everyone had found the messages too strong for adults yet alone children as young as three years old. I made it my goal to always follow my predecessor's instructions after that incident.

When it came to Scottish County Dancing competition, I came unstuck with his warnings in the first year. I knew no steps and had no contacts for tuition. The two elderly volunteers who had helped for years decided to take this opportunity, with a new headteacher arriving, to retire from their duties. We did not enter the competition and I felt sick at the thought of the incomer failing. I was mortified that I was helpless. By the second year I had secured a volunteer and the children practising steps for months before the competition. The costumes were found and washed ready for the evening at another local primary school. Off went the dancers, in twos, threes, sixes and even eights: the 'Military Two Step', the 'Gay Gordons', the 'Pride of Erin' or 'Strip the Willow'. We did not win but we took part, and I was relieved. The children were not up to the standards expected by the previous headteacher because I simply could not teach the steps myself. I had 'two left feet' when it came to listening to dance instructions, as Fiona, my tutor, had told me all those years ago at college. All I could do was to ensure the dancers were turned out smartly and had refreshments when needed. We always competed after that first year.

I had also been dreading the arrival of Burns Night. As soon as Hogmanay was over, the days flew by quickly, and 25th January approached. Grace had invited me to the wee school for a special lunch to celebrate the annual event. As soon as she mentioned food, I dreaded it. The children were all to wear tartan. Having visited Scotland so many times I had loads of Chisholm tartan so that was not a problem. The issue was haggis! When she had invited me to the meal, I could not stop myself from blurting out,

'You mean I must eat haggis?'

Whilst I am not a vegetarian, I eat very little meat. I kept telling myself that haggis must be like black pudding, and I could just about tolerate the little black circles on my breakfast plate if I didn't dwell too long on what was in them. Haggis was an unknown territory. Grace nodded,

'Just try a little. I'm sure you'll like it.'

I did not want to look foolish in front of the children or staff at Tarn, so we got a haggis from Lidl when we next went shopping. It could be microwaved. After following the instructions, the haggis was heated. The smell was horrendous and neither I nor Mark could stand the odour. The haggis was binned, and I resolved that I should have to say I was a vegetarian or had a food intolerance. The day arrived that I had been dreading. I really did not want to offend anyone but as I placed the Chisholm clan scarf around my neck, I knew I needed to be honest. I boke easily at food that I cannot eat so there would be no hiding or trying to fake enjoyment at the meal.

Preparations were in full swing when I arrived at the school. Shona, the clerical, who also doubled as a classroom assistant, started to prepare the dishes as soon as she arrived. At the allotted time we all went into the room where we normally ate. Plates were laid out ready for the festivities. The oldest child in school read a Robbie Burn' poem, the one about addressing the haggis. In went the knife to slit the haggis open when she reached the appropriate part of the poem. I watched the ceremony with interest. All the children knew what was to come and they all readily accepted a pile of haggis, neeps and tatties on their plates. The air was full of the smell of the food, and I was surprised that it did not smell the same as my Lidl haggis. Grace must have realised my hesitation. She gave me a large portion of vegetables and a small amount of haggis.

'Try this, Emma. I think you will be surprised but it's not to everyone's taste.'

I sank back into my chair. Oh, thank goodness she had said these words! I would take one mouthful and politely leave the rest. The fork sank into the haggis and as I lifted it to my mouth, I could smell the meat. I expected to swallow without really tasting anything. This would be my brave attempt as an English woman to try the Scottish delicacy. As soon as the haggis touched my tongue there was no need to swallow without chewing. It was delicious. When I told Shona and Grace about my Lidl purchase, and the disaster it had been, they both laughed. Grace offered me some advice,

'Never buy haggis from a supermarket. This is a prize winning one from a local butcher.'

That was it; I was smitten with haggis. A couple of years later, when a supply teacher was at the school for the Burns lunch, I proudly cooked the usual meal … and it was still delicious!

I started to appreciate the magic of small schools. Everything was more personal. There was a familiarity with children and families which larger schools could never replicate. Although there were fewer children, parents and staff, all the same paperwork needed to be completed even in the tiniest of schools. When I first started working in this area of Scotland, there were still a few headteachers who were class committed. They had to teach full time and complete the same tasks as those of a headteacher in a city or town.

The major advantage of working in a tiny school such as Tarn was the opportunities that sometimes came along. One morning I saw an email about an event that was planned for a few weeks' time, down in the nearest city which was seventy miles away. I was elated Tarn had been chosen even though it meant a Saturday trip to the city. Train tickets were booked as part of the adventure for the children. They were used to be transported everywhere by 4x4 vehicles as the area was remote. There was no public transport. The parents agreed to drive the children down to the railway station over twenty miles away from Tarn.

It was strange to be back in the hustle and bustle of a city. There were people and traffic everywhere. The sight of a busy shopping centre and row upon row of shops took me aback. We negotiated our way to a museum and spent an hour looking at the exhibits. After eating our packed lunches, we made our way to the theatre where the special guest would be welcomed by the children before he entered the building to give a speech. We were ushered into our position in a carpark, along with other schools and waited. First some cars carrying local dignitaries arrived, then came a couple of black cars bringing people who were security. They jumped out and immediately were surveying the scene, earpieces in place, listening to instructions, ready for any occurrence should it happen.

Finally, one silver vehicle arrived and out got an elderly gentleman, dressed in dark red and orange robes, with a black scarf around his neck. His spectacles and face were immediately recognised. The crowd went silent. An indescribable peace came upon us all in those minutes in his presence. It was incredible. He put his two hands together in prayer as he greeted the crowd, then came directly towards the children. As he went along the line, he touched every child's head with his hands or placed their hands in his, blessing them. When he came to the children from Tarn, he spoke quietly to each one, blessing them as he done to every child he had met. I was two metres away from the 14th Dalai Lama. It was an experience I shall never forget.

Afterwards the whole school, seven children and two teachers, went to a restaurant in the city centre. It was an incredible day in so many ways. On the train back home, I just wanted to pinch myself that I had this job. I lived in an amazing place and worked in two lovely schools. That afternoon I had felt the deepest peace imaginable.

✓✓✓✓✓

As the months went on, I began to feel settled. All the education terminology of working in Scotland was different to the English system but in the classroom, it was practically identical. The teaching methods were up to date, which surprised me at times, as the texts books and furniture used were not. Curriculum for Excellence, the Scottish education curriculum, had been introduced a couple of years before. Just as National Curriculum evolved from the early days of the endless subject folders, Curriculum for Excellence was also evolving. Having been a veteran of the English system and the many changes witnessed, I foretold of how assessments and league tables would eventually come. Within a few short years, my prophesy would sadly come true, although league tables are perhaps a description too harsh, but all the data for any school with more than fifty pupils is published each year for primary one, four and seven. It is easy to make comparisons.

I loved most aspects of living and working at Loch Dubhglas and Tarn but in May, I faced my biggest battle ever. How such tiny wee beasties can cause such bother is beyond me, but those damn midges could find their way into any orifice, nook or cranny. By June, when I collected the children from the playground in the mornings, if there was no breeze, the air would be filled with a black haze. Children would run into school slapping their faces, arms and legs to rid themselves of the pests. As the last one in before closing the door, I should be bitten to pieces just in the couple of minutes I remained outside. At Tarn, an area covered in forests and heathery bogs, the wee beasties would multiply by the millions. The children had to wear midge jackets to get any outdoor play. I became uneasy when I felt the little blighters at the start of each midge season.

In the weeks leading up to the summer holidays, I was told it was tradition to hold a prize giving assembly in the last week of term. I looked at some old notes and programmes that the headteacher had left. There were certain prizes that had to be given out at Loch Dubhglas each year which had been donated over time by members of the community. Some were memorial trophies. I did not want to do away with such a service but knew I had to do it my way. I kept my plans a secret for fear someone would say they were too modern. A large screen and projector were placed in the school hall early on the last morning of term., together with some loudspeakers I had acquired. Hours were spent perfecting a PowerPoint slide show to celebrate the year. When I had looked at the musical items mentioned in the old notes, they bored me to tears. There seemed no fun. Prize giving should be a celebration, not a funeral service, of the past year.

So, in true spirit I started the presentation. Images came onto the screen which the children, staff and parents had not seen. I had taken photographs for months, a habit I formed many years before when Gerald insisted that we documented all work with photos. Music began to play, 'Proud' by M People. There was laughter at the funny images and tears for some of the special moments captured. The tradition of a final assembly on the last morning began. Always there was music. One year it was 'Hall of Fame' by The Script, another it was Rihanna singing 'Diamonds' or One Direction with 'Story of My Life'. Sometimes there was a homage to older music such Cyndi Lauper's 'True Colors'. Often it was bang up to date with Jess Glynn's 'I'll Be There.' There had to be music … always.

The summer holiday arrived. I had survived my first three terms and one week as a cluster headteacher. In the next six weeks we finalised the sale of our cottage in Derbyshire and found a house in buy in a village a few miles away from Loch Dubhglas. We moved all our furniture, the cats and ourselves into our new home towards the end of September. It had taken a year almost to find a permanent home. We could finally settle and were landowners in Scotland; it might be just an average sized house and garden, but we felt like lairds.

The End

Chapter 11
Swansong

One day Isla knocked on my office door and asked to speak to me, closing the door quickly behind her. I knew instantly, call it a sixth sense, that she wanted to discuss something important. She was a quiet lady, never causing fuss. When she announced she was pregnant I was not entirely surprised. The thought in my head immediately was about supply cover but I would deal with that later. I offered my congratulations and wished her well, before I was asked to keep her secret for a little while longer until she told staff.

On the next day I visited Tarn as usual. All seemed well until breaktime when Grace disappeared for a couple of minutes. She came back into the room slightly flustered and rather red in the face. I smelt just a faint odour of mints and something else. We were alone as it was not yet time for Shona to arrive. As soon as she began to speak, again my sixth sense took over. She was pregnant! Before the words came out of her mouth, she was apologising for dropping me into a difficult situation. Isla had text her the evening before to give her the good news. I was stunned. Two thirds of the teaching staff in the cluster were pregnant, due to have their babies within a few days of each other. I could not let Grace see my anxiety of finding two supply teachers, especially for Tarn. I congratulated the poor teacher in front of me who was more worried about my reaction than the joy of announcing her pregnancy.

I set to work straight away to start the process of recruitment. Unlike my English school where there was complete autonomy to place my own adverts in the authority vacancy listings, here there were forms to fill out. In the end, after a series of complicated questions, I gave up and phoned the staffing department who helped me through the process. When the time came to hold interviews, I had three applicants, one for Tarn and two for Loch Dubhglas. My luck at filling the posts still shocks me, even now. Both posts were covered. I breathed a sigh of relief.

With pregnancy in the air, or perhaps in the water, it was ironic that a few weeks later the school nurse and her sex education session to the older junior children was due. It had been in the diary for weeks. I was intrigued as to how the talk would go and was glad, for once, that I hadn't got to deliver the lesson. The group were an eclectic mix of children, some very streetwise who would know everything there was to know about sex and others who were little innocents who still believed in the tooth fairy. The school nurse was going to be the lamb to the slaughter!

The group piled into the spare classroom, away from the younger children in their class. In they walked: the *'Streetwise'* giggling and laughing loudly at some rude joke they had all just shared, the *'Little Innocents'* with red faces and the *'Fainters'*, a few who looked so pale they might pass out. At least there was a nurse in the room if they did. I positioned myself with the *'Streetwise'* where I thought there would be more need for intervention, should it be needed, and who had all chosen to take the back row of seats.

The sex education talk commenced with the school nurse describing body changes in puberty. Apart from a couple of nervous giggles from the *'Little Innocents'* no one spoke to my great surprise. In fact, if the truth was known, all the children were paying full attention and were all keen to learn. The nurse was a confident speaker with endless enthusiasm to impart her messages to her audience. With her natural, light-hearted manner, I sensed that the group had relaxed, even the potential *'Fainters'*. My only fear was that the *'Streetwise'* group, well known for inappropriate comments in other lessons, might start with some rude innuendo, but so far all was going well. Perhaps I had been wrong. Perhaps the lesson would pass without incident. Perhaps I could hold it together without blushing.

The nurse continued her talk moving on to changes in hormones and explained, in simple terms, that boys have one major hormone change in puberty whilst girls have two. Without a blink of an eye, the boy next to me, one of the *'Streetwise'*, said,

'Miss, that must be why you can multi-task!'

A roar of laughter filled the room, a belly aching roar that would not stop. When you really try to cease laughing, when something is so funny and unexpected, the more you try to stop, the laughter gets stronger and more uncontrollable. I shook from head to toe, my stomach aching with agony. My chest felt crushed as I gasped for air and to calm down, to control myself. My cheeks, now beetroot in colour were covered with my tears. The *'Streetwise'*, the *'Little Innocents'*, the *'Fainters'* and the school nurse all looked at me in despair. Luckily, just as all hope was lost,

228

the bell went for morning break. The nurse dismissed the children, as I was in no fit state to do so. They walked down the corridor, starting to mingle with their younger classmates as one of the staff exited her classroom, eager for a cup of coffee. She overheard one child asking his pal how the talk had gone as he was keen to hear some juicy highlights of the lesson, he would have the next year.

'It was okay, I learned loads of sex stuff, but it was too much for the headteacher.'

One of the pleasures of being a primary school teacher was always the things children said. Donnie had lived in Loch Dubhglas most of his life. I had known him first when he had been a tiny lad in nursery and now, he was still three years away for high school. One day when Caitlin was on a course, Donnie had critiqued my lesson at the end of the day.

It was praise indeed from the most critical of inspectors.

'You're not a bad teacher. In fact, you were quite good for a headteacher.'

Donnie was an old head on young shoulders. Every now and again he would ask to leave the classroom for the toilet, mainly to avoid work. If I was in the corridor he loved to chat, until I reminded him that he needed to return to his lesson. He always amused me with his philosophy on life.

'Have you seen the news about Avicii, Miss?'

'Yes, I have, Donnie. It's very sad. I loved 'Wake Me Up.'

'It was my favourite track too. He was a great artist. They are saying he committed suicide.'

I did not feel particularly comfortable where the conversation was heading but I allowed him to continue.

'Why would a multi-millionaire kill himself? That's the question. It just shows money doesn't bring happiness. Tragic, just tragic!'

Off he went down the corridor to the toilet, a young head full of wisdom.

Isla and Grace went on maternity leave a few months later. Both schools got used to the new teachers and life settled down again. Then came a phone call. It was the from one of the managers in the area. Could I take on a third school for just a few weeks? There had been a recruitment drive to find a new headteacher, but it had failed, and the authority needed to advertise again. I did not want to have a third school. It was hard enough running two and have two thirds of my permanent teaching staff on maternity leave. I was given little choice. The choking part of this conversation was that despite already having two schools, I should receive the grand total of zero extra pay for the added responsibility. It would be for six weeks.

On the first visit to Brae Primary, the staff greeted me at the door with their tales of woe, wanting me to solve their problems immediately. An acting headteacher had been at the school for a while and his actions had been cause for concern in many ways but no one was brave enough to tell any managers. It was an unhappy place. Morale was low and worse still; the school was in a mess with the way it had been run. There were no records for the children, no data on their attainment, no lesson observations on staff and no school action plan. The staff were hard working and clearly the relationships with the children were excellent. I hoped that these two things would help to make rapid changes.

What on earth could I do in six weeks? I got started with getting to know everyone. It did not take long. The school was smaller than Loch Dubhglas but larger than Tarn. There were twenty- three pupils which meant it was a two-teacher school. Every few years the magic number of needing twenty-one pupils or more on roll fluctuated. This meant there was no real stability in staffing. If a school went under that number, a full-time teacher would be taken away. If numbers went down to fifteen or less, the school would have a single teacher like at Tarn. The policy of the Scottish government had been made years ago on staffing ratios. I had known none of this when I had first arrived in Scotland. I was naïve about how staffing worked.

When the manager asked me to continue with three schools for the rest of the term until Christmas I reluctantly agreed. With no permanent headteacher in place I continued, in total for two terms before I completely refused the task. The effort and workload of running three schools had nearly killed me. Apart from clocking up the miles in the car to visit each school each week, I could not focus on school improvement matters. I was always crisis managing some situation over the phone to staff. No-one had been happy with this arrangement and when there had been a fire at Brae, with me at Tarn, over an hour away, all hell broke loose.

Whoever arrived earliest would enter the code to open the key box, extract the key and open the main door. On this morning, as the teacher entered the building, she smelt smoke instantly. Oxygen rushed into the little hallway. Nearby was an ancient tweed chair, made long before fire retardant materials were used. It had been left too close to a night storage heater the afternoon before, becoming hotter and hotter overnight. As the oxygen filled the building, the chair began to smoulder. With adrenaline flowing, she found the strength to drag it outside just before the material burst into flames.

Another member of staff, just arriving, ran into the building and grabbed a fire extinguisher. The flames were put out within a second or two but there was acrid smoke in the air. No fire brigade was called. I got the news half an hour later when the children were arriving at school. I ordered that everyone left the building, and that children and staff should be sent home. The whole horrendous story led to the school being closed for four days. The building was deep cleaned to rid the furniture, carpets and walls of any smoke damage. The school hallway and staffroom were rapidly painted but the fallout from the fire lasted a long time in form filling and endless health and safety visits. Although the teacher had put herself in danger, she had saved the school from more than flames. Had the building caught fire, the school would have been permanently closed.

I know that I visited Brae Primary sixteen times in all, except for the endless hours spent there in the aftermath of the fire. That is what was explained to Her Majesty's Inspectorate for Education (HMIe) just after Easter when I was no longer the acting headteacher. In the feedback I received from my line manager a few days later, I was told that even though I had only made sixteen visits, the school had begun to have systems in place to function as it should. My work had counted, and the school did not get a repeat visit.

✓✓✓✓✓

Life went back to normal for a time. It was wonderful to be able to concentrate on two schools again. We celebrated the birth of two children, both boys and after a time the ladies came back from maternity leave.

231

When things were quiet in both schools, I worried something would happen; that my luck would run out. After peace always came chaos and the struggles would be relentless. I dreaded that anyone would phone in sick at either school as I knew I could not be in two places teaching at the same time. Supply was a luxury most days and there was rarely anyone available to cover. Some weeks were harder than others. I could be covering for someone to go on a course and be in nursery on Monday. On Tuesday I might teach in the primary four to seven room to give Caitlin some time out of class. By Friday I might be teaching at Tarn so that Grace could be given her Class Contact Reduction time, known by staff as C.C.R. In England, the same time out of class is called Planning, Preparation and Assessment, shortened to P.P.A. Life was rarely dull and always busy but I loved the challenge of teaching a range of three- to twelve-year-olds within a few days. It was also a way of finding out about each child in the cluster and all the staff.

✓✓✓✓✓

Peace was shattered in the late summer of 2014 when the villagers in and around Loch Dubhglas went to war. I had an email from the council to inform staff there should be no banners or signs in staff cars, nor should *the event* be discussed on school premises. *The event* was the Scottish Referendum. In the days leading up to the vote, the temperature in the village rose steeply, due to the heat generated by debates in the streets, shop and local hotel. Placards and banners were everywhere and there was no avoiding the fact that this was *the event* of the century.

It was hard to keep the staffroom neutral, but most people avoided the conversation as it was officially off limits. It did not stop villagers accosting me, outside the school gate, with badges for each side of the political spectrum. Pamphlets went straight in the bin, and I refused to open the door to any canvassers, of which there were many! One person told me that I should not have a vote because I was English and that this was a Scottish decision to make. I thought it best to keep my opinions to myself and my mouth firmly closed.

On the day of the referendum, the tension in the air was palpable. Gone were the gentle, placid folk of the village. They were replaced by savages, warring over their country. Cars with Scottish Saltire flags cruised the six streets in the village, honking their horns. Posters were ripped down by one campaigner, so someone from other side ripped the lamp post signs in protest. It was even reported that the old folk were up to fisty cuffs in the shop and told to calm down or be banned by the shop keeper.

There was no avoiding the issue amongst the children. Even some of the primary ones got into the debate at playtime.

'Is your dad voting for or against?'

'What do you think? Against of course!'

'Your dad's a numpty!'

'No, your dad's the numpty!'

A fight broke out and the two five-year-olds ended up scraping on the grass. A few minutes later the sound of crying could be heard in the corridor, followed by a knock on the staffroom door. Caitlin got up from her chair to see what the commotion was all about. An older child had brought the pair of dishevelled little politicians for first aid and a referee. As I got up to deal with them, Caitlin returned to her chair. Through frustration and bewilderment as to when the mayhem would stop, she groaned,

'It's the fourth lot this week, for pity's sake!'

When the results were in that Scotland would remain part of the UK, life quietened down. The surface of the water on Loch Dubhglas looked still and pretty once more but it took weeks for some villagers to speak to others

✓✓✓✓✓

For some reason there was an influx of new children to Loch Dubhglas from other counties across the world, other parts of Scotland, and some from England. Loch Dubhglas grew to three classes. One lad had arrived who was very streetwise beyond his years, compared with the children at Loch Dubhglas. Although he was shorter than others in his year group, he spoke as if he was in his late teens. He was highly intelligent but extremely lazy. He knew much about the world when his classmates knew little. His name was Lachlan, but everyone called him Lachie. For some reason I liked his cheek when he toned it down. He reminded me so much of Larkshill pupils.

A residential visit had booked to an outdoor learning centre, specialising in water sports. Off the older class went with Caitlin, me and a volunteer parent. We piled into a minibus and away we went for the week. It was a beautiful place, situated on a loch and surrounded by hills and mountains. Although I feared all the things that could go wrong on such a residential, the centre's staff were experienced and safety conscience. The days were spent mainly on the water, canoeing, wind surfing or sailing.

Lachie and his mother had naturally abandoned any rules about taking sweets and snacks in his suitcase. On the second night a boy came running down the stairs to my bedroom, a few yards away from the boys' dormitory. He was out of breath but excitedly told me that someone was being sick in the bathroom. I leapt up the stairs to get to the sick child only to find my cheeky little friend vomiting at the highest volume possible. Lachie retched and retched even after bringing up the disgusting brown contents of his stomach.

'What on earth have you eaten?'

I was sharp with the boy. I was tired. It was two o'clock in the morning and my patience was thin.

'Well, it was eight double Twix packets, three lots of Quavers, two packets of Wotsits, six Mars bars and three big blocks of Cadbury's milk chocolate,' came Lachie's reply.

I felt like telling him that he had been greedy little devil, and, in some ways, I wanted Lachie to suffer for his gluttony but all that came out of my mouth was a smirk. Then I quipped,

'Serves you right. You never offered me anything!'

There was no point in chastising him, getting him to take some punishment such as missing breaks, doing lines or telephoning his parent. Lachie had had his punishment for being so greedy after stashing all his snacks. He smirked for a second before his head went into the toilet pan again for another retching session. After that I always called him *'Twix Boy'*.

Whilst we were on the residential stay, Donnie the philosopher was put into my group for an archery activity. He was never much trouble, so I was delighted he was with me. It wasn't long before he began his usual deep conversations.

'Have you ever thought how a fish learned to swim?'

'Well, I guess it was the way the creatures evolved, maybe?'

'You could be right, Miss. It's an interesting thing to ponder.'

234

I was about have my first ever attempt at archery. It was not a question I had foreseen thinking about that morning. I fired my arrows, missing the target, probably because of the distraction. Donnie was not finished. As I walked away from the safety area to the hut where children were seated, he appeared again.

'Miss, here's another thing to ponder. Why do the English hate the Scots so much? We should live and let live.'

'Well, Donnie. I cannot speak for all English people but most of the problems have been about who owned land and money hundreds of years back. This English woman does not hate the Scots.'

'What English woman?'

'Me, Donnie. I'm English, of course.'

'Are you English?'

'Yes!'

'Well, that's a shock. I hate the English … but I like you.'

'I'm glad to hear that. Did you not realise I was English by my voice?'

'No. I'm still in shock. I thought you had a funny accent because you were Irish.'

For the most part, pupils at Loch Dubhglas and Tarn who had gone on the trip were used to outdoor life. Being brought up in the countryside gave them a massive advantage over children at schools I had previously worked at. They threw themselves into make rafts and racing across lochs with ease. They excelled at adventures in the sailing boats, worked hard in keeping the canoes afloat, yet when asked to mix with other schools on the last evening for a disco, most were painfully shy. Life was never boring when working with children, no matter where they grew up.

✓✓✓✓✓

Not long after we had returned from a long summer holiday, Isla knocked on my office door and shut it behind her again. I knew as soon as she sat down that she was pregnant for a second time. Within twenty-four hours, whilst visiting Tarn, I joked with Grace.

'So, Isla is pregnant again. Don't get giving me a heart attack, will you?'

Grace's eyes filled with tears, and she shook.

'I am so sorry. I'm … pregnant again. I was going to tell you today, but Isla got in first.'

'This is a joyous occasion. Wipe your tears. Things will work out. They did before.'

Supply in the area was almost non-existent now. For weeks I taught fifty percent of the timetable to cover part of the teaching needed at Loch Dubhglas. Somehow, just as predicted, both maternity leaves were covered. When supply was found I felt it had been a miracle. Grace returned from having her baby girl in time for the new school year in August.

The three older children at Tarn were now in P7. In less than a year, they would be leaving. Only three others would remain at the school. There would be two little ones from the same family and a new primary one. If either family moved, Tarn would close. Grace also had this on her mind as it was a topic that came up in conversation whenever I visited the wee school. When I thought about the situation Tarn was in, it was hard to imagine a future.

The local authority started talks about the viability of the school just before the Easter holidays. I was informed that I should be taking a different cluster arrangement, Loch Dubhglas and Brae. Tarn was to close. It was no longer viable, financially or for the social aspect of schooling for three children.

The battle amongst the parents of Tarn began to save the school. They argued their children would have to travel many miles if it was closed. In winter the single-track roads could be lethal in ice and snow. Meetings were held between parents and officers from the education department. When I was excluded from meetings, I remembered Gary's fate at Larkshill when he had been banned too. The *'Men in Grey Suits'*, it appeared, sometimes had Scottish accents.

If Tarn was saved, I was offered a three-school cluster permanently for no extra financial reward. This time I refused when pressure was placed upon me to give the arrangement a chance. When asked why I could not have my two schools as normal, there was a barrier of silence. Parents at Brae had already been told of the new arrangements. There was no going back. Grace was asked to be Tarn's acting headteacher. I was delighted for her but sensed this was the school's swansong.

The battle was initially won, and Tarn remained open from the next August to February. When the family with two children moved away from the hamlet, there was just one tiny child left. She was taken to an establishment sixteen miles away. Grace was redeployed to a school closer to home, saving her the long and often dangerous journeys to the wee school. There was something in both of our hearts that died when Tarn was closed for ever.

Just as the final arrangements for the new cluster were formally announced, Caitlin knocked the office door one morning. She informed me that she and her family were moving to Glasgow. She was hoping to secure a job there as her husband had gained a promotion in his work and needed to relocate to the Central Belt. I knew she would be successful. She was a popular teacher at Loch Dubhglas and her confidence had grown since I had met her years before. She would gain much experience from working in a bigger, city school.

There were three vacancies at Loch Dubhglas. Isla was still on maternity and would only return part-time; Caitlin was leaving, and another teacher was needed to take a third class. The school had grown considerably since I had become head. These young teachers, Isla and Caitlin, together with Grace, had been such stable influences in making the cluster work. It was the end of an era. On leadership courses I had often heard speakers talking of how change scared staff. I had always embraced change and had even enjoyed it. Tarn was closing. I had a new cluster school and I needed three teachers for Loch Dubhglas. Dark thoughts entered my head. I could see no light. I was afraid of change.

✓✓✓✓✓

The new school year began with Loch Dubhglas and Brae as my cluster. After four weeks of the term, I already felt exhausted. There were so many major changes of staff at the big school that my head was spinning. The authority had staffed Loch Dubhglas with two probationary teachers and a teacher who was being redeployed from a desk job after his service had been deleted with financial cuts. He hadn't taught in a classroom for well over ten years and had been told that he would only be at the big school until Isla had returned from maternity leave. The man was an absolute bag of nerves and his teeth chattered as he spoke. I wasn't sure if he would ever stop shaking.

How the hell was I going to support and mentor two probationers and a teacher so inexperienced and so nervous? These were my teaching staff! The sheer thought of this made me ill with worry. What happened if we

237

had the call from HMIe? I shuddered to think what they would say. I kept telling myself that this situation was not my fault. Surely, any inspector would see this …

The probationary teachers were bubbly and brought life to the school with their young ways in the classrooms and in the staffroom where they both quickly built rapport with the support staff. One was a country lass; one had a posh southern accent. Both probationers fitted in well and started their year in different ways. One started a 'bucket filler' display, encouraging children to fill their imaginary buckets with positive thoughts and actions for confidence building. I knocked on the door of the second probationer's classroom, as I did with all teachers as a sign of politeness when entering their space. There he was wearing a pair of bright yellow Marigolds, scrubbing tables, chairs and every surface in sight. In his very posh voice, he told me that classrooms were breeding grounds for germs, and he meant to start off his teaching career with a very clean room. Three thoughts went through my head as I watched this privately educated young man scrub the tables. *I hoped the cleaners were not offended. No COSHH sheets had been filled in for the chemicals in the cleaning products. Did this man have a cleaning fetish?* So, I had three teachers at the big school that year, *'Mr Bag of Nerves,'* *'Miss Bucket Filler'* and *'Mr Marigolds.'*

✓✓✓✓✓

There was no doubt I was tired and longing for the 'tattie fortnight' to arrive. I had a new cluster, the emotions of losing Tarn still, three inexperienced teachers and many other issues floating in my mind. No wonder I was tired and stressed. I sat in Loch Dubhglas, sipping my coffee and listened to the blethering of the young teachers as they were telling tales of their weekend antics. I suddenly felt a strange feeling in my chest as if there were butterflies floating between my breasts. I felt slightly dizzy, and odd. I sensed something was not right but said nothing, hoping no-one had noticed. Perhaps it was a panic attack or the menopause? I had had hot flushes before, but this felt different. The feeling stopped a few seconds later. I decided to avoid the filter coffee for a few days.

The next time I remember experiencing the feeling was four weeks later as I was walking on a beach in Cornwall. I felt my chest flutter again, just as it had a few weeks before. This was completely different circumstances to the first time of experiencing these butterflies. I was relaxed, on a beautiful beach, not thinking of school or anything remotely linked to it. I dismissed the feeling, thinking I was tired.

The next term came and went. I got into a system of mentoring the probationers and keeping up to date with all the all observations and paperwork. Both interim reports had been positive. *'Miss Bucket Filler'* had filled twenty little buckets and *'Mr Marigolds'* had not worn his gloves since we had the conversation about leaving hygiene to the cleaning staff. There were the obligatory Christmas parties, plays and lunches in each school. All seemed to pass without much effort, and I had somehow managed to survive the whole two terms unscathed. In total I had four incidents of chest flutters, but I was stressed with all the staff changes, the cluster changes and the loss of the wee school.

As usual Christmas at home was an anti-climax after spending the best part of a month being jolly and celebrating the festive season twice already. The holiday came and went. I was exhausted, the chest flutters hadn't made a reappearance. I was delighted I had lost loads of weight in the last year without even trying so I had much to be cheerful about. When I looked in the mirror my eyes seemed to bulge. The sight of them reminded me of *Wilma the Witch* from my third teaching practice. I shuddered at the thought of her and ignored what I saw reflecting back at me.

I struggled to get through the first week of term but on the Friday afternoon I was at Brae, and I felt awful. I was so tired that I sat staring at my computer screen watching the seconds tick away until home time. On Monday I felt so awful that I phoned in sick and went to the doctor's surgery thinking I probably had a virus. Within minutes of speaking to the GP a blood sample was taken and I was booked in for an ECG, just to be on the *'safe side.'* On Wednesday morning I was asked to pop into the surgery for my blood test results. I panicked. What on earth was the matter with me? The odd cold, cough or virus was usual for a teacher, but this felt different. When the doctor went through my results everything was normal, white blood cell count fine, not diabetes; the list of my fears lessened. Then he hit me with the whammy.

'I suspected this from the symptoms you described but had to confirm with a blood test. You have hyperthyroidism. I have contacted the endocrinologist at the hospital, and he will be in touch with you.

239

However, we need to put you onto Carbimazole immediately as you can die if left unmedicated from something called a thyroid storm.'

He then asked me if any of my family had thyroid issues. I hated this question because I could only give half of an answer. In my mother's side of the family, I knew there was none. As for my father and his side of the family, I had no clue. He then asked me if there had been any stress lately as that can also be a contributing factor if there is no family history. I stared into space and didn't answer for a few seconds. I have been under some incredible stress at work with three temporary teachers and a new cluster school. For the first time ever, I swore in a doctor's surgery.

'The bloody job's killing me, isn't it?'

The GP stared at me and nodded. When I looked up hyperthyroidism on the internet it sounded serious but could be controlled by medication. The downside of the condition was that Carbimazole should only be taken for a short time as these little pink pills could affect the white blood cell count. About four or five weeks later, I was given a hospital appointment with a consultant endocrinologist. I returned to work feeling empty, with no energy. Somehow, I got through the rest of the year with no more time off school, although I regularly had to have blood tests or see the consultant.

✓✓✓✓✓

I had been the headteacher at Brae for three terms when I received a call from one of the managers. I thought perhaps they were telling me that we should be having an HMIe inspection at Loch Dubhglas, as it was long overdue. I was shocked to be told the authority was re-clustering yet again. The news was stressful. More importantly it was unsettling for the children and staff. I was sad to leave Brae as I was beginning to settle and starting to move forward with improvements after so many years of changes for the school. The new cluster arrangements made sense. Loch Dubhglas was to be clustered with a school much closer to home than either Brae or Tarn. I should be working with Grace again. I was delighted.

When I visited my new cluster school Ericoid Primary, I felt like I was returning home. The school had twelve pupils. It was in the middle of a forest with red squirrels regularly seen from the classroom windows. As part of the restructuring of clusters, the two schools would also have a principal teacher. This person would be promoted from within the cluster and would support me with aspects of curriculum development. When the selection process began it was clear only one member of teaching staff was interested in the post. Just a term after I began at Ericoid Primary, Grace became the principal teacher for the new cluster. Both schools were staffed finally with permanent teachers. '*Mr Bag of Nerves*', '*Miss Bucket Fille*r' and '*Mr Marigolds*' had all moved out of the area. The biggest and brightest news of all was that clearing snow had been taken away from heads by a new janitorial system. I could finally hang up my shovel!

There would be no more changes. I had been headteacher of four primary schools in the time I had been in Scotland. I was tired of change; I felt as if I had been on a roller coaster for the past few years. The emotions of leaving Tarn had taken its toll. There had been great stress at staff changes but joy at the babies born. I had felt frustrated with the politics of the change in the area. My illness was a millstone around my neck. Perhaps even the whole move north had taken a toll on me. I can't remember the exact moment when I decided time had come to finish. It was an idea in my head, rather like the feeling that I had hidden away years before about wanting to be a teacher. The thoughts made me restless at night. I had only ever wanted to be a teacher. The jokes about being a nun, Debbie Harry or the more serious ideas about an accountant or librarian had all been distractions from the only idea in my mind. Now, whenever I tried to distract myself from the thoughts in my head, they always led back to the idea of retiring early.

✓✓✓✓✓

One day, I took a call from the cluster's education officer. She wanted to know if I could help her out with an authority inspection of a school. The officers liked to have headteachers involved as part of the process. It was also training so that headteachers understood how these internal assessments worked. One experience led to another. Eventually I was involved with an inspection which took me away from home for several days. It was strange to be on the other side of the coin. I was one of the '*Men in Grey Suits*'. The nervousness on teachers' faces was apparent when I walked into their classrooms. I knew those glances to see if an observer was writing. Giving feedback to staff was easy if I had witnessed a good lesson. When the teaching was poor, I found myself being diplomatic, but I never lied. What was the point? For a few days after the last inspection, I wondered if I could be an advisor or even an HMIe. The more I pondered my future, the more I felt like a traitor. No! This role was not for me. If there was to be a change, it would be to retire.

A grand distraction from the ideas in my mind, came again from the education officer. She had become a good friend and I think she sensed I was unhappy. She recommended applying to take part in an Education Scotland programme called 'Excellence in Headship'. I wondered if reigniting my leadership skills might be the answer. I had been on many courses over the years since gaining the N.P.Q.H. qualification but had done nothing on my own specific leadership skills for a while. I agreed and took part in several residential experiences which were very thought provoking and exceptionally good. When I saw a module within the programme to take part in a project on small schools with Irish colleagues, I was instantly attracted to the study.

In the 'tattie fortnight' in October, Mark and I travelled to a part of Ireland we had not visited before, near the Great Atlantic Way. I met a wonderful headmistress (in Ireland called a principal) who made me welcome. Bridget was the head of a two-teacher school, smaller than Loch Dubhglas. She was a class teacher, with little time out of class for leadership duties. Some of the systems felt very different to Scotland or England but others were more familiar. Bridget had managed to get some supply cover to take me to other small schools and to show me a teacher's centre where courses were held. It reminded me of the days back in my old authority where there had been a dedicated centre for training many years before. With cuts it had closed and been demolished. I hoped the Irish principals would keep this facility.

I sat in a room full of strangers. The course was about preparing the older children in primary for their first holy communion. There were many prayers said before the session got underway together with the warmest of welcomes when one of the speakers introducing me as a visitor from Scotland. The greeting took me back. To them I was not an 'incomer', I was representing my country. I was proud of my Scottish heritage, the Chisholm blood running through my veins. A nun began the first session and I tried to block out Julie Andrews singing in my head.

When Bridget came to visit my two schools, I proudly showed her around. She spotted some Scottish Gaelic words on display and discussed

242

the differences between them and Irish Gaelic. We travelled to Glasgow to attend a meeting to discuss the project and what we had discovered about being leaders of small schools with other colleagues from Ireland and Scotland. The whole experience had been a wonderful one, Bridget was a friend for life. I wanted to believe the ideas of retirement, nagging away in my head, would go away but they did not.

✓✓✓✓✓

Almost at the end of the school year, it was someone's bright idea to have a whole school trip. The staff sold the notion to me by saying there would be just one risk assessment and just one coach needed so it would be the cheapest trip. I liked the plan straight away as the thought of just one risk assessment pleased me immensely. I completely understood the need for planning a trip and considering the risks involved, unlike Mr MacDougall, years back. However, I always felt buried alive in risk assessment forms during the summer term, year in year out, so the prospect of just one thrilled me. The logistics of a single coach and the cost made my heart flutter even more. I must admit I continued with a ploy of saying I would consider it for a few minutes longer than needed. By the time I had agreed the staff were virtually begging for my consent.

A few weeks later all the staff, children and parents gathered an hour before normal school time. It was a pleasant, sunny morning, with a slight breeze so no midges thankfully. Everyone stood or sat outside. We were due to leave at eight o'clock but there was no sign of the coach. After a phone call, we were reassured that it was on the way. The children went off to play and the parents and staff blethered. The coach finally arrived at half past eight. We gathered everyone quickly, did yet another toilet run and after a head count onto the vehicle, off we went.

After around an hour and a half of travelling, the coach pulled into a layby. Sensing something was wrong I moved to the front and spoke to the driver. He told me to get the children off the coach as quickly as possible, so with the help of a parent who was ex-army the evacuation of the coach took just a few seconds. '*Mr Army Parent*' and I scouted around the back of a hedgerow and luckily, we were able to place the whole group behind it, a safe distance away from the dual carriageway in front of us. So began '*Operation Layby.*'

Black, acrid smoke and hot water spewed out the back of the vehicle. It was clear that the coach was knackered. Frantic calls were made by the

243

driver for a replacement. I made a call to Moira, still at work in the office. It was her day for finishing at lunch time and she was elated that she hadn't gone on the trip. I asked her to phone the centre where we were going as we would be slightly delayed. There was nothing to do but make sure the children were safely away from the road and they were told to have a snack. The rays of the sun were powerful, and all jackets and jumpers were abandoned. It was now important to check that children had brought sun cream and sunhats.

Forty-five minutes later another bus arrived. We all climbed onto the new coach and the children started to sing as we set off. I am not quite sure why they chose to sing 'Let it go' from the film *Frozen* as they had red, sweaty faces from sitting in the sun but they sounded happy to be on their way again. We had not gone ten minutes along the road when the driver pulled into yet another layby. This time, I stood up instantly knowing something was wrong again. So did *'Mr Army Parent'* who kicked into *'Operation Layby Two'* immediately. He was brilliant, directing us all out of the coach and organising a chain of adults to make sure children disembarked onto a safe place in the layby. It was the same problem as with the first coach; the engine was overheating due to the temperature rising and the water pump had failed. This time we were further away from the coach depot, so a replacement bus took longer than before. *'Mr Army Parent'* was an engineer but even he couldn't fix the gaping hole that was discovered in the water pump, which was again spewing out hot water.

Unfortunately, this layby had no hedge to move the children behind so adults formed a line on the outside of the group. The youngsters were told to sit on their jackets and to eat their lunch. No one was silly. Everyone remained sitting and chatting away about the adventure. They had all been early risers for the trip, so they were starving, and they needed drinks urgently. Although the group were safely away from the dual carriageway there was the problem if any other vehicles wanted to use the layby. Adults were vigilant for any on-coming traffic that might pull off the road. The thermometer had risen rapidly. There was no shade of any kind. The staff stood and the children sat. We all baked in the sun, and I worried that we should all have sunstroke.

When the third bus eventually turned up, we had been in the layby for an hour and a half. This time it was not a plush coach, speakers for music, a toilet and a dodgy water pump. The coach came into sight and my heart sank. It was worse than I thought when I boarded the coach to speak to the driver. It looked like something out of a motoring museum. The seats were more like benches, some of which faced sideways into the coach rather than facing forwards. Worse still I spotted an immediate problem. There for all to see was the passenger capacity displayed just to the left above the driver's seat. I ran a mental check on the number again before speaking.

'I am right in saying this coach takes forty-nine people?'

'Yes Madam. That is correct,' answered the new driver who had replaced the first one.

'The problem is we are a party of fifty!'

I couldn't get the number out quickly enough. At first, I thought the driver was a *'Jobsworth'* who would leave one person stranded in the layby. However, he quickly got on his phone and got permission for one person to stand. Although my feet and legs were sore from standing in the heat for so long, I knew it was my place to volunteer. However, *'Mr Army Parent'* refused to allow me to stand, and he immediately took up a position holding a pole, talking to the driver.

When we arrived at the centre, we were all exhausted from the heat but elated we had finally got there. Everyone was hot and sweaty as we got off the bus, delighted to breathe fresh air again. The staff at the centre had managed to rearrange our booking so despite having arrived over three hours late we were able to see all the animals, take a ride into an enclosure where more dangerous ones were kept and still had time to relax at the end of the day in the play park with an ice cream. For days afterwards, parents reported their children elated at our adventure. Everyone declared it was the best trip ever. I can safely announce that I acquired a few more grey hairs after our day out!

It would be my last educational visit. Just a couple of weeks before, I had applied for early retirement after speaking to a financial pensions' expert. I should lose some money in the grand scheme of things, but it would be possible to retire at the age of fifty-six. I told few people for fear something would stop my plans. I also was facing some time away from work for some treatment for my thyroid condition. It meant I should be in isolation for around four weeks, away from Mark and my pets as well as anyone in school. I was given a date which worked well with my retirement plans. I should return for four weeks after the summer holiday, then have four weeks off work for my treatment. After that it would be the 'tattie fortnight' and then I should retire.

The final assembly of the year came swiftly. As always it was a celebration of the academic year. As the speakers blared out 'This is Me' from *The Greatest Showman,* photographs of the children flashed across the screen. I tried hard not to show any emotion, rushing through the presentation for fear of showing the world what was in my thoughts and in my heart. Little did anyone know that I was picturing hundreds of children as I stared at the images.

✓✓✓✓✓

In mid-August staff were told when we returned for the new year. I think they were shocked, but the decision had been made long before. Grace agreed to be acting cluster headteacher when the authority approached her. With some fine negotiation skills, she secured a teacher to work at Ericoid, in her absence. My final five days came quickly in the end. The three previous weeks of the new school year had been spent tidying. I was determined to complete the job I had begun years before, to rid the school of all items dating back to the 1920s. Why do teachers accumulate so much junk? It was a question Mark asked many times!

I felt numb as I ticked off the lasts; the last assembly, last staff meeting, last visits to see headteacher colleagues. I had presentations, presents and parties at both schools. Past colleagues and friends wished me luck which brought memories flooding back, many of which I have recalled in these pages. There was a lot of cake and many lovely mementoes to keep forever including a book of 'Bucket List' suggestions by the primary three to five class on what I could do in my retirement.

Holidays
'Dreaming of snoozing in a hammock supported by with two palm trees on an exotic beach' - *What a clever child!*

'Swimming in a holiday pool'- *Another clever child.*

'Staying in a luxury hotel in Luxor' - *Heat! Glorious, after all the rain we had been having in Scotland!*

I turned the pages, eagerly thinking of my own 'Bucket List'. However, at this point, the book took a nosedive …

'Having a farm holiday' - *Err, no!*

'Camping in a local wood' - *Forget it! I like a bed and radiators!*

Heights

'Going on a roller coaster' - *Highly unlikely, given my fear of heights!*

'Visiting a local trampoline park' - Same answer as roller coaster!

'Doing a climbing wall' - *I have imagined myself climbing quite a few walls especially since being a senior leader, so no!*

'Flying over the big school and village in a hot air balloon'- *I am sure the teacher has put them up to this!*

'Wing Walking' - *Now you really are taking the p***!*

Animals

'Looking after monkeys at a Monkey Adventure Park' - *No chance as I had worked with little monkeys for years!*

'A keeper at a reptile rescue centre' - *Have met a few reptiles, mainly inspectors and education officers in my time, so a big fat no!*

'Owning a Wild Animal Rescue Centre' - *The answer is still no!*

Big Ambitions

'Moving to Hollywood' - *Well, if this book sells and I become a multi-millionairess ... perhaps?*

'Have a new job working in the local ice cream parlour selling ice creams' - *Finally a child who knew me well!*

The final day went quickly. I checked emails and made sure I had left every instruction, password and gems of advice I could give to Grace. I talked through every document and folders prepared for HMIe. I was convinced the *'Men in Grey Suits'* would come to the big school during that session, even before Christmas. She looked overwhelmed but I knew she would cope. She had the ability as all those headteachers I had met along my journey in teaching had. She just had to believe in herself and trust her instincts, something no course could ever teach. Seven weeks later Grace would face the inspectors and, a few months after that, home-schooling because of the Covid 19 pandemic. As I closed the outer door of Ericoid Primary behind me I whispered,

'Over to you Grace ...'

I did not look back as Mark drove out of the gate. My emotions ran wild. I had been the summer gift my father had not wanted. I had been the shyest child, the one who wet herself, too scared to ask an unfamiliar teacher for the loo. I had been too reticent to speak in class. I had been told I should never be a teacher but to sell cakes instead. I had been the child expected by my family to follow her mother into teaching, but I had taught because a passion burnt in my soul. I had worked in some of the most deprived schools in the United Kingdom and some with the most beautiful of settings. I had taught some incredible children and worked with adults who shaped my thoughts and taught me to judge people fairly without prejudice of their skin colour, their nationality, or their home backgrounds.

Why did I need to retire early from a job I had loved? Was it my illness? Was the job too stressful? In truth, there is just one simple answer which might not make sense to anyone but me. I could no longer hear music and I did not want to sing.

I had held the tears for months. Now saltwater ran onto my tongue. I was so relieved. Five words came in my head from a few years before …

'I can, and I will.'

I had and I did!

Did The Fat Lady Sing?

Encore

Dear Reader,

I guess you might be wondering what life is like on *'the other side'* so here is a quick catch up on how things have gone so far.

Two days after leaving school for the last time, I received some treatment for my thyroid problems. I went into isolation away from Mark, our pets or anyone else. He visited once a day and spoke to me through a window. Staying in a caravan by the sea for four weeks, alone with my thoughts, I wondered how I would cope without education being in my life after six decades. I had been in school from the age of two to fifty sixth years and thirty-four days.

It could have been the treatment or pure exhaustion but, for the first two weeks, I slept for many hours. My dreams were vivid, as if I was reliving the beginning, middle and end of my teacher's tales. When I began to feel better, thoughts of school simply drifted away. Retirement didn't feel strange or too soon. It felt perfectly timed.

When I finally found freedom and emerged into the outside world, it was as if I was playing truant to visit a cafe or restaurant in the middle of a school day. I could also stop up late to watch a film, instead of having an eye on the clock for bedtime. I loved the lie-ins but most of all, I could visit the toilet when I wanted. There was no longer a need to pee at the end of break, just in case I needed the toilet in the middle of the next lesson. It was bliss!

In less than five months, the world went into Covid 19 lockdown. I had not expected that much of my first year of retirement would be spent in isolation. Any thoughts of travel were out of the question. We were confined to walking around the village once per day with our three rescue dogs. The rest of the time was taken in shopping online, baking and cuddling our old cats. From having no creative bone in my body for fifty odd years, I found a passion for photography and writing. When lockdown ended, I even took up golf!

I had no plans to ever return to the classroom as a supply teacher, something that lots of teachers do when they retire. As if it was fate, I could not have gone back if I had wanted. Schools were closed because of the pandemic and when they re-opened there were constraints on who could enter schools. I had cancelled my teaching union fees and was no longer licenced to teaching after deciding not to renew my membership of the General Teaching Council of Scotland.

Despite these decisions I felt guilt. It was a guilt for Grace and what I had left her to cope with. It was a guilt for all my friends and ex-colleagues who still taught. They went through hell, working in horrendous conditions. There were certainly no parties in staffrooms as the M.P. Michael Fabricant suggested, in his defence of numerous Downing Street staff and the Prime Minister being fined for breaking lockdown restrictions. The virus spread rapidly in schools. All my teacher friends had Covid at least once. It has been two years since Boris Johnson told us that we must 'stay home' and Captain Tom inspired the world walking his laps, raising millions of pounds. So much has changed for children and school staff.

One day, last summer, Mark spotted an advert for an occasional holiday cottage cleaner. He got the job and often I help him. The irony is not lost. Teacher or cleaner; it was always going to be one or the other. It turns out both were my dynasty and destiny.

I often joked that one day when I retired, I should write a story about the things that happened in schools and the characters I met. After many years of pondering what and how to write, I sat and typed. Memories flowed, words poured out, and there were many tears of joy and despair. My book has now been read, not just by me, but by you too. Thank you for getting to the end. I was a teacher but am now a published author because you read my tales.

You have shared some of the best and worst times in my life. I hope you felt my passion. Teaching was my life and stole my heart. It was like a lover. It swept me off my feet, wooed me and I embraced it. Our relationship lasted many years but, finally I grew tired, and my beau did too. We were no longer compatible, and our love affair ended. I am, however, pleased to say that one of my greatest loves is back in my life. Music is, once again, loud and clear. Once in a while I laugh when I say,

'Alexa! Play Blondie, 'Heart of Glass' …'

Go on … play it and listen to the words. You'll understand!

Much love,

Emma

Acknowledgements

This book would not exist without the help and encouragement of some special people.

Firstly, thanks to my devoted husband for being a writing widower. Your patience is unending, and the cups of coffee kept me going, along with jam sandwiches!

Thanks to my mum for reminding me of stories from my childhood and talking about the past.

Thank you to the 'Write That Book' tribe, friends and family who supported and encouraged the writing and publication of this book from its origins in October 2021. Thank you to Michael Heppell for writing a foreword for my first book and for his enthusiasm, time, and brilliance. Thank you to Anne, Deb, Nia, Tracey, Alison, Eileen, and Megan for all the countless hours of beta reading put in to support me in my journey into writing.

Finally, last but not least, sincere thanks to all the children, parents and staff who inspired me. From the heart of the Midlands to the glens of Scotland, life would have been dull without you. Whilst the characters in this book are all fictional, you gave me material for characters galore to write about. A special mention goes to Helen for her wisdom, support, and friendship, leaving our world far too soon.

R.K.J. Adams

R.K.J. Adams was born in part of the industrial West Midlands, rich in the heritage of the Black Country, taking great pride in saying she is not a Brummie although she married one! She lived and worked in the area until settling in a small hamlet in Derbyshire. After five years of renovating a three hundred year old cottage in the heart of the countryside, she moved with her husband and two cats to a small village in northern Scotland. Having rescued three dogs, the household is full of animals. There is never a dull moment or an empty lap!

She trained to be a teacher in the early 1980s and spent more than thirty-five years in primary schools, teaching Nursery children to Year 6/Primary 7. She steadily rose through the leadership ranks to headship. Over the years she was the headteacher of five primary schools ranging in size from more than two hundred and fifty children to one that had just five.

Following a lifetime in teaching, she retired in late 2019. She now has a life full of writing, music and photographing nature's gems. Finally, now able to stay up late, she loves being a night bird, aurora borealis hunting or gazing at the wonders of the night sky.

'Wasn't Me, Miss!' is her first published book. To find out more about her future writing projects and news, subscribe to her website, **https://www.rkjadams.com**. She also has a private Facebook page **RKJ Adams** readers are welcome to join and is on both Instagram and Twitter with the username **@rkjadams**.

Wasn't Me, Miss!
WASN'T ME, MISS!
Wasn't Me, Miss!
Wasn't Me, Miss!

Wasn't Me, Miss!

Wasn't Me, Miss!
Wasn't Me, Miss!
Wasn't Me, Miss!